OXFORD READINGS IN POLITICS
AND GOVERNMENT

PRESSURE GROUPS

OXFORD READINGS IN POLITICS AND GOVERNMENT

General Editors: Vernon Bogdanor and Geoffrey Marshall

The readings in this series are chosen from a variety of journals and other sources to cover major areas or issues in the study of politics, government, and political theory. Each volume contains an introductory essay by the editor and a select guide to further reading.

ALSO PUBLISHED IN THIS SERIES

PRESSURE GROUPS

EDITED BY

JEREMY J. RICHARDSON

OXFORD UNIVERSITY PRESS

Oxford University Press, Walton Street, Oxford OX2 6DP
Oxford New York
Athens Auckland Bangkok Bombay
Calcutta Cape Town Dar es Salaam Delhi
Florence Hong Kong Istanbul Karachi
Kuala Lumpur Madras Madrid Melbourne
Mexico City Nairobi Paris Singapore
Taipei Tokyo Toronto
and associated companies in
Berlin Ibadan

Oxford is a trade mark of Oxford University Press

Published in the United States by
Oxford University Press Inc., New York

First published 1993
Reprinted in paperback 1994

British Library Cataloguing in Publication Data
Data available

Library of Congress Cataloging in Publication Data
Pressure groups / edited by Jeremy J. Richardson.
p.   cm.—(Oxford readings in politics and government)
Includes bibliographical readings (p.   ) and index.
1. Pressure groups. I. Richardson, J. J. (Jeremy John) II. Series.
JF529.P717 1993   324.4—dc20   92-42267
ISBN 0-19-878051-6
ISBN 0-19-878052-4 (Pbk)

Printed in Great Britain
on acid-free paper by
Biddles Ltd, Guildford and King's Lynn

To
Sammy Finer

CONTENTS

FIGURES

TABLES

INTRODUCTION
PRESSURE GROUPS AND GOVERNMENT

JEREMY J. RICHARDSON

DEFINITIONS

As Graham Wilson notes, one of the basic problems for interest group studies is the problem of definition.[1] He notes that a wide variety of organizations are described as interest groups or pressure groups and he, therefore, asks the question 'Are we to conclude that any organization which seeks to any degree to influence public policy is therefore to be regarded as an interest group?'[2] His approach is to 'rely on the requirements that interest groups be *organizations* which have some autonomy from government or political parties and that they try to influence policy'.[3] In an earlier work we identified over twenty terms for what is essentially the same phenomenon—namely organizations pressing government to act (or not). Amongst the terms we discovered were: political group, lobby, political interest group, special interest group, organized group, voluntary association, pressure group, protective group, defensive group, anomic group, institutional group, associational group, non-associational group, formal-role group, exclusive group, and political group![4] As a working definition, we suggested the following: 'A pressure group may be regarded as any group which articulates demands that the political authorities in the political system or sub-system should make an authoritative allocation.' In order to exclude from this definition political parties and other groups whose objective is to take over the government, it is usual to add a note that such groups do not themselves seek to occupy the position of authority.[5]

© Jeremy J. Richardson 1993.

[1] Graham K. Wilson, *Interest Groups* (Oxford: Basil Blackwell, 1991), 6.
[2] Ibid. 7.
[3] Ibid. 8.
[4] Richard Kimber and Jeremy J. Richardson (eds.), *Pressure Groups in Britain* (London: Dent & Co., 1974), 1.
[5] Ibid. 3.

THE FUNDAMENTAL IMPORTANCE OF INSTITUTIONS AND INTERESTS

If we are not to live in anarchy, then we have to devise some means by which society can agree both on a set of institutions and processes by which laws and rules are to be decided and on those laws and rules which govern the workings of society at any one time. Both sets of decisions invariably give rise to conflict. This is because institutions and processes for deciding rules are not neutral in their effects. Different kinds of institutions and processes benefit or disbenefit different sectors of society. One only has to look at conflicts over rules in sport—and conflicts over the interpretation of the rules—to see that, in reality, there is no such thing as a 'level playing field'. The pitch itself may be flat, but the rules governing the playing of the game on that field can benefit one team or another. Similarly, a biased referee can assist one side in winning. Motor-racing is a classic example of a sport being contested both on the track and off it. As soon as a particular constructor develops an innovation which presents his/her team with an advantage, other constructors will lobby the sport's governing body to restrict the use of that innovation as giving an unfair advantage to one team, until they all have time to redesign their cars. Similarly, in the market-place, it is increasingly common for manufacturers to press the state for new and tougher regulations, once they have invented a product or process which might give them a market advantage. For example, Volkswagen the German motor manufacturer, was very successful in 1990–1 in persuading the European Community to adopt Europe-wide emission standards based on catalytic converters. This gave VW an immediate market advantage over its competitors—such as Ford and Rover Group—who had been addressing the pollution problem via the so-called 'lean burn' technology. Their own costly investments were overtaken by the new regulations and they quickly had to develop their own catalytic converters.

Because rules and laws do matter (e.g. emission controls and the global warming problem, the safety of consumers, the rights of women, etc.), *institutions* matter also—because rules are decided via institutions. For nearly forty years in Political Science, it has been fashionable to de-emphasize the importance of institutions and to stress the importance of behaviour and processes. Yet more recently, the so-called 'new institutionalism' has re-emerged as a fashion in the discipline. As Johan P. Olsen argues,

An institutional perspective assumes that the organization of political life makes a difference. Political institutions are the building blocks of political life. They influence available options for policy-making and for institutional change. They also influence the choices made among available options.[6]

In a telling passage Olsen draws our attention to a central feature of modern political institutions, of special relevance to the focus of this volume. Thus he notes that

contemporary formal organizations are not easily captured by distinctions between a private and public sphere, between hierarchies and markets, or by distinctions based on the legal status of organizations . . . government is often described . . . as a conglomerate of semi-federal, loosely allied organizations, each with a substantial life of its own, interacting with one another and interacting separately with civil groups.[7]

The reader only has to reflect on the importance of whether we live under a federal or unitary system of government, or under an executive or parliamentary dominated system, or under a multiparty or single-party system to realize that institutions do indeed 'matter'.

In focusing on the role of pressure or interest groups in this volume, we must always, therefore, be aware that different countries have quite different institutional structures and different sets of rules governing the internal working of these institutions. (For example, many Scandinavian democracies have a very open bureaucracy giving citizens free access to information—Britain has a very closed bureaucracy.) Pressure groups, of course, have played and continue to play a key role in the formation of these institutions, in the rules governing them and in the way that they change. To a considerable degree, the current institutional arrangements for governing any one country reflect the outcome of past battles between opposing pressure groups—they are the institutionalized peace treaties of past battles. Equally, the *existing* institutional arrangements are very difficult to change, without further battles, if only because 'agency capture' is quite common in all societies. Indeed, new agencies—such as state bodies created to reduce racial discrimination, encourage equal opportunities, counter unemployment, or deal with pollution—become the centre of whole industries consisting of the agency and its 'client' groups. Thus, old agencies, like old soldiers, rarely die. They and their clients have a strong self-interest in the survival and expansion of the agency.

---

[6] Johan P. Olsen, 'Political Science and Organization Theory: Parallel Agendas but Mutual Disregard', in Roland M. Czada and A. Windhoff-Heritier (eds.), *Political Choice: Institutions, Rules, and the Limits of Rationality* (Frankfurt: Campus Verlag, 1991), 95.

[7] Ibid. 96.

Thus whilst institutions do change—and new institutions are set up—the pressure group game at any one time is played out in the context of existing institutional structures and processes. For example, Italian groups must take account of the chronic instability of Italian government and of the importance of the Italian parliament. British groups must take account of the phenomenon of strong, centralized and stable government faced by a very weak yet well disciplined parliament. In the USA, pressure groups take account of (and exploit) the multiplicity of access points which is so characteristic of the American system of government—the Presidency, the bureaucracy, both Houses of Congress, the powerful Congressional Committees, the Judiciary and state and local government. In contrast, in the former Soviet Union and newly democratized Eastern bloc countries, one institution which was hitherto absolutely central—the Communist Party—has all but disappeared from the landscape, leaving an institutional vacuum which is often at the centre of the new group struggle. A similar example of institutional change was in France when the Fifth Republic was set up in 1958. There was then a major shift in the locus of power moving France from a parliamentary dominated system of government to a presidential system. Like a weather vane when the wind changes, pressure group activity quickly adjusted to the new institutional arrangements. These new arrangements were, however, of benefit to certain kinds of groups—particularly those professional and business interests having good contacts with the bureaucracy—and were disadvantageous to those groups having stronger contacts with the French Assembly—such as farmers and trade unions.

We must also note, as Robert Salisbury has argued, that institutions are not always *governmental* institutions. In a seminal paper, he has argued that interest group theory has focused too heavily on interest groups (along with political parties) as part of the articulation–aggregation process in society. In contrast he argues that *non-governmental institutions* have 'come to dominate the process of interest representation in American national politics'.[8] He makes a central distinction between an institution and an interest group by arguing that 'institutions have interests that are politically and analytically independent of the interest of particular institutional members'.[9] The types of institutions with which he is concerned include think-tanks, corporations, local governments, churches, and even universities. He concludes that the importance

[8] Robert Salisbury, 'Interest Representation: The Dominance of Institutions', *American Political Science Review*, 78 (1984), 64.

[9] Ibid. 68.

of institutional representation has significant implications for public policy, as 'institutional representation may be expected to be a more durable or persistent in policymaking circles than most purposive groups or even membership groups based on material incentives'.[10] Finally, he warns that much of the conservative bias which writers such as Schattschneider[11] have identified in the American system is more due to the activities of institutional representation than it is of ordinary membership groups.[12]

In practice, public policy in all societies is probably decided as a result of a complex and often unpredictable interplay between governmental institutions, non-governmental institutions (of the type analysed by Salisbury) and conventional membership groups which have been the main attention of pressure group studies so far. As Walker warns us, however, it would be wrong to see public policy as solely an outcome of group pressure. Thus, in considering the American interest group system, he suggests that,

A pressure model of the policymaking process in which an essentially passive legislature responds to petitions from groups of citizens who have spontaneously organized because of common social or economic concerns must yield to a model in which influences for change come as much from inside government as from beyond its institutional boundaries, and in which political entrepreneurs operating from bases in interest groups, from within the Congress, the presidency, or many private institutions, struggle to accomodate citizen discontent, appeal to emerging groups, and strive to generate support for their own conceptions of the public interest.[13]

Walker's observation suggests that we also need to address the range of *interests* that are involved in the processes of governing society. For any one issue or policy problem, we can usually identify a wide range of actors who have a very direct interest—*in the sense that they stand to gain or lose significantly by the decision.* These actors can be politicians whose electoral fortunes may be affected, bureaucrats whose career opportunities and budgets may be affected, private institutions, such as churches and universities, conventional membership interest groups—and, of course, citizens. Each policy problem, as it reaches the agenda, brings with it a whole *constellation of interests* who then engage in political activity in order to ensure that the processing of that issue is to their advantage. Indeed, the very agenda-setting process is often at the centre of the power

---

[10] Ibid. 75.

[11] E. E. Schattschneider, *The Semi-Sovereign People: A Realist's View of Democracy in America* (New York: Holt, 1960).

[12] Salisbury, 'Interest Representation', 75.

[13] Jack L. Walker, 'The Origins and Maintenance of Interest Groups in America', *American Political Science Review*, 77 (1983), 403.

struggle in society with pressure groups playing a central role in the struggles to attract the attention of decision-makers and the public at large. As Schattschneider has suggested, determining what politics is actually about is perhaps the supreme exercise of political power.[14] Equally, influencing what politics is *not* about is the focus of much activity. If we see public policies as in some sense the equilibrium of the various struggles over issues which have reached the agenda, then we should not be surprised to learn that those pressure groups and other interests in society who are *benefiting* from existing public policies have no desire to see the issue reopened for discussion. For example, farmers in all Western democracies have, historically, achieved very favourable public policies which distribute benefits to them at the expense of consumers. Farmers have, therefore, been very active in trying to prevent non-agricultural groups from participating in the making of agricultural policy, for fear that this would open up the whole question of agricultural subsidies for debate. Indeed, over time, this is just what has happened as environmentalists, food health groups and even taxpayers have begun to demand participation in the processes by which agricultural policies are determined. Grenson's classic study of 'non-decision-making' compared two American cities with similar air pollution problems—Gary and East Chicago in Indiana—yet which exhibited marked differences in the way that they dealt with them. It was not until the mid-1950s that air pollution became a public issue in Gary, yet East Chicago passed an ordinance relating to air pollution in 1949. The explanation, according to Grenson, is that industrial interests in Gary were more influential in preventing air pollution from becoming an issue than were industrialists in East Chicago.[15]

At the theoretical level, power theorists have introduced the concepts of two (and subsequently, three) faces of power. Bachrach and Baratz argue that by concentrating on decisions, we are ignoring a vital element in the power structure—the power not to make decisions in given policy areas. Thus, 'power is exercised when A participates in decisions that affect B' but it is 'also exercised when A devotes his energies to creating or reinforcing social and political values and institutional practices that limit the scope of the political process to public consideration of only those issues which are comparatively innocuous to A'.[16]

[14] Schattschneider, *The Semi-Sovereign People*.

[15] M. Grenson, *The Un-Politics of Air Pollution* (Baltimore, Mo.: Johns Hopkins Press, 1971).

[16] P. Bachrach and M. S. Baratz, *Power and Poverty: Theory and Practice* (New York: Oxford University Press, 1970), 7.

The agricultural case, cited above, may be an example of a much broader modern phenomenon, identified in 1978 by Hugh Heclo in the United States. At that time it was conventional wisdom to see American politics as dominated by so-called 'Iron Triangles' of public bureaucracies, congressional committees, and pressure groups. Yet he identified a trend in American politics which lead to an important qualification of this simple but convenient model. Thus he emphasized the fact that the number of participants in the policy process has increased considerably over time, eroding the rather closed system of decision-making (which in Britain we identified as the private management of public business),[17] and transforming it into a system of issue networks. Heclo argued that, 'Looking for the closed triangles of control, we tend to overlook the fairly open networks of people that increasingly impinge upon government').[18] He warned that, with increasing complexity, it has become more difficult to identify 'leaders' in policy areas.

This phenomenon—essentially a tendency for policy-making to become more complex and less predictable because of the widening of participation—can possibly be traced back to the increased mobilization of *interests* in society. Indeed, McFarlane sees Heclo's issue networks as yet another example of the emergence of countervailing power to limit the excesses of existing (usually producer) groups.[19] As people become more educated, articulate, and wealthier, and as knowledge and information become more widespread, more people come to recognize their own interests in issues which hitherto they were happy to ignore and leave to others to resolve. Thus, new interests are constantly being formed in society, to press for policy change. There are two very spectacular examples of this process in all Western democracies since the 1970s: the rise of environmentalists and of women's groups. The origins of these two movements are rather different. In the case of the environmentalists, the emergence of new and more vociferous organized pressure groups is linked to the progress of scientific discovery. Once scientists discover more about the effects of certain processes—e.g. the burning of carbon fuels, the emission of waste gases by cars, the use of artificial fertilizers, or the effects of smoking, then so either completely new groups are formed or existing groups

---

[17] Jeremy J. Richardson and A. G. Jordan, *Governing Under Pressure: The Policy Process in a Post-Parliamentary Democracy* (Oxford: Martin Robertson & Co., 1979).

[18] Hugh Heclo, 'Issue Networks and the Executive Establishment', in A. King (ed.), *The New American Political System* (Washington, DC: American Enterprise Institute, 1978), 88.

[19] Andrew S. McFarland, 'Interest Groups and Theories of Power in America', *British Journal of Political Science*, 17 (1987), 146.

become more active. As a result of this mobilization of groups, the existing policy area becomes 'overcrowded' and it becomes much more difficult to agree on policy outcomes or solutions. In a different policy area—health—Fritschler's study of smoking and politics in the USA is now a classic study of this process at work. He concludes that

The tobacco subsystem was changed completely in eight years. The small group of people in Congress, in the agencies, and in the tobacco groups lost control of the policymaking processes. As they did, very remarkable changes in public policy occurred . . . The new tobacco subsystem is likely to be a much different one from that which preceded it and was powerful until the early 1960s.[20]

Essentially, new participants entered the policy-making arena because they began to recognize that they had a direct *interest* in the policy process which determined the regulation of the tobacco industry. The rise of women's groups is rather different as it is difficult to relate this to the scientific and technological developments in society. The phenomenon appears to be more to do with a developing consciousness and awareness amongst women worldwide—literally, a (belated) recognition by women that they too had an *interest* in many public policies (and in securing new public policies) which previously had been ignored or left to men. Thus, despite the concern expressed earlier by those theorists concerned with non-decision-making, we might take some reassurance from the relevance of *interest* in all human activity. This was recognized by David Truman, writing about the USA, as long ago as 1951. In his *The Governmental Process: Political Interests and Public Opinion* he introduced the very useful concept of 'potential group'. He observed that if a disequilibrium occurs in society, new groups may form in order to restore the balance. For Truman, this was a very important aspect of group politics 'especially if a considerable number of individuals is affected, since these new groups are likely to utilize political means of achieving their objectives. They are likely to become political groups although they need not do so'.[21] He cited a number of instances of this phenomenon at work—for example, farm movements throughout American history have developed during times of economic difficulties such as the 1870s and early 1920s. He also cites examples from simpler (*sic*) societies such as New Guinea, as follows:

[20] A. Lee Fritschler, *Smoking and Politics: Policymaking and the Federal Bureaucracy* (Englewood Cliffs, NJ: Prentice Hall, 1969), 152.

[21] David B. Truman (1951), *The Governmental Process: Political Interests and Public Opinion* (New York: Knopf, 1951), 31.

When government officials and missionaries arrived in the Papua Territory, New Guinea, in the 1920s, they attempted to alter the ways of the natives and particularly to keep them from holding some of their customary religious ceremonies. The resulting disturbance in the established patterns of interaction was followed by the development of a series of religious movements that spread over New Guinea.[22]

Much later, in 1980, James Q. Wilson, having studied the regulatory process in the USA, also emphasized the role of countervailing interests in the policy process. The regulatory process was not entirely dominated by economic producer interests, as many had believed. Both producer interest and countervailing interests played a significant role in influencing the type of regulation adopted.[23] In a sophisticated reformulation of Wilson's ideas in terms of a 'power triad', McFarland has identified five elements derived from Wilson's analysis of the regulatory process, as follows:

1. the government policy process may be viewed in terms of specific areas of policies;
2. economic producer groups (abbreviated as P) normally organize to lobby government agency policy-makers in the area of production;
3. but countervailing groups (abbreviated as CV) will also be normally organized to oppose some of the interests of P;
4. state agencies are normally assumed to have a significant degree of autonomy (abbreviated by P or by CV);
5. this power triad is assumed to be a basic analytical unit, which is then complicated by adding such factors as legislators, presidential policy-makers, and the judiciary.[24]

McFarland also points to the emergence of social movements as a source of countervailing power. As he notes, resource mobilization theory is a combination of interest group theory with the sociologists' interest in mass behaviour: 'This theory posits a supply of "movement entrepreneurs", eager to gain influence and social position through the management of social movement organizations (SMOs) to further some cause or other. Many of these become lobbies, and thus a fertile source of countervailing groups.'[25] Interestingly, McFarland also echoes Truman's earlier work, cited above, when he suggests that another source of countervailing power 'results from the public recognition that elite control of a sub-system

[22] Ibid. 32.
[23] James Q. Wilson, *The Politics of Regulation* (New York: Basic Books, 1980).
[24] Amended from McFarland, 'Interest Groups and Theories of Power', 146.
[25] Ibid. 145.

has got out of hand, which in American vocabulary is called "special interest power"'.[26]

Before we turn to a discussion of another major feature of pressure group politics—the routinization of contacts between pressure groups and government—it is useful to remind ourselves that we are discussing a *dynamic* system. Many of the contributions in this volume point to a process of change in the system of government/group relations. It is important not to lose sight of the possibility of change in the balance of power between government and groups and between groups. We need look no further than the march of regulation in the modern state for evidence of this truth. Over the past thirty years, every Western democracy has witnessed a tightening of the regulatory grip by the state. Thus, for example, we have better consumer protection, better environmental protection, better safety protection for workers, and better regulation of workers' rights and conditions. All of these have been achieved via a shift in the balance of power between groups. Even the fashion for 'deregulation' in the 1980s and 1990s has actually seen much re-regulation, designed to protect the consumer from the adverse effects of the (now fashionable) market forces unleashed by deregulation.

REGULARIZING THE RELATIONS BETWEEN GOVERNMENTS AND GROUPS

Much of the preceding discussion has been designed to convince the reader of the centrality of groups in society. Whether we call them pressure groups, interest groups, or lobbies makes relatively little difference to the actual phenomenon under discussion—namely, the processes by which *interests* become *organized* in society and the processes by which those organizations participate in public policy-making.

As the passage from Bentley reproduced in this volume suggests, much of the 'stuff' of governing is to do with the management of the interface between governments and groups. Indeed pre-democratic governance had as one of its central features the bargaining between government and barons. This has continued throughout the processes and barons. This has continued throughout the processes of industrialization, democratization, and especially in post-industrial societies where we have possibly seen the final stages in interest mobilization. Pressure groups are the new barons with

---

[26] Amended from McFarland, 'Interest Groups and Theories of Power', 146.

which governments have to deal. In this latter stage, interests which were previously ignored or were unorganized have mobilized to a degree which often equals that of traditional producer groups. Thus, the existence of groups is a constraint on governmental action in all political systems. The institutions, structures, and processes of intermediation between groups and government vary considerably, as the subsequent chapters in this volume demonstrate. Yet the process of governing societies always involves some accommodation of the wishes of pressure and interest groups, even in totalitarian systems.

Indeed, one of the surprising aspects of pressure group studies is the frequency with which authors describe their own national systems as almost unique! In practice, the similarities between nations in the way that their governments manage the interface with groups in the policy process are striking—especially in Western Europe. One of the best researched European studies is that conducted by Johan P. Olsen and his colleagues in Bergen, Norway. Drawing on the results of the now famous Norwegian 'power project' they conclude that, despite the fact that styles of mobilization and confrontation will occur in the Norwegian political system from time to time, the main tendency will still be peaceful coexistence and revolution in slow motion. In their view:

The Norwegian situation will be influenced by a long tradition of political compromises; by the fact that most (but not all) interests are organised; by the willingness of ad hoc groups to avoid violence; and by a certain ability to adapt political institutions to new circumstances. Certainly, there are limits to what can be achieved through organisational means, but those limits are not given.[27]

Much earlier, another Norwegian political scientist, Stein Rokkan, produced an analysis of Norwegian democracy that has now been generalized to capture the essence of democracy in Western Europe as a whole. In what may have originally appeared to be a rather esoteric comment, seemingly highly specific to Norway, he wrote as follows:

the crucial decisions on economic policy are rarely taken in the parties or in Parliament: the central area is the bargaining table where the government authorities meet directly with the trade union leaders, the representatives of the farmers, the smallholders and the fishermen, and the delegates of the Employers' Association. These yearly rounds of negotiations have in fact

[27] Johan P. Olsen, Paul Roness, and Harald Saetren, 'Norway: Still Peaceful Co-existence and Revolution in Slow Motion?', in Jeremy J. Richardson (ed.), *Policy Styles in Western Europe* (London: Allen & Unwin, 1932), 76.

come to mean more in the lives of rank-and-file citizens than formal elections.[28]

In fact this captures the essence of European democracy—the so-called 'co-optation' of groups into the policy process in which the interrelationship between groups and government, depending on the policy area or issue, can often be of greater significance for policy outcomes than elections. Martin Hessler and Robert Kvavik have summarized what they term the 'European Polity' as follows:

We would emphasise as a characteristic of the European polity a common denominator of all polities . . . *a decision-making structure characterized by continuous, regularized access for economically, politically, ethnically, and/or subculturally based groups to the highest levels of the political system, i.e. the decision-making subsystem.*[29]

As they correctly suggest, most European countries have had some experience with the co-optive arrangements of the sort outlined for Norway, even though variations occur in the level and extent and the formal structures of co-optation. Despite these variations, they observe that 'The dominant pattern [of co-optation] consists of the emergence of commissions, permanent and ad hoc, as extensions of the formal government bureaucracy'.[30] They also emphasize both the *institutionalization* of this process and the cross-cutting linkages within it. Thus,

by viewing the decision-making structure in the European polity as a linkage structure, we wish to convey a picture of an established, vigorously structured—perhaps even institutionalised . . . entity. The decision-making subsystem that characterises the European polity is in no way ad hoc. It underpins the 'elite cartel' with massive bureaucratic infrastructures, comprised not only of the governmental administration formally viewed (i.e. the civil service), but of the numerous . . . commissions and committees as well. Inasmuch as the rule sets that comprise the decision-making subsystem are so numerous, diverse, and broadly encompassing (of the society as a whole), the linkage structure forms a substantial segment of the overall political structure in the European polity.[31]

As Grant Jordan's contribution to this volume indicates, so far-reaching is the system of group co-optation in Europe that for much

[28] Stein Rokkan, 'Numerical Democracy and Corporate Pluralism', in R. A. Dahl (ed.), *Political Opposition in Western Democracies* (New Haven, Conn.: Yale University Press), 164.

[29] Martin O. Heisler and Robert B. Kvavik, 'Patterns of European Politics: The European Polity', in Martin O. Heisler (ed.), *Politics in Europe: Structures and Processes in Some Postindustrial Democracies* (New York: David McKay & Co., 1974), 48.

[30] Ibid. 63.

[31] Ibid. 66.

of the 1970s and 1980s there was a growing literature on the corporatist 'tendencies' of the European model. Looking back on that debate, it seems that the proponents of the corporatist model (as the most accurate description of the European polity) were mistaken. Even one of its main advocates—Philippe Schmitter—has now reformulated his analysis.

The original core description of corporatism by Schmitter listed its main features as follows: 'the constituents' units . . . organised into a limited number of singular, compulsory, non-competitive hierarchically ordered and functionally differentiated categories . . .'.[32] This corporatist model was, of course, in sharp contrast to the pluralist American literature of the 1950s and 1960s which had emphasized the open, competitive, disaggregated, and essentially democratic nature of the policy process. The corporatist model was an ideal type and it was never found in the wild! Writing over a decade later, in the context of a discussion of the possibility of *neo-*corporatism at the level of the European Community, Schmitter and his colleague, Wolfgang Streeck, admitted that there had been a

decay of national corporatism in the late 1970s and in the 1980s (that) was rooted in domestic developments like qualitative changes in social structures, in the economy, and in domestic political systems that had imperceptibly at first eaten away at corporatism's structural and perhaps cultural foundations.[33]

They conclude that a combination of three trends was important: increasing differentiation of social structures and collective interests in advanced capitalist societies; market instability and volatility and pressures on firms to increase 'flexibility' of their product ranges, technologies and social organization; and changing roles and structures of interest organizations. In combination these trends apparently add 'to the reasons why a restoration of neocorporatism at either national or supranational level has become unlikely now and in the future'.[34] They see the processes of intermediation at the European level as moving towards an American pattern of 'disjointed pluralism' or 'competitive federalism' organized over three levels: regions, nation-states, and 'Brussels'. Thus, 'as in the United States and perhaps more so, this system would be

---

[32] Philippe C. Schmitter, 'Still the Century of Corporatism?', in G. Lehmbruch and P. Schmitter (eds.), *Trends Towards Corporatist Intermediation* (London: Sage), 13, also quoted by Jordan later in this volume.

[33] Wolfgang Streeck and Philippe C. Schmitter, 'From National Corporatism to Transnational Pluralism: Organized Interests in the Single European Market', *Politics & Society*, 19/2 (1991), 146.

[34] Ibid.

characterised by a profound absence of hierarchy and monopoly among a wide variety of players of different but uncertain status'.[35] At the Euro-level at least, the picture they paint is unrecognizable from Schmitter's original definition (and prediction) of corporatism. Now there is 'no mechanism in sight that could rationalize its political system, help crystallize its *mélange* of actors and processes, and establish corporatist monopolies of representation, interassociational hierarchies or for that matter, a predominant position for the (EC) Commission's hierarchy and technology'.[36] Could anything be further from the 'limited number of singular, compulsory, non-competitive, hierarchically ordered, and functionally differentiated categories' as the core elements of corporatism cited above? Even at the national level, Schmitter now appears pessimistic about the chances of corporatism. Thus, he now believes that 'especially when viewed from the macro- or national-level, it (corporatism) looks too small in scale to be of much help in the restructuring of sectoral and regional patterns'.[37] Finally, he concedes that 'There are many ways of handling these problems of conflicting interest and policy compromise in capitalist societies and none is a priori necessarily more efficient than others.'[38]

We may conclude, then, on this theme of a *multiplicity* of patterns of state–group relations. They vary from state to state, from policy sector to policy sector, and over time. In an attempt to disaggregate general models of state–group relations, Atkinson and Coleman suggest that, by concentrating on the sectoral level of the policy process, we may more effectively capture the nuances of the specific bureaucratic arrangements and the relationships with key societal actors. Thus, they conclude that policy networks 'may take in a variety of forms and hence their study requires a more nuanced categorization than the strong–weak state or pluralist–corporatist formulations'.[39] They also conclude that the relative frequency of different types of policy networks will 'vary systematically across democratic polities depending on the macropolitical institutions'.[40] Gerhard Lehmbruch has also emphasized the *variation* in 'standard

---

[35] Philippe C. Schmitter, 159. See also Mazey and Richardson in this volume, and S. P. Mazey and Jeremy J. Richardson, 'Interest Groups and European Integration' (forthcoming).

[36] Streeck and Schmitter, 'From National Corporatism', 159.

[37] Philippe C. Schmitter, 'Corporatism is Dead! Long Live Corporatism!', *Government & Opposition*, 24/1 (1989), 72.

[38] Ibid. 67.

[39] Michael M. Atkinson and William D. Coleman, 'Strong States and Weak States: Sectoral Policy Networks in Advanced Capitalist Economies', *British Journal of Political Science*, 19 (1989), 66.

[40] Ibid. 67.

operating procedures'.[41] For example, he suggests that 'the degree to which the participation of organized interests in general is considered legitimate varies considerably'.[42] He identifies a number of factors which may produce differences in national approaches to interest group intermediation, including the degree of discretion which the bureaucracy has in determining whether and whom to consult and the degree of sectoral segmentation.[43] He concludes that future research needs to address what he terms the 'configurative' aspect of interest intermediation. This is 'a structure made up of complex linkages between organizations, agencies, and other institutions . . .'. He sees the policy network concept, cited above (see also the chapter on Britain in this volume) as of the greatest potential in identifying cross-national variations in the intermediation process.

The main purpose of this brief volume, therefore, is to sketch for students these macro-political institutions in their broad characteristics and in terms of their relationship to national and sometimes transnational interest group systems. In selecting our contributions, we have tried to include both a theoretical perspective and a wide range of political systems. One overriding theme emerges, however. Despite structural differences in political systems—for example, contrast the US, Australian, German, and Canadian federal systems, with unitary systems like Britain, Denmark, and France—and despite differing degrees of interest organization, it is clear from this volume that as Bentley put it in 1908, the 'process of government' is centrally concerned with managing the vast variety of groups which exist in modern societies in such a way as to secure stability and a reasonable level of consensus. At its most basic, the task of government is to hold societies together. In practice this is possible only if the major sections of society are somehow 'accommodated'. If these interests are excluded from the policy process then society itself is threatened.

---

[41] See A. G. Jordan and Jeremy J. Richardson, 'The British Policy Style or the Logic of Negotiation?', in Jeremy J. Richardson (ed.), *Policy Styles in Western Europe* (London: Allen & Unwin, 1982), 81.

[42] Gerhard Lehmbruch, 'The Organization of Society, Administrative Strategies and Policy Networks: Elements of a Developmental Theory of Interest Systems', in Roland M. Czada and A. Windhoff-Heritier (eds.), *Political Choice: Institutions, Rules and the Limits of Rationality* (Frankfurt, Campus Verlag, 1991), 123.

[43] Ibid. 124.

PART I

PRESSURE GROUP THEORY

I

THE PROCESS OF GOVERNMENT

A. F. BENTLEY

I have set forth our raw materials as consisting entirely of the group activities of men; activities that always embody an interest, that never define themselves except in terms of other group activities of the existing society, that in many cases are differentiated in such a way that they become representative of other group activities; and I have made a preliminary examination of leadership and public opinion, important elements of the governing process, to show that they are themselves only to be understood as such representative group activities. By these steps the way has been prepared to take up systematically the phenomena of government and study them in group terms.

The phenomena of government are from start to finish phenomena of force. But force is an objectionable word. In the first place, it is apt here, as in the natural sciences, to lead its users into metaphysical quagmires. In the second place, it is too closely identified with so-called 'physical force', and too apt to be understood as in opposition to non-force factors of a sympathetic or moral or ideal nature; and this even while these latter factors are actually being treated as themselves very powerful agents in social process.

I prefer to use the word pressure instead of force, since it keeps the attention closely directed upon the groups themselves, instead of upon any mystical 'realities' assumed to be underneath and supporting them; and since its connotation is not limited to the narrowly 'physical'. We frequently talk of 'bringing pressure to bear' upon someone, and we can use the word here with but slight extension beyond this common meaning.

Pressure, as we shall use it, is always a group phenomenon. It indicates the push and resistance between groups. The balance of the group pressures *is* the existing state of society. Pressure is broad

Reprinted in abridged form by permission of the publishers from *The Process of Government* by Arthur F. Bentley, edited by Peter H. Odegard, Cambridge, Mass.: The Belknap Press of Harvard University Press, © 1967 by the President and Fellows of Harvard College.

enough to include all forms of the group influence upon group, from battle and riot to abstract reasoning and sensitive morality. It takes up into itself 'moral energy' and the finest discriminations of conscience as easily as bloodthirsty lust of power. It allows for humanitarian movements as easily as for political corruption. Groups exert their pressure, whether they find expression through representative opinion groups or whether they are silent, not indeed with the same technique, not with the same palpable results, but in just as real a way. The tendencies to activity are pressures as well as the more visible activities.

Political phenomena have no peculiar technique of pressure not possessed by other social phenomena; that is, no technique qualitatively or fundamentally all their own. They have, of course, specialities of organization which are themselves technique; but these, from the present point of view—pressure itself—are merely a special forming or working-up of the common material. . . .

The term political phenomena does not square exactly with the term government. From one point of view the former is the broader, as when we talk of certain party or subparty activities as political, but hesitate to include them under government proper. From another point of view, however, government is much the broader term; this is where political is limited in its meaning to activities having to do with the organized government, and government is given a still wider meaning. I wish next to describe three senses in which the word government may be used, not because our study has to do equally with all of them, but because they indicate different ranges, or types, of the pressure process between groups; because similar specific contents of activity may be handled in all of them and make clear transitions from one to the others; and because we cannot get an adequate understanding of the particular facts we shall have before us, without taking a glance at them in their broader setting. I shall call these three senses of the word government simply the broadest, the narrowest, and the intermediate.

In the broadest sense—a very broad sense indeed—government is the process of the adjustment of a set of interest groups in a particular distinguishable group or system without any differentiated activity, or 'organ', to centre attention on just what is happening. We must recognize that there is such a thing as genuine government in this very broad sense, because societies showing adjusted interest groups without a differentiated 'government' are actually found in corners of the earth—their government is called 'anarchy' by political scientists who find it in primitive communities; because an immense mass of such adjustments not mediated by government organs underlies the work of the differentiated government in our familiar societies—this is the habit background already discussed; and because interest groups, identical with those that are adjusting themselves or that have become fully adjusted in the ways just described, work through the differentiated government, and give that government its characteristic forms and movements, whether that government be despotic or 'pure democracy'; or, in other words, whether it is as near to what somebody thinks would be abstract despotism or pure democracy as can be found. I shall return to this sense of government, to illustrate it, in a moment.

In the narrowest sense—except for the British technical use of 'the Government'—government is a differentiated, representative group, or set of groups (organ, or set of organs), performing specified governing functions for the underlying groups of the population. I may well say now, and be done with it, that 'organ' is merely an inept word to indicate a peculiar kind of representative group, and that if I occasionally lapse into using it, the word has no other meaning than that. Government in this sense is not a certain number of people, but a certain network of activities. The most absolute monarch that ever ruled does not himself under exact analysis enter as a physical man entirely into the government; he always takes part in many activities that are not governmental. Nor is he ever under exact analysis all by himself the whole of the government: he always is a part of it, a most spectacular part, of course, but still a part. And so with other official personages, no matter what the type of government. It is always their specialized activity that is the government itself in the present sense.

Now between the broadest and the narrowest sense of the word government there lies an intermediate sense to which we must attend. We get to it when we have clearly passed beyond the limits of the differentiated governing activities, but are still among phenomena that are specialized with reference to the government, or let us say, among political phenomena. A particular form of political party may or may not be regarded as part of the government in the narrowest sense, but even when it is not it is decidedly a phenomenon of government, that is, of the governing process. And behind that are organized movements of a political nature, or tending toward political activity. We cannot shut them out. The directors of a corporation may finish their ordinary business and turn at the same meeting to discuss the part the corporation will take in the next political campaign. Their activity, which a moment before was industrial or economic, then becomes at once

political—a part of the governing process of the country—and is to
be studied specifically as such. Moreover, the corporation as activity
will be represented through its members, along with other corporations, in various organizations, which operate in the political field;
and the activity of all these organizations is part of government in
the intermediate sense.

2

THE LOGIC OF COLLECTIVE ACTION

MANCUR OLSON

It is often taken for granted, at least where economic objectives are involved, that groups of individuals with common interests usually attempt to further those common interests. Groups of individuals with common interests are expected to act on behalf of their common interests much as single individuals are often expected to act on behalf of their personal interests. This opinion about group behaviour is frequently found not only in popular discussions but also in scholarly writings. Many economists of diverse methodological and ideological traditions have implicitly or explicitly accepted it. This view has, for example, been important in many theories of labour unions, in Marxian theories of class action, in concepts of 'countervailing power', and in various discussions of economic institutions. It has, in addition, occupied a prominent place in political science, at least in the United States, where the study of pressure groups has been dominated by a celebrated 'group theory' based on the idea that groups will act when necessary to further their common or group goals. Finally, it has played a significant role in many well-known sociological studies.

The view that groups act to serve their interests presumably is based upon the assumption that the individuals in groups act out of self-interest. If the individuals in a group altruistically disregarded their personal welfare, it would not be very likely that collectively they would seek some selfish common or group objective. Such altruism, is, however, considered exceptional, and self-interested behaviour is usually thought to be the rule, at least when economic issues are at stake; no one is surprised when individual businessmen seek higher profits, when individual workers seek higher wages, or when individual consumers seek lower prices. The idea that groups tend to act in support of their group interests is supposed to follow logically from this widely accepted premiss of rational, self-interested behaviour. In other words, if the members of some group have a common interest or objective, and if they would all be better off if that objective were achieved, it has been thought to follow logically that the individuals in that group would, if they were rational and self-interested, act to achieve that objective.

But it is not in fact true that the idea that groups will act in their self-interest follows logically from the premiss of rational and self-interested behaviour. It does not follow, because all of the individuals in a group would gain if they achieved their group objective, that they would act to achieve that objective, even if they were all rational and self-interested. Indeed, unless the number of individuals in a group is quite small, or unless there is coercion or some other special device to make individuals act in their common interest, rational, self-interested individuals will not act to achieve their common or group interests. In other words, even if all of the individuals in a large group are rational and self-interested, and would gain if, as a group, they acted to achieve their common interest or objective, they will still not voluntarily act to achieve that common or group interest. The notion that groups of individuals will act to achieve their common or group interests, far from being a logical implication of the assumption that the individuals in a group will rationally further their individual interests, is in fact inconsistent with that assumption. This inconsistency will be explained in the following chapter.

If the members of a large group rationally seek to maximize their personal welfare, they will not act to advance their common or group objectives unless there is coercion to force them to do so, or unless some separate incentive, distinct from the achievement of the common or group interest, is offered to the members of the group individually on the condition that they help bear the costs or burdens involved in the achievement of the group objectives. Nor will such large groups form organizations to further their common goals in the absence of the coercion or the separate incentives just mentioned. These points hold true even when there is unanimous agreement in a group about the common good and the methods of achieving it.

The widespread view, common throughout the social sciences, that groups tend to further their interests, is accordingly unjustified, at least when it is based, as it usually is, on the (sometimes implicit) assumption that groups act in their self-interest because individuals do. There is paradoxically the logical possibility that groups composed of either altruistic individuals or irrational individuals may sometimes act in their common or group interests. But, as later, empirical parts of this study will attempt to show, this logical possibility is usually of no practical importance. Thus the customary view that groups of individuals with common interests tend to further those common interests appears to have little if any merit.

None of the statements made above fully applies to small groups, for the situation in small groups is much more complicated. In small groups there may very well be some voluntary action in support of the common purposes of the individuals in the group, but in most cases this action will cease before it reaches the optimal level for the members of the group as a whole. In the sharing of the costs of efforts to achieve a common goal in small groups, there is however a surprising tendency for the 'exploitation' of the great by the small. . . .

The kinds of organizations that are the focus of this study are expected to further the interests of their members.[1] Labour unions are expected to strive for higher wages and better working conditions for their members; farm organizations are expected to strive for favourable legislation for their members; cartels are expected to strive for higher prices for participating firms; the corporation is expected to further the interests of its stockholders;[2] and the state is expected to further the common interests of its citizens (though in this nationalistic age the state often has interests and ambitions apart from those of its citizens).

Notice that the interests that all of these diverse types or organizations are expected to further are for the most part common interests: the union members' common interest in higher wages, the

[1] Philanthropic and religious organizations are not necessarily expected to serve only the interests of their members; such organizations have other purposes that are considered more important, however much their members 'need' to belong, or are improved or helped by belonging. But the complexity of such organizations need not be debated at length here, because this study will focus on organizations with a significant economic aspect. The emphasis here will have something in common with what Max Weber called the 'associative group'; he called a group associative if 'the orientation of social action with it rests on a rationally motivated agreement'. Weber contrasted his 'associative group' with the 'communal group' which was centred on personal affection, erotic relationships, etc., like the family. (See Max Weber (1947 translation), *Theory of Social and Economic Organisation*, trans. Parsons, Talcott, and Henderson (New York: Oxford University Press), 136–9, and Grace Coyle, *Social Process in Organized Groups* (New York: Richard Smith Inc., 1930), 7–9.) The logic of the theory developed here can be extended to cover communal, religious, and philanthropic organizations, but the theory is not particularly useful in studying such groups.

[2] That is, its members. This study does not follow the terminological usage of those organization theorists who describe employees as 'members' of the organization for which they work. Here it is more convenient to follow the language of everyday usage instead, and to distinguish the members of, say, a union from the employees of that union. Similarly, the members of the union will be considered employees of the corporation for which they work, whereas the members of the corporation are the common stockholders.

farmers' common interest in favourable legislation, the cartel members' common interest in higher prices, the stockholders' common interest in higher dividends and stock prices, the citizens' common interest in good government. It is not an accident that the diverse types of organizations listed are all supposed to work primarily for the common interests of their members. Purely personal or individual interests can be advanced, and usually advanced most efficiently, by individual, unorganized action. There is obviously no purpose in having an organization when individual, unorganized action can serve the interests of the individual as well as or better than an organization; there would, for example, be no point in forming an organization simply to play solitaire. But when a number of individuals have a common or collective interest—when they share a single purpose or objective—individual, unorganized action (as we shall soon see) will either not be able to advance that common interest at all, or will not be able to advance that interest adequately. Organizations can therefore perform a function when there are common or group interests, and though organizations often also serve purely personal, individual interests, their characteristic and primary function is to advance the common interests of groups of individuals. . . .

Even when unorganized groups are discussed, at least in treatments of 'pressure groups' and 'group theory', the word 'group' is used in such a way that it means 'a number of individuals with a common interest'. It would of course be reasonable to label even a number of people selected at random (and thus without any common interest or unifying characteristic) as a 'group'; but more discussions of group behaviour seem to deal mainly with groups that do have common interests. As Arthur Bentley, the founder of the 'group theory' of modern political science, put it, 'there is no group without its interest'.[3] The social psychologist Raymond Cattell was equally explicit, and stated that 'every group has its interest'.[4] This is also the way the word 'group' will be used here.

Just as those who belong to an organization or a group can be presumed to have a common interest,[5] so they obviously also have

[3] Arthur Bentley, *The Process of Government* (Evanston, Ill.: Principia Press, 1949), 211. David B. Truman takes a similar approach; see his *The Governmental Process* (New York: Alfred A. Knopf, 1958), 33–5. See also Sidney Verba, *Small Groups and Political Behaviour* (Princeton, NJ: Princeton University Press, 1961), 12–13.

[4] Raymond Cattell, 'Concepts and Methods in the Measurement of Group Syntality', in *Small Groups*, ed. A. Paul Hare, Edgard F. Borgatta, and Robert F. Bales (New York: Alfred A. Knopf, 1955), 115.

[5] Any organization or group will of course usually be divided into subgroups or factions that are opposed to one another. This fact does not weaken the assumption made here that organizations exist to serve the common interests of members, for the assumption does not imply that intragroup conflict is neglected. The opposing groups

purely individual interests, different from those of the others in the organization or group. All of the members of a labour union, for example, have a common interest in higher wages, but at the same time each worker has a unique interest in his personal income, which depends not only on the rate of wages but also on the length of time that he works.

The combination of individual interests and common interests in an organization suggests an analogy with a competitive market. The firms in a perfectly competitive industry, for example, have a common interest in a higher price for the industry's product. Since a uniform price must prevail in such a market, a firm cannot expect a higher price for itself unless all of the other firms in the industry also have this higher price. But a firm in a competitive market also has an interest in selling as much as it can, until the cost of producing another unit exceeds the price of that unit. In this there is no common interest; each firm's interest is directly opposed to that of every other firm, for the more other firms sell, the lower the price and income for any given firm. In short, while all firms have a common interest in a higher price, they have antagonistic interests where output is concerned. This can be illustrated with a simple supply-and-demand model. For the sake of a simple argument, assume that a perfectly competitive industry is momentarily in a disequilibrium position, with price exceeding marginal cost for all firms at their present output. Suppose, too, that all of the adjustments will be made by the firms already in the industry rather than by new entrants, and that the industry is on an inelastic portion of its demand curve. Since price exceeds marginal cost for all firms, output will increase. But as all firms increase production, the price falls; indeed, since the industry demand curve is by assumption inelastic, the total revenue of the industry will decline. Apparently each firm finds that with price exceeding marginal cost, it pays to increase its output, but the result is that each firm gets a smaller profit. Some economists in an earlier day may have questioned this result,[6] but the fact that profit-maximizing firms in a perfectly

within an organization ordinarily have some interest in common (if not, why would they maintain the organization?), and the members of any subgroup or faction also have a separate common interest of their own. They will indeed often have a common purpose in defeating some other subgroup or faction. The approach used here does not neglect the conflict within groups and organizations, then, because it considers each organization as a unit only to the extent that it does in fact attempt to serve a common interest, and considers the various subgroups as the relevant units with common interests to analyse the factional strife.

[6] See J. M. Clark, *The Economics of Overhead Costs* (Chicago: University of Chicago Press, 1923), 417, and Frank H. Knight, *Risk, Uncertainty and Profit* (Boston: Houghton Mifflin, 1921), 193.

competitive industry can act contrary to their interests as a group is
now widely understood and accepted.[7] A group of profit-maximizing
firms can act to reduce their aggregate profits because in perfect
competition each firm is, by definition, so small that it can ignore the
effect of its output on price. Each firm finds it to its advantage to
increase output to the point where marginal cost equals price and to
ignore the effects of its extra output on the position of the industry. It
is true that the net result is that all firms are worse off, but this does
not mean that every firm has not maximized its profits. If a firm,
foreseeing the fall in price resulting from the increase in industry
output, were to restrict its own output, it would lose more than ever,
for its price would fall quite as much in any case and it would have a
smaller output as well. A firm in a perfectly competitive market gets
only a small part of the benefit (or a small share of the industry's
extra revenue) resulting from a reduction in that firm's output.

For these reasons it is now generally understood that if the firms
in an industry are maximizing profits, the profits for the industry as
a whole will be less than they might otherwise be.[8] And almost
everyone would agree that this theoretical conclusion fits the facts
for markets characterized by pure competition. The important point
is that this is true because, though all the firms have a common
interest in a higher price for the industry's product, it is in the
interest of each firm that the other firms pay the cost—in terms of
the necessary reduction in output—needed to obtain a higher price.

About the only thing that keeps prices from falling in accordance
with the process just described in perfectly competitive markets is
outside intervention. Government price supports, tariffs, cartel
agreements, and the like may keep the firms in a competitive market
from acting contrary to their interests. Such aid or intervention is
quite common. It is then important to ask how it comes about. How
does a competitive industry obtain government assistance in
maintaining the price of its product?

Consider a hypothetical, competitive industry, and suppose that
most of the producers in that industry desire a tariff, a price-support
programme, or some other government intervention to increase the
price for their product. To obtain any such assistance from the
government, the producers in this industry will presumably have to
organize a lobbying organization; they will have to become an active
pressure group.[9] This lobbying organization may have to conduct a

[7] Edward H. Chamberlin, *Monopolistic Competition*, 6th edn. (Cambridge, Mass.:
Harvard University Press, 1950), 4.

[8] For a fuller discussion of this question see Mancur Olson, Jr. and David
McFarland, 'The Restoration of Pure Monopoly and the Concept of the Industry',
Quarterly Journal of Economics, 76 (1962), 613–31.

[9] Robert Michels contends in his classic study that 'democracy is inconceivable
without organization', and that 'the principle of organization is an absolutely

considerable campaign. If significant resistance is encountered, a great amount of money will be required.[10] Public relations experts will be needed to influence the newspapers, and some advertising may be necessary. Professional organizers will probably be needed to organize 'spontaneous grass roots' meetings among the distressed producers in the industry, and to get those in the industry to write letters to their congressmen.[11] The campaign for the government assistance will take the time of some of the producers in the industry, as well as their money.

There is a striking parallel between the problem the perfectly competitive industry faces as it strives to obtain government assistance, and the problem it faces in the market-place when the firms increase output and bring about a fall in price. Just as it was not rational for a particular producer to restrict his output in order that there might be a higher price for the product of his industry, so it would not be rational for him to sacrifice his time and money to support a lobbying organization to obtain government assistance for the industry. In neither case would it be in the interest of the individual producer to assume any of the costs himself. A lobbying organization, or indeed a labour union or any other organization, working in the interest of a large group of firms or workers in some industry, would get no assistance from the rational, self-interested individuals in that industry. This would be true even if everyone in the industry were absolutely convinced that the proposed programme was in their interest (though in fact some might think otherwise and make the organization's task yet more difficult).

Although the lobbying organization is only one example of the logical analogy between the organization and the market, it is of some practical importance. There are many powerful and well-financed lobbies with mass support in existence now, but these lobbying organizations do not get that support because of their legislative achievements. The most powerful lobbying organizations

essential condition for the political struggle of the masses'. See his *Political Parties*, trans. Eden Paul and Cedar Paul (New York: Dover Publications, 1959), 21–2. See also Robert A. Brady, *Business as a System of Power* (New York: Columbia University Press, 1943), 193.

[10] Alexander Heard, *The Costs of Democracy* (Chapel Hill, NC: University of North Carolina Press, 1960), esp. 95–6 n. 1. For example, in 1947 the National Association of Manufacturers spent over $4.6 million, and over a somewhat longer period the American Medical Association spent as much on a campaign against compulsory health insurance.

[11] 'If the full truth were ever known . . . lobbying, in all its ramifications, would prove to be a billion dollar industry.' US Congress, House Select Committee on Lobbying Activities, *Report*, 81st Cong., 2nd Sess. (1950), as quoted in the *Congressional Quarterly Almanac*, 81st Cong., 2nd Sess., VI, 764–5.

now obtain their funds and their following for other reasons, as later parts of this study will show.

Some critics may argue that the rational person will, indeed, support a large organization, like a lobbying organization, that works in his interest, because he knows that if he does not, others will not do so either, and then the organization will fail, and he will be without the benefit that the organization could have provided. This argument shows the need for the analogy with the perfectly competitive market. For it would be quite as reasonable to argue that prices will never fall below the levels a monopoly would have charged in a perfectly competitive market, because if one firm increased its output, other firms would also, and the price would fall; but each firm could foresee this, so it would not start a chain of price-destroying increases in output. In fact, it does not work out this way in a competitive market; nor in a large organization. When the number of firms involved is large, no one will notice the effect on price if one firm increases its output, and so no one will change his plans because of it. Similarly, in a large organization, the loss of one dues' payer will not noticeably increase the burden for any other one dues' payer, and so a rational person would not believe that if he were to withdraw from an organization he would drive others to do so.

The foregoing argument must at the least have some relevance to economic organizations that are mainly means through which individuals attempt to obtain the same things they obtain through their activities in the market. Labour unions, for example, are organizations through which workers strive to get the same things they get with their individual efforts in the market—higher wages, better working conditions, and the like. It would be strange indeed if the workers did not confront some of the same problems in the union that they meet in the market, since their efforts in both places have some of the same purposes.

However similar the purposes may be, critics may object that attitudes in organizations are not at all like those in markets. In organizations, an emotional or ideological element is often also involved. Does this make the argument offered here practically irrelevant?

A most important type of organization—the national state—will serve to test this objection. Patriotism is probably the strongest non-economic motive for organizational allegiance in modern times. This age is sometimes called the age of nationalism. Many nations draw additional strength and unity from some powerful ideology, such as democracy or communism, as well as from a common religion, language, or cultural inheritance. The state not only has many such powerful sources of support; it also is very important economically. Almost any government is economically beneficial to its citizens, in that the law and order it provides is a prerequisite of all civilized economic activity. But despite the force of patriotism, the appeal of the national ideology, the bond of a common culture, and the indispensability of the system of law and order, no major state in modern history has been able to support itself through voluntary dues or contributions. Philanthropic contributions are not even a significant source of revenue for most countries. Taxes, compulsory payments by definition, are needed. Indeed, as the old saying indicates, their necessity is as certain as death itself.

If the state, with all of the emotional resources at its command, cannot finance its most basic and vital activities without resort to compulsion, it would seem that large private organizations might also have difficulty in getting the individuals in the groups whose interests they attempt to advance to make the necessary contributions voluntarily.[12]

The reason the state cannot survive on voluntary dues or payments, but must rely on taxation, is that the most fundamental services a nation-state provides are, in one important respect, like the higher price in a competitive market: they must be available to everyone if they are available to anyone. The basic and most elementary goods or services provided by government, like defence and police protection, and the system of law and order generally, are such that they go to everyone or practically everyone in the nation. It would obviously not be feasible, if indeed it were possible, to deny the protection provided by the military services, the police, and the courts to those who did not voluntarily pay their share of the costs of

[12] Sociologists as well as economists have observed that ideological motives alone are not sufficient to bring forth the continuing effort of large masses of people. Max Weber provides a notable example: 'All economic activity in a market economy is undertaken and carried through by individuals for their own ideal or material interests. This is naturally just as true when economic activity is oriented to the patterns of order of corporate groups . . . Even if an economic system were organized on a socialistic basis, there would be no fundamental difference in this respect . . . The structure of interests and the relevant situation might change; there would be other means of pursuing interests, but this fundamental factor would remain just as relevant as before. It is of course true that economic action which is oriented on purely ideological grounds to the interest of others does exist. But it is even more certain that the mass of men do not act in this way, and it is an induction from experience that they cannot do so and never will . . . In a market economy the interest in the maximization of income is necessarily the driving force of all economic activity' (Weber, *Theory*, 319–20). Talcott Parsons and Neil Smelser go even further in postulating that 'performance' throughout society is proportional to the 'rewards' and 'sanctions' involved. See their *Economy and Society* (Glencoe, Ill.: Free Press, 1954), 50–69.

government, and taxation is accordingly necessary. The common or collective benefits provided by governments are usually called 'public goods' by economists, and the concept of public goods is one of the oldest and most important ideas in the study of public finance. A common, collective, or public good is here defined as any good such that, if any person X_i in a group $X_1, \ldots, X_i, \ldots X_n$ consumes it, it cannot feasibly be withheld from the others in that group.[13] In other words, those who do not purchase or pay for any of the public or collective good cannot be excluded or kept from sharing in the consumption of the good, as they can where non-collective goods are concerned.

Students of public finance have, however, neglected the fact that the achievement of any common goal or the satisfaction of any

[13] This simple definition focuses upon two points that are important in the present context. The first point is that most collective goods can only be defined with respect to some specific group. One collective good goes to one group of people, another collective good to another group; one may benefit the whole world, another only two specific people. Moreover, some goods are collective goods to those in one group and at the same time private goods to those in another, because some individuals can be kept from consuming them and others can't. Take, for example, the parade that is a collective good to all those who live in tall buildings overlooking the parade route, but which appears to be a private good to those who can see it only by buying tickets for a seat in the stands along the way. The second point is that once the relevant group has been defined, the definition used here, like Musgrave's, distinguishes collective good in terms of infeasibility of excluding potential consumers of the good. This approach is used because collective goods produced by organizations of all kinds seem to be such that exclusion is normally not feasible. To be sure, for some collective goods it is physically possible to practise exclusion. But, as Head has shown, it is not necessary that exclusion be technically impossible; it is only necessary that it be infeasible or uneconomic. Head has also shown most clearly that non-excludability is only one of two basic elements in the traditional understanding of public goods. The other, he points out, is 'jointness of supply'. A good has 'jointness' if making it available to one individual means that it can be easily or freely supplied to others as well. The polar case of jointness would be Samuelson's pure public good, which is a good such that additional consumption of it by one individual does not diminish the amount available to others. By the definition used here, jointness is not a necessary attribute of a public good. As later parts of this chapter will show, at least one type of collection good considered here exhibits no jointness whatever, and few if any would have the degree of jointness needed to qualify as pure public goods. None the less, most of the collective goods to be studied here do display a large measure of jointness. On the definition and importance of public goods, see John G. Head, 'Public Goods and Public Policy', *Public Finance*, 17/3 (1962), 197–219; Richard Musgrave, *The Theory of Public Finance* (New York: McGraw-Hill, 1959); Paul A. Samuelson, 'The Pure Theory of Public Expenditure', *Review of Economics and Statistics*, 36 (1954), 387–90; 'Diagrammatic Exposition of a Theory of Public Expenditure', ibid. 37 (1955), 350–6; and 'Aspects of Public Expenditure Theories', ibid. 40 (1958), 332–8. For somewhat different opinions about the usefulness of the concept of public goods see Julius Margolis, 'A Comment on the Pure Theory of Public Expenditure', ibid. 37 (1955), 347–9, and Gerhard Colm, 'Theory of Public Expenditures', *Annals of the American Academy of Political and Social Science*, 183 (1936), 1–11.

common interest means that a public or collective good has been provided for that group.[14] The very fact that a goal or purpose is common to a group means that no one in the group is excluded from the benefit or satisfaction brought about by its achievement. . . .

A state is first of all an organization that provides public goods for its members, the citizens; and other types of organizations similarly provide collective goods for their members.

And just as a state cannot support itself by voluntary contributions, or by selling its basic services on the market, neither can other large organizations support themselves without providing some sanction, or some attraction distinct from the public good itself, that will lead individuals to help bear the burdens of maintaining the organization. The individual member of the typical large organization is in a position analogous to that of the firm in a perfectly competitive market, or the taxpayer in the state: his own efforts will not have a noticeable effect on the situation of his organization, and he can enjoy any improvements brought about by others whether or not he has worked in support of his organization. . . .

Whether a group will have the possibility of providing itself with a collective good without coercion or outside inducements therefore depends to a striking degree upon the number of individuals in the group, since the larger the group, the less the likelihood that the contribution of any one will be perceptible. It is not, however, strictly accurate to say that it depends solely on the number of individuals in the group. The relation between the size of the group and the significance of an individual member cannot be defined quite that simply. A group which has members with highly unequal degrees of interest in a collective good, and which wants a collective good that is (at some level of provision) extremely valuable in relation to its cost, will be more apt to provide itself with a collective good than other groups with the same number of members. The same situation prevails in the study of market structure, where again the number of firms an industry can have and still remain oligopolistic (and have the possibility of supracompetitive returns) varies somewhat from case to case. The standard for determining whether a group will have the capacity to act, without coercion or

[14] There is no necessity that a public good to one group in a society is necessarily in the interest of the society as a whole. Just as a tariff could be a public good to the industry that sought it, so the removal of the tariff could be a public good to those who consumed the industry's product. This is equally true when the public-good concept is applied only to governments; for a military expenditure, or a tariff, or an immigration restriction that is a public good to one country could be a 'public bad' to another country, and harmful to world society as a whole.

outside inducements, in its group interest is (as it should be) the same for market and non-market groups: it depends on whether the individual actions of any one or more members in a group are noticeable to any other individuals in the group.[15] This is most obviously, but not exclusively, a function of the number in the group. . . .

Only a separate and 'selective' incentive will stimulate a rational individual in a latent group to act in a group-oriented way. In such circumstances group action can be obtained only through an incentive that operates, not indiscriminately, like the collective good, upon the group as a whole, but rather selectively towards the individuals in the group. The incentive must be 'selective' so that those who do not join the organization working for the group's interest, or in other ways contribute to the attainment of the group's interest, can be treated differently from those who do. These 'selective incentives' can be either negative or positive, in that they can either coerce by punishing those who fail to bear an allocated share of the costs of the group action, or they can be positive inducements offered to those who act in the group interest. A latent group that has been led to act in its group interest, either because of coercion of the individuals in the group or because of coercion of the individuals in the group or because of positive rewards to those individuals, will here be called a 'mobilized' latent group. Large groups are thus called 'latent' groups because they have a latent power or capacity for action, but that potential power can be realized or 'mobilized' only with the aid of 'selective incentives'. . . .

THE 'BY-PRODUCT' THEORY OF LARGE PRESSURE GROUPS

If the individuals in a large group have no incentive to organize a lobby to obtain a collective benefit, how can the fact that some large

---

[15] The noticeability of the actions of a single member of a group may be influenced by the arrangements the group itself sets up. A previously organized group, for example, might ensure that the contributions or lack of contributions of any member of the group, and the effect of each such member's course on the burden and benefit for others, would be advertised, thus ensuring that the group effort would not collapse from imperfect knowledge. I therefore define 'noticeability' in terms of the degree of knowledge, and the institutional arrangements, that actually exist in any given group, instead of assuming a 'natural noticeability' unaffected by any group advertising or other arrangements. This point, along with many other valuable comments, has been brought to my attention by Prof. Jerome Rothenberg, who does, however, make much more of a group's assumed capacity to create 'artificial noticeability' than I would want to do. I know of no practical example of a group or organization that has done much of anything, apart from improve information, to enhance the noticeability of an individual's actions in striving for a collective good.

groups are organized be explained? Though many groups with common interests, like the consumers, the white-collar workers, and the migrant agricultural workers, are not organized,[16] other large groups, like the union labourers, the farmers, and the doctors have at least some degree of organization. The fact that there are many groups which, despite their needs, are not organized would seem to contradict the 'group theory' of the analytical pluralists; but on the other hand the fact that other large groups have been organized would seem to contradict the theory of 'latent groups' offered in this study.

But the large economic groups that are organized do have one common characteristic which distinguishes them from those large economic groups that are not, and which at the same time tends to support the theory of latent groups offered in this work. This common characteristic will, however, require an elaboration or addition to the theory of groups developed in this study.

The common characteristic which distinguishes all of the large economic groups with significant lobbying organizations is that these groups are also organized for some other purpose. The large and powerful economic lobbies are in fact the by-products of organizations that obtain their strength and support because they perform some function in addition to lobbying for collective goods. . . .

The lobbies of the large economic groups are the by-products of organizations that have the capacity to 'mobilize' a latent group with 'selective incentives'. The only organizations that have the 'selective incentives' available are those that (1) have the authority and capacity to be coercive, or (2) have a source of positive inducements that they can offer the individuals in a latent group.

A purely political organization—an organization that has no function apart from its lobbying function—obviously cannot legally coerce individuals into becoming members. A political party, or any purely political organization, with a captive or compulsory membership would be quite unusual in a democratic political system. But if for some non-political reason, if because of some other function it performs, an organization has a justification for having a compulsory membership, or if through this other function it has obtained the power needed to make membership in it compulsory, that organization may then be able to get the resources needed to support

---

[16] 'When lists of these organizations are examined, the fact that strikes the student most forcibly is that *the system is very small*. The range of organized, identifiable, known groups is amazingly narrow; there is nothing remotely universal about it.' E. E. Schattschneider, *The Semi-Sovereign People* (New York: Holt, Rinehart & Winston, 1960), 30.

a lobby. The lobby is then a by-product of whatever function this organization performs that enables it to have a captive membership.

An organization that did nothing except lobby to obtain a collective good for some large group would not have a source of rewards or positive selective incentives it could offer potential members. Only an organization that also sold private or non-collective products, or provided social or recreational benefits to individual members, would have a source of these positive inducements.[17] Only such an organization could make a joint offering or 'tied sale' of collective and non-collective good that could stimulate a rational individual in a large group to bear part of the cost of obtaining a collective good.[18] There are for this reason many organizations that have both lobbying functions and economic functions, or lobbying functions and social functions, or even all three of these types of functions at once.[19] Therefore, in addition to

[17] An economic organization in a perfectly competitive market in equilibrium, which had no special competitive advantage that could bring it a large amount of 'rent', would have no 'profits' or other spare resources it could use as selective incentives for a lobby. None the less there are many organizations that do have spare returns they can use for selective incentives. First, markets with some degree of monopoly power are far more common than perfectly competitive markets. Second, there are sometimes important complementaries between the economic and political activities of an organization. The political branch of the organization can win lower taxes or other favourable government policies for the economic branch, and the good name won by the political branch may also help the economic branch. For somewhat similar reasons, a social organization may also be a source of a surplus that can be used for selective incentives. An organization that is not only political, but economic or social as well, and has a surplus that provides selective incentives, may be able to retain its membership and political power, in certain cases, even if its leadership manages to use some of the political or economic power of the organization for objectives other than those desired by the membership, since the members of the organization will have an incentive to continue belonging even if they disagree with the organization's policy. This may help explain why many lobbying organizations take positions that must be uncongenial to their membership, and why organizations with leaders who corruptly advance their own interests at the expense of the organization continue to survive.

[18] The worth of the non-collective or private benefit would have to exceed its cost by an amount greater than the dues to the lobbying branch of the organization, or the joint offering would not be sufficient to attract members to the organization. Note that selective incentives were defined to be values larger in absolute magnitude than an individual's share of the costs of the collective good.

[19] An organization that lobbied to provide a collective good for a large group might even obtain its selective incentives by lobbying also for non-collective 'political' goods, like individual exceptions to (or advantageous interpretations of) a general rule or law, or for patronage for particular individuals, etc. The point is not that the organization must necessarily also be economic or social as well as political (though that is usually the case); it is rather that, if the organization does not have the capacity to coerce potential members, it must offer some non-collective, i.e. selective, benefit to potential members.

the large group lobbies that depend on coercion, there are those that are associated with organizations that provide non-collective or private benefits which can be offered to any potential supporter who will bear his share of the cost of the lobbying for the collective good.

The by-product theory of pressure groups need apply only to the large or latent group. It need not apply to the privileged or intermediate groups, because these smaller groups can often provide a lobby, or any other collective benefit, without any selective incentives. . . . It applies to latent groups because the individual in a latent group has no incentive voluntarily to sacrifice his time or money to help an organization obtain a collective good; he alone cannot be decisive in determining whether or not this collective good will be obtained, but if it is obtained because of the efforts of others he will inevitably be able to enjoy it in any case. Thus he would support the organization with a lobby working for collective goods only if (1) he is coerced into paying dues to the lobbying organization, or (2) he has to support this group in order to obtain some other non-collective benefit. Only if one or both of these conditions hold will the potential political power of a latent group be mobilized.

3

INTEREST GROUPS AND THE FALLACY OF THE LIBERAL FALLACY

RICHARD KIMBER

What is the role of interest groups in society? How and why do they come into existence? The answer to these questions offered by orthodox group theory, as exemplified by the work of David Truman,[1] has been much criticized on a variety of grounds.[2] Not one of these criticisms, however, has proved quite as damaging as the apparently crippling blow aimed by Mancur Olson at the theory's underlying logic.[3] He suggests that Truman and other 'analytical pluralists' committed what Brian Barry later refers to as 'the standard liberal fallacy'. That is, they subscribed to the argument that, 'if a collective good is genuinely beneficial to all there is no need to secure it by compulsion since all those benefited will have an incentive for contributing to the cost of providing it'.[4]

Olson, on the contrary, argues that, 'unless there is coercion or some other special device to make individuals act in their common interest, *rational, self-interested individuals will not act to achieve their common or group interests.*[5] Thus, Olson maintains that interest group membership must be accounted for, not by the rational, self-interested choices of individuals, but by their being compelled, or offered inducements, to belong.

In the introduction to the second edition of *The Governmental Process*, Truman seems to view this development with remarkable

This is a revised version of an article that first appeared in *World Politics*, 33/2 (1981), 178–95. I should like to thank Bob Goodin for his comments.

[1] B. Truman, *The Governmental Process: Political Interests and Public Opinion* (New York: Alfred Knopf, 1951; 2nd edn., 1971). Reference will be made to the second edition.

[2] See e.g. Roy C. Macridis, 'Interest Groups in Comparative Analysis', *Journal of Politics*, 23 (1961), 25–45; Peter H. Odegard, 'A Group Basis of Politics: A New Name for an Ancient Myth', *Western Political Quarterly*, 11 (1958), 689–702; Stanley Rothman, 'Systematic Political Theory: Observations on the Group Approach', *American Political Science Review*, 54 (1960), 15–33.

[3] M. Olson, *The Logic of Collective Action* (Cambridge, Mass.: Harvard University Press, 1965; 2nd edn., 1971). Reference will be made to the second edition.

[4] B. Barry, *The Liberal Theory of Justice* (Oxford: Clarendon Press, 1973), 118.

[5] Olson, *Logic of Collective Action*, 2; emphasis in original.

equanimity, arguing that the economic model applies only to a limited range of phenomena, and that 'for groups characterized by a low level of rationality, in the technical sense, economics is a less satisfactory source of theory than social psychology, which is, of course, the chief reliance of *The Governmental Process*'.[6] But Truman here underestimates the fundamental importance of Olson's argument and the fact that, although it appears to rest on an economic analogy, the argument—if valid—has a much wider significance. In an influential article,[7] Russell Hardin took the debate a stage further by arguing from a game-theoretic perspective that the problem is a Prisoners' Dilemma[8] for large and intermediate groups, and that any analysis which prescribes a solution for the Prisoners' Dilemma must prescribe a similar solution for the game of collective action. Most writers dealing with the problem of collective action seem to accept the 'non-cooperative' solution; that is, like Olson, they conclude that rational individuals will not contribute to the provision of a collective good.

Thus, only a direct assault on the logic of the new orthodoxy can save Truman's theory from collapsing. It is the purpose of this paper to attempt to show that the logic of Truman's underlying assumption about individual behaviour is not defective, and that it is the new orthodoxy which is unsatisfactory.

Although his argument is not logically dependent upon them, Olson approaches the problem by drawing analogies on the one hand with a perfectly competitive market, and on the other hand with the state.[9] I wish not only to argue against Olson's position, but also to show that the two analogies are misleading.

In a perfectly competitive market (where there is a uniform price) there is a conflict between common and individual interests. The large number of firms all have a common interest in maintaining a high price by restricting output and thereby maximizing their aggregate profits; yet for individual firms it will be advantageous to increase output until marginal cost equals price. Although each firm is so small that it can ignore the effect of its increased output on the price, the overall effect is to reduce the price, and therefore to reduce aggregate profits. The crucial point is that no individual firm will

[6] Truman, *Governmental Process*, p. xxix.

[7] R. Hardin, 'Collective Action as an Agreeable n-Prisoners' Dilemma', *Behavioral Science*, 16 (1971), 472–81, also *Collective Action* (Baltimore, Md.: Johns Hopkins University Press, 1982).

[8] For an explanation of the Prisoners' Dilemma, see Richard Kimber, 'Collective Action and the Fallacy of the Liberal Fallacy', *World Politics*, 33/2 (1981), 178–96.

[9] Olson, *Logic of Collective Action*, 9–16.

voluntarily reduce its output in order to help keep up the price. A similar situation obtains with the state: the rational individual will not, Olson argues, voluntarily contribute taxes when he can benefit from, say, government defence spending whether or not he has contributed. As with a perfectly competitive industry and with the state, so with large economic groups. Analytical pluralists have built their theory around an inconsistency.

They generally take for granted that such groups will act to defend or advance their group interests, and take it for granted that the individuals in these groups must also be concerned about their individual economic interests. But if the individuals in any large group are interested in their own welfare, they will not voluntarily make any sacrifices to help their group attain its political (public or collective) objectives.[10]

In order to examine the soundness of Olson's argument, we must remind ourselves of the main assumptions involved. Olson approaches the problem from the point of view of an existing interest group and attempts to show that it could not have existed unless inducements were offered or compulsion was applied. Thus, we postulate a large group which is organized to provide a collective good and which comprises individuals all of whom are assumed to act out of rational self-interest. Each individual is assumed to derive a net benefit from the provision of the good; and no one can be excluded from benefiting from the good, regardless of whether or not they are members of the organization.

A given individual who would derive a net benefit from the provision of the good would be better off outside the organization, according to Olson, because he can receive the benefit of the collective good without having to pay the subscription (i.e. he can free-ride). Thus, rational self-interest causes the individual to leave the organization; and since all the individuals are assumed to act in this way, the organization fails and the good is not provided.

Olson tries to head off the obvious objection that someone would support the group 'because he knows that if he does not, others will not do so either, and then the organization will fail, and he will be without the benefit that the organization could have provided' by asserting that this argument 'shows the need for the analogy with the perfectly competitive market', and that

it would be quite as reasonable to argue that prices will never fall below the levels a monopoly would have charged in a perfectly competitive market, because if one firm increased its output, other firms would also, and the price would fall; but each firm could foresee this, so it would not start a chain of price destroying increases in output.

---

[10] Olson, *Logic of Collective Action*, 126; emphasis in original.

In fact, Olson says,

> it does not work out this way in a competitive market; nor in a large organization. When the number of firms involved is large, no one will notice the effect on price if one firm increases its output, and so no one will change his plans because of it. Similarly, in a large organization, *the loss of one dues payer will not noticeably increase the burden for any other one dues payer,* and so *a rational person would not believe that if he were to withdraw from an organization he would drive others to do so.*[11]

Thus, at the moment of decision, Olson is not relying on the same self-interested calculation for all the individuals. A given individual, A, is said to examine the effects of his action on the others, and the others are assumed by him to be motivated in their actions by whether or not their burden is noticeably increased. The individual himself is assumed to predict the behaviour of the others on this basis and to arrive at the conclusion that they will not leave the organization, and that therefore the continued supply of the good is certain. Since only if the others remain in the organization will the given individual actually be better off when he leaves it, this step is crucial.

Others

	Pay	Not Pay
A Pay	1.1	−2.0
Not Pay	3.1	0.0

FIGURE 3.1 Prisoners' Dilemma Analogue[a]

[a] Based on a hypothetical example in which a good is valued at 3 units per head, with a subscription of 2 units per head.

Much has been made in the literature of an analogy with the Prisoners' Dilemma (PD) in both its 2-person and n-person forms. Olson, of course, is concerned with an n-person game. I would argue that there are two reasons for rejecting the 2-person PD as an analogue for this type of group action [see Fig. 3.1]. First, the upper right-hand cell in the matrix (in which the individual appears to make a loss), although it has dire consequences for A if he is a prisoner, is meaningless in the group context: A cannot pay a subscription to a non-existent organization in the event of the others not paying. Thus, if anything, A's entry in this cell of the matrix should become zero, thereby removing any vestige of an analogy with the PD. Second, unlike in a PD, the individual and the others are not involved in an independent decision-making process. We are

---

[11] Olson, *Logic of Collective Action,* 12, emphasis added.

dealing with a situation in which their objective is to obtain the collective good (there is no problem about explaining the non-contribution of people who don't want the good). Thus, it would not be rational for an individual to opt for a course of action which he thought might lead to the non-provision of the good he wanted. It follows that the individual must take into account the consequences of the choices of the others. It is whether or not the others pay that determines whether the good is provided. He would only act in the independent, isolated, manner of the PD if he were indifferent between the provision and non-provision of the good. He is not.

Thus, he must consider how likely is it that the good will be supplied, given a group of people who all want it. He must also assume that the others are making the same analysis of the situation as he is. Olson, on the other hand, makes the individual base his prediction on the assumption that the others are motivated differently from him—that is, on the assumption that they will only leave if they notice that their burden has increased. Were we to accept this motivation, whether they would leave the organization would depend on how much the good was valued relative to the slightly increased burden.[12]

Moreover, although A may not believe that the others will notice the effect of his leaving, he is not entitled further to conclude that they will remain in the organization *because* they have not noticed. In fact, if they do not notice anything, and yet continue their membership, they must be making a calculation that is different from the one involved in the increased-burden approach. That is, there are two components to A's perception of the others' calculation: (1) the calculation that it is worth being in the organization at the subscription level which operates while A is a member, and (2) the calculation the others are perceived to make after A has withdrawn his support. According to Olson, because the group is a large one, A does not believe that the others will notice any increased financial burden. That is, A assumes that (2) is not noticeably different from (1). In other words, if the others remain in

---

[12] With this approach there is a difficult extreme case in which, if the net value is sufficiently small, the increased burden of one individual leaving transforms a small net benefit for the others into a net loss, thus causing them to leave the organization. Consider a large group of, say, 10,000 individuals providing a good at a total cost of £999,000. The cost per head is thus £99.90. If the value to each individual is £99.90½, then each individual has a net benefit of ½p; small but perceptible. If one person now leaves, the new cost per head becomes £999,000 divided by 9,999 which is £99.91. Thus, the original net benefit is transformed into an equally small but perceptible net loss, and the organization should fail. This may not be a major objection to the increased-burden approach, but any deductive theory should be consistent across all cases.

the organization, it must be because their first calculation suggested that membership was worth while, and the zero increased-burden argument is irrelevant.

The individual can therefore not rely on the others staying for the reason Olson gives; if they stay, they do so for other reasons (which A must share). The size of the group *per se* does not entail either that they stay in or leave the organization. Olson's mistake lies in supposing that it does—or rather in supposing that A thinks that it does. The organization only fails because Olson makes each member of the *n*-person game systematically attribute the same wrong motive to the others. Wrong, because A perceives the motivation of the others to be the increased burden (which it cannot be) whereas it is in reality exactly the same as his own (*ex hypothesi*). Thus A can actually only be made better off if he is put in a privileged position by introducing an assumption that gives the others a different motivation so that they will not leave; the good will therefore continue to be provided, and A can ride free.

The key question here is: what can we reasonably say about A's perceptions? Under conditions of ignorance (i.e. when the 'game' has never been played before), A would not know whether the others were going to make the same calculation as he, and would have to make an assumption about this. He must assume either that his reasoning is different from the others, or that it is the same. If he assumes the others are not making the same rational calculation (and therefore assumes that the others will stay in the organization), he will leave, thinking that the supply of the good is certain—only to find that everyone else has in fact left, since he was mistaken about their motivation. If he assumes that his motivation is like that of everyone else (i.e. that they too will calculate rationally), A will not leave: he will realize that everyone else is making the same calculation he is and that, if acted upon, this leads to the good not being provided. The possibility of further levels of strategic second-guessing only serves to strengthen the perception that the supply of the good is uncertain.

I maintain that A will only choose to be a free-rider of a good he values if he is certain that there will be something to ride free. 'Free-riding' means benefiting from a good without paying your share of its production costs. It does not simply mean 'not paying', and choosing not to pay is not the equivalent of choosing to free-ride, as the PD analysis implies. In choosing to free-ride the individual is assuming that the good will continue to be provided, otherwise it would be irrational to choose this option. Of course, once A is allowed to take previous experience into account (which is more realistic anyway), he will induce the others' approach from their actions, and will be in a position to estimate how likely it is that the collective good will actually be provided.

Thus, only under the somewhat unrealistic assumptions both that *A* has no information about the behaviour of others and that he arbitrarily (and wrongly) assumes he is different from the others, can we conclude that the organization will fail and that the collective good will not be provided. Indeed, regardless of the consideration of the level of information, it could be argued that it is not unreasonable to assume that in a theory in which individuals are assumed to behave out of rational self-interest, a given rational individual assumes that the others also act out of rational self-interest.

Even when *A* lacks information, there are some contexts in which, if the individual assumes he is different, the consequences of being wrong are so dire that he would choose to subscribe to the organization. For example, if the only water available to a group was highly toxic, the rational, self-interested individual would presumably be better off helping to pay for a purification plant than taking the risk of it not being provided. The individual is sufficiently threatened here that circumstances force co-operation.

As the argument stands so far, the only situation in which the rational, self-interested individual finds he is better off outside the organization is when the continued provision of the good is *guaranteed* in some way. Thus, key factors (though not the only ones) in the calculation determining what the individual will do are whether, at the moment of an individual's decision, the provision of the good seems certain or uncertain, coupled with whether the individual is inside or outside the organization. It is important to distinguish the idea of a good being supplied from that of the supply of a good being *certain*, particularly for those inside the organization. As we have seen, if the provision of a good seems certain, the rational self-interested individual is better off not subscribing; he leaves because he knows the good will still be provided. An individual outside an organization that provides a collective good will not join if there is no risk of the supply of the good being discontinued—that is, if the supply is effectively certain as far as he is concerned. Once the supply of the good is threatened, however, the rational individual will join the organization. The individual thus appears to follows the maxim:

if the supply of the good is uncertain, join; if it is certain, do not join

The certainty or uncertainty of the provision of the good affects the question of how satisfactory the market and the state are as analogies for the group. As we have seen, where the organization does not exist, the rational calculation (with the aforementioned proviso about the assumption concerning the motives of others, and the existence of enough people who will reap a net benefit) leads to the formation of the organization. Where it does exist, those inside seek to maintain it while those outside do not—unless the supply of the good is threatened. Coercion is not a necessary feature of this situation, in the sense that the good could not be provided without it. If there is coercion in such a context, its justification would be on some ideological or moral basis extraneous to the model. (Usually that is the case with the 'closed shop', which is rarely sought in order to prevent the collapse of an organization, but is more commonly justified on moral grounds.)

With the state, the argument is different. Where the state does not exist, coercion is a consequence of the existence of any individuals who either put no value on the creation of the state, or who will have no net benefit and who are unable to create their own state; that is so because of the state's inclusive nature. Once the state has been created, a different situation arises. Exactly how the argument proceeds depends upon what one assumes about the decision-making process, and in particular on whether the provision of the good is certain or not. Although in the real world there often appears to be public money seeking a spending programme, the underlying logic of government decision-making is to the effect that revenue is raised in order to pay for a specific programme. That is, the authorities take a decision to supply a particular good, and legislation is passed authorizing it. The authorities then seek to raise the necessary taxes to fund the programme. In this situation, the provision of the good has become certain from the individual's point of view; it then becomes rational for even an individual who obtains a net benefit to seek to obtain the good without paying his taxes. The state is therefore obliged to resort to coercion. Thus the individual is placed in a different strategic context in the two arguments; this makes the state a poor analogy.

In the case of the perfect market, the collective good in the economic model does not bear the same relationship to the calculation of the rational individual as it does in the group model. Where there is perfect competition, the collective good is the price, which is available to all and is uniform throughout the market. However, unlike the collective good in the case of the group, it is always available. A firm will always obtain the current price for its goods. When Olson speaks of the price being 'destroyed' as a result of rational calculation,[13] this is in no sense analogous to the collapse

---

[13] Olson, *Logic of Collective Action*, 12.

of an organization and the consequent non-provision of the collective good. What happens is that each producer increases output so long as price exceeds marginal cost. Neither the price nor the market cease to exist. The strategic context is therefore quite different. Similarly, Olson's beguilingly simple objection to Marx's theory of class action[14] (namely, that the rational prole will not willingly support a revolution to establish a proletarian government because he would get the benefit anyway) does not hold, because of the uncertainty of the establishment of the proletarian government.

SUMMARY AND CONCLUSION

I have argued that the problems of orthodox group theory are a special case of the problem of collective goods, and that the analogy with the Prisoners' Dilemma is not appropriate. Nor are Olson's analogies with perfect competition and the state helpful, and his basic argument is mistaken. In the context considered here, the good is not provided only if the individual arbitrarily and wrongly assumes that he is different from the others. Otherwise the rational, self-interested individual will voluntarily contribute to a group organized to provide collective benefits.

This approach does not rule out 'free-riding' altogether. The conclusion about voluntary subscription clearly does not hold for all conceivable circumstances; the argument would need to be reworked in different situations, depending on such factors as whether at the given moment the group is organized; whether A is inside or outside the organization; and in particular, whether the supply of the good is certain. For example; if the organization exists, the good is being provided, and A is outside, it is rational for A to be a free-rider until such time as the supply of the good becomes uncertain. Nor does the argument completely rule out the use of inducements or coercion. Such incentives, if part of the rational calculation about joining (i.e. where they are not introduced for, say, moral reasons), would be expected to be used as supplements to the basic rational, self-interested calculation (e.g. where there are not enough takers on the basis of rational self-interest to realize the cost of the good)—perhaps as an alternative to accepting an inferior good.

This picture of interest-group formation and membership seems to be quite consistent with that presented by orthodox group theory, and obviates the need for some of the more artificial devices for

[14] Olson, *Logic of Collective Action*, 106.

explaining interest-group formation—such as that of the organization being created by a professional political entrepreneur who is himself indifferent to the collective good in question.[15]

Indeed, one could go further and suggest that the logic argued for in this paper can be used as the basis for an explanation of the entire pattern of interest groups existing in society at a given moment. In other words, we can say that individuals in society have a constantly (though not necessarily quickly) changing set of perceptions about the net benefits which accrue from the provision of a range of goods, and which are the crucial components in calculations that determine membership, and therefore the configuration of organized groups in society. In so far as the relevant components of the calculation do not change much, the result is a relatively stable pattern of interest groups. As the political context changes and individuals are forced to revise their perceptions, there may be a period of uncertainty until a new set of relatively stable strategies is established.[16] Under the new conditions, the new set of strategies may be such that, whereas a group did not organize under the previous circumstances, it now does. This, surely, is what Truman had in mind when he discussed the idea of potential groups coming into existence.[17] A group of rational individuals with given valuations in one set of circumstances remains unorganized because there is no net benefit to be derived from organization; in the new situation, they consider their interest to be threatened so that their new perceived net benefit results in a change of strategy, and a new interest group is formed. Of course, this type of change is not the only way in which a new organization might arise. For example, the total cost of providing the good is also important. A change in this could also have the effect of producing a new organization. Thus, explanations of the emergence of new interest groups will not necessarily be the same in each case.

I suggest that this approach is both more realistic and more satisfying than the conventional 'economic' one. An explanation that rules out the possibility of individuals voluntarily joining interest groups is not only intuitively odd, but also conflicts with much of our day-to-day experience. There is surely something

[15] See e.g. Robert H. Salisbury, 'An Exchange Theory of Interest Groups', *Midwest Journal of Political Science*, 13 (1969), 1–32.

[16] 'Strategy' here refers to the decision at which an individual arrives when he has completed his calculation based on the relevant factors. The societal process envisaged here has some similarity with the ethologists' view in which evolution takes place against a background of an evolutionarily stable set of genes. See Richard Dawkins, *The Selfish Gene* (Oxford: Clarendon Press, 1976), 93.

[17] Truman, *Governmental Process*, 159.

absurd in the idea that a revolutionary would never find it worth while to overthrow a government and establish a new regime, and also something whimsical in the idea that the Council for the Protection of Rural England was really organized, not to protect rural England, but to provide wine and cheese parties for its members. If lobbying is merely a by-product of whatever function enables an organization to secure its membership, as Olson maintains,[18] then one might ask, as David Marsh does, 'why any interest group continues to attempt to supply the collective good if potential members only join to obtain selective benefits. Why don't interest groups merely supply selective incentives?'[19] They don't because the argument that the rational self-interested individual would voluntarily contribute to the provision of a collective good was wrongly characterized as fallacious.

[18] Olson, *Logic of Collective Action*, 133. The process that gives rise to the by-product is unclear. The problem is not so much to explain how large groups come to be organized, but rather to explain how they come to provide collective goods.

[19] Marsh, 'More on Joining Interest Groups', *British Journal of Political Science*, 8 (1978), 384.

4

THE PLURALISM OF PLURALISM: AN ANTI-THEORY?

GRANT JORDAN

The initial purpose of this paper is simply to define, if possible, the term 'pluralism'. It starts from the assumption that pluralism has been an under-explicit theory; an evolving or (less flatteringly) a mutating theory; an inconsistent theory. These inconstant qualities perhaps explain why pluralism has been 'in the ring' with such different alternatives as élitism, corporatism and totalitarianism. Thus the first issue is whether or not it is possible to recognize pluralism. Is there an agreed description of the suspect? Since pluralism is so vague a set of ideas it is difficult to understand how opponents can have rejected it with such confidence. It is also suggested that pluralism has been a lucky theory to the extent that the empirical developments of the past decades make pluralism a more tenable option than it was in the 1950s. Pluralism also looks more respectable in the 1980s than the 1950s as the idea of the 'market' has regained popularity.

However, although this paper seeks to restore pluralist sources to the centre of the discipline it is not argued that as they stand they offer a satisfactory and final account of how decisions are made in western democratic societies. The work is surprisingly patchy, even when approached sympathetically. It needs integration and development. Moreover, apart from the quality of the pluralist accounts, there is a separate issue of whether any *single* model is likely to be adequate. This is not to say that there is an obviously superior account with which to replace pluralism, but to express suspicion of the notion that we should expect to find any adequate model that does not feature explicit variety as its core.

WHAT DO PLURALISTS SAY ABOUT PLURALISM?

It is difficult to cite an authoritative statement of the theory of pluralism. Who exactly are the pluralists? Pluralism just might be

Reprinted by permission of Blackwell Publishers, Journals Department.

an exceptional theory in the sense of being exceptionally useful. It is certainly an exceptional theory in the sense that everyone who writes about it wants to make their exceptions to any generally accepted conclusions.

It is all too often and too readily assumed that modern pluralism is some kind of straight-line development from turn-of-the-century philosophies of that label. Certainly it has something to do with their concerns about limiting the all-powerful state but the relationship is more of retrospective recognition than a positive steering of modern research by historical precedent. To stress the role of interest groups, the modern pluralist does not rely upon anti-statism to reach conclusions about the importance of interest groups in interaction with bureaucracies. This new empirical orientation was perhaps encouraged by the anti-institutionalism of earlier writers but it was not fundamentally dependent on these sources.

Dahl's Account

The obvious place to look for the precise meaning of the term 'pluralism' is the work of Robert Dahl, but disturbingly we discover that he himself looks back on his early work and recognizes that the concept seemed to develop a life of its own. It was not carefully defined. About *Who Governs* he wrote, '*Pace* some interpretions, the book was not written to advance a general "pluralist theory of politics" . . . In hindsight, it might have been better to set out a more explicit theory. But perhaps not.'[1] None the less, the citation for Dahl's Woodrow Wilson Foundation Award for *Who Governs* commended his, 'Dynamic, *pluralist* [emphasis added] theory of local power structure . . .'.

Dahl did define another term—polyarchy—with some care. It was introduced as a label for a rough approximation to the democratic goal, in that non-leaders exercise a relatively high degree of control over leaders. This concept of polyarchy allowed Dahl and Lindblom to distinguish between the ideal type of democracy and the practices of imperfect approximation to democracy found in actual societies, which could be more or less democratic.[2] It was polyarchy rather than pluralism that was Dahl's primary concern and he did not satisfactorily relate the one term to the other. It is plain that he did not see himself as developing a formal pluralist

[1] R. A. Dahl, *Who Governs* (New Haven, Conn.: Yale University Press, 1961); id., 'Polyarchy, Pluralism and Scale', *Scandinavian Political Studies*, 7/4 (1984).

[2] R. A. Dahl and C. E. Lindblom, *Politics, Economics and Welfare* (New York: Harper & Row, 1976).

theory. If we, with hindsight, see him subconsciously performing that role it is something that we read into his account.

In *Who Governs* his first sentence was: 'In a political system where nearly every adult may vote but where knowledge, wealth, social position, access to officials, and other resources are unequally distributed, who actually governs?' He noted that running counter to the legal equality of citizens in the voting booth was an unequal distribution of the resources that could be used to influence voters or, between elections, officials. Dahl then reviews several possible ways in which, given these inequalities, the question of who actually governs in a democracy can be answered. He slips—by his own terminology—into the conflating of polyarchy with democracy.

Dahl's guiding questions in *Who Governs* included:

Are the inequalities in resources of influence 'cumulative' or 'noncumulative'? That is, are the people who are better off in one resource also better off in others? In other words, does the way in which political resources are distributed encourage oligarchy or pluralism?

How are important political decisions actually made?

Do leaders tend to cohere in their policies and form a sort of ruling group, or do they tend to divide, conflict, and bargain? Is the pattern of leadership, in short, oligarchical or pluralistic?[3]

These questions show that Dahl was using pluralism in a way that is much more 'normal' than his efforts—before and afterwards—to present pluralism as some ingredient of polyarchy. His next chapter confirms this. It was *not* entitled 'From Oligarchy to Polyarchy' but 'From Oligarchy to Pluralism'. It begins:

In the course of the past two centuries, New Haven [*his focus of study*] has gradually changed from oligarchy to pluralism. Accompanying and probably causing this change—one might properly call it a revolution—appears to be a profound alteration in the way political resources are distributed among the citizens of New Haven. This silent socioeconomic revolution has not substituted equality for inequality so much as it has involved a shift from cumulative inequalities in political resources . . . to noncumulative or dispersed inequalities.

He picks this point up much later

This change in New Haven is fully consistent with three of the key hypotheses in this study. First, a number of old American cities . . . have passed through a roughly similar transformation from a system in which resources of influence were highly concentrated to a system in which they

3 Dahl, *Who Governs*.

are highly dispersed . . . *the present dispersion does not represent equality of resources but fragmentation.*[4]

He lists the characteristics of the system of dispersed inequalities as:

1. Many different kinds of resources for influencing officials are available to different citizens.
2. With few exceptions, these resources are unequally distributed.
3. Individuals best off in their access to one kind of resource are often badly off with respect to many other resources.
4. No one influence resource dominates all the others in all or even in most key decisions.
5. With some exceptions, an influence resource is effective in some issue-areas or in some specific decisions but not in all.
6. Virtually no one, and certainly no group of more than a few individuals, is entirely lacking in some influence resources.[5]

It could hardly be more clear that for Dahl the essential feature of political resources in a polyarchy or a pluralist society was that they were dispersed, not that they were equal. While the above list represents what would for many be a definition of pluralism, Dahl did not so label it, though since this was part of his 'Pluralist Democracy: An Explanation' we can reasonably see his notion of pluralism as connected with dispersed inequality.

For Dahl the question was: 'Who then, rules *in* a pluralist democracy?'[6] It seems that such a label as 'pluralist' is more appropriate as a *conclusion* than as a starting-point. Dahl himself seemed to envisage such a use when he posed another question: 'In other words, does the way in which political resources are distributed encourage oligarchy or pluralism?'[7]

There is ambiguity in Dahl's account of the role of elections as an expression of political conflict. He claims that no sooner had the importance of the political party as an instrument of democracy been discovered by political scientists, than other analysts reduced the political party to little more than a collection of 'interest groups'. He summarized this approach in terms that if the party was the molecule the group was the atom, 'everything could be explained simply by studying the atoms. Neither people nor parties but interest groups, it was said, are the true units in the political system.' He claimed that this theory of democracy postulated that the group could unite the resources of the weak. He concludes this description—which we might again label pluralist but Dahl does not—by saying:

---

[4] Dahl, *Who Governs*, 227 (emphasis added).   [5] Ibid. 228.
[6] Ibid. 86.   [7] Ibid. 7.

Thus some theorists would answer our question by replying that interest groups govern; most of the actions of government can be explained . . . as the result of struggles among groups of individuals with differing interests and varying resources of influence.[8]

Thus Dahl recognizes very well what was to be labelled modern pluralism but he did not identify himself with it and indeed his tone was sceptical.

Polsby's Version

For Polsby pluralism was clearly a methodology to discover who ruled in a community. In Polsby's hands—more so than for Dahl—the New Haven exercise was part of academic combat with élitist interpretations of American politics. Polsby claims a lineage for his 'pluralist presumptions' that includes Bentley, Herring, Truman, and others. Dahl seems to have resisted this idea of a coherent school. Nor does Dahl so boldly and baldly set out the features of pluralism as Polsby:

Pluralists . . . see American society as fractured into congeries of hundreds of small special interest groups, with incompletely overlapping memberships, widely differing power bases, and a multitude of techniques for exercising influence on decisions salient to them . . .[9]

Dahl, of course, worked with Polsby in related studies of New Haven, but Polsby was making clearer the methodology that Dahl was using. This was to test the fashionable élitist theory. The essence of the pluralist approach—used initially for discovering community rather than national-level power—was that it did not make a prior assumption that *some* group necessarily dominates. The first research question was thus not 'Who runs this community?' but 'Does anyone at all run this community?'[10] Polsby then suggests that it is necessary to study several significant issue areas in some depth to discover if the same pattern of outcomes is found in all areas. If the same pattern was found in all areas studied, Polsby recognized that an élitist conclusion would have been reached. He did admit, however, that the expectation was—from past research—that it was unlikely that the same power-holders dominated all issue areas. He argued that, none the less, 'the presumption that a power élite is unlikely does not . . . prevent finding one'. Thus in theory at least,

    [8] Ibid. 5.
    [9] N. Polsby, *Community Power and Political Theory* (New Haven, Conn.: Yale University Press, 1971), 118.
    [10] Ibid. 113.

there was a distinction between pluralist assumptions, pluralist methodology and pluralist conclusions.

However, Polsby's concluding chapter admitted: 'I do not mean to imply that a pluralist theory has emerged which successfully explains the shaping and sharing of values in American local life.'[11] Pluralist theory is thus again a tentative offering. This is mentioned not to minimize the value of the approach but to note that it is a difficult target to criticize—and that critics often redefine in more positive and exaggerated form when they seek to dispute it. He noted that instead of constructing theory, pluralist orientated researchers had focused upon case studies or had indulged in metaphors about 'the ecology of game' or 'the contest for prizes'. Polsby complained that neither of these substitutes for theory had performed the function of theory. He forecast that we might anticipate 'the differentiation of a few or several different forms of pluralistic decision-making . . .'.[12] This still seems necessary. He also noted that the desirability for a developed theory of pluralism was not lessened by the fact that it could be converted by the unwary into an ideology, thus imprisoning rather than disciplining thought.[13]

In his 1980 second edition, Polsby argues that the intellectual development that he had looked for had not occurred. He suggested that anyone entering this field was in danger of augmenting a scholarly morass and subtracting from the sum total of human knowledge.

Truman's Contribution

If Dahl, unlike Polsby, has not really been engaged in a debate about the pluralist approach—and indeed has added weight to his own reservations over the years—a similar lack of interest in discussing the history and content of the idea was shown by David Truman. The second edition in 1971 of *The Governmental Process* was reprinted word for word, reference for reference from the first edition.[14] A new introduction provided an opportunity to relate his work to that of Dahl. Instead he said that, 'once a book leaves the author's hands it has a life of its own that has to be respected'.[15]

It is now uncontroversial to regard Truman as a pluralist. If he is, he is a subconscious one. Like Molière's M. Jourdain who had talked

---

[11] N. Polsby, *Community Power and Political Theory*, 122.
[12] Ibid. 138.   [13] Ibid. 123.
[14] D. B. Truman, *The Governmental Process: Political Interest and Public Opinion* (New York: Alfred Knopf; 2nd edn., 1971).
[15] Ibid. p. xviii.

prose for 40 years without realizing it, Truman was describing pluralism without ever seeing himself as a pluralist. The term 'pluralist' is used to mean 'them' rather than 'us'. For him the pluralists were that rejected school which reached its height in the first quarter of the twentieth century. He argued that the pluralists were so bent on discrediting the state-centred conception of politics that they overlooked the significance of their own central ideas. Perhaps the same might be said of Truman: he did not notice the significance of his neopluralism.

Truman's major contribution was perhaps his proposition that it is the overlap of interests held by any individual or group that mediates the conflict. Overlapping membership is thus put forward as a factor limiting extremism. This was to be a feature of pluralist thought, although not advanced by Truman in the context of a shared set of ideas with Dahl and others. Instead of discovering and aligning himself with a coherent neopluralist school, Truman discussed his work in terms of the group literature that had developed in the US in the 20 years between his editions. He did not like what he found. He was not prepared to be a self-confessed group theorist, far less a pluralist. He argued:

The interest group focus of *The Governmental Process* has, in the intervening years, become a major emphasis—perhaps a predominant one—in political science, especially as practised in the United States. What in 1950 was a somewhat unusual way of looking at the governmental scene has become a part of the conventional wisdom of the discipline.[16]

One might more accurately say that dissent from pluralism became the academic orthodoxy.

Several points can be retrieved from Truman's brief comments on the literature of the two decades between his editions. Truman complains that critics confuse two types of objection. There are some who do not accept pluralist theory as it seems to fail to 'fit' when there is change. There are some who dislike the operating system of the US; they dislike the practice of pluralism. We might further distinguish complaints that the US is criticized as being imperfectly pluralist.

He too was not a believer in the existence of equality between groups: 'Any system . . . tends to discriminate in favour of established groups and interests, and it may deny to new groups access to points of decision.'[17] Truman in 1971 also pointed out that although he found the phrase 'the public interest' in danger of being

---

[16] D. B. Truman, *The Governmental Process: Political Interest and Public Opinion*, p. xxv.
[17] Ibid. p. xii.

meaningless for analytical purposes, he did not intend to endorse the view that we should be happy to be left with nothing other than a process of contention, bargaining and pressure by organized groups.[18]

Truman raps the fingers of those pressure-group writers who had mechanically and narrowly ascribed too much to the interest group:

A third weakness associated with this research vogue is a simplistic conception of the process, one that assigns to interest groups a monopoly of political initiative. In this view governmental actors . . . are no more than referees of group conflict . . . The obvious error of this superficial viewpoint is that it treats an extreme situation as if it were typical . . . Locating the sources of initiative and identifying the variable roles of governmental actors are among the most challenging assignments of the political scientist. Therefore, to assume these problems out of existence is a kind of intellectual abdication.[19]

Truman includes himself in the general behavioural camp and literally underlines that the book was about *process*. The emphasis that he gives to the sense of process links up with a series of interwar studies by Odegard and others which simply tried to establish how policy was made. Truman described how the experience in government of various political scientists in the Second World War contributed to an appreciation that constitutional formalities alone could not show how the system actually operated.

Arguably, much of the pluralist approach is connected with the empirical observation of decisions that came from the reaction against institutionalism in political science. Pluralism seems to be a theory acceptable to those engaged in empirical observation and to be criticized by those who reject the notion that one can satisfactorily report on the structure of power by decision-making studies.

Lindblom's Discussion

Lindblom has addressed the topic of pluralism more directly than did Dahl and both say more about it in their revisionist work in the late 1970s.[20] Lindblom distanced himself from other pluralists.[21] He admits that his discussion of mutual adjustment could be described

[18] D. B. Truman, *The Governmental Process: Political Interest and Public Opinion*, p. xlvi.
[19] Ibid. p. xxv.
[20] e.g. R. A. Dahl, *A Preface to Economic Democracy* (Cambridge: Polity Press, 1985); C. E. Lindblom, *Politics and Markets* (New York: Basic Books, 1977).
[21] C. E. Lindblom, *The Intelligence of Democracy* (New York: Free Press, 1965).

as attending to some unfinished business in pluralist thought but he immediately goes on to say that he either rejected or did not employ the key features of English pluralist thought of Maitland, Figgis, Laski, and Cole which challenged the sovereignty of the state. Lindblom establishes that the state in his scheme was more than the passive register of the competition between interests. He similarly dissents from what he presents as American pluralism. 'The emphasis that Bentley and others give to the interest group goes too far'. He says that

Bentley, Truman, Latham and Herring, to mention a representative sample, all recognize that public agencies or groups of public officials can themselves constitute interest groups . . . For the most part, however, the prime movers in the pluralist tradition are private groups . . .[22]

For Lindblom, government was often the major participant. He wanted to distance himself from the belief that all interaction of groups was beneficial. He thought this general endorsement was as unwise as a general condemnation. He also argued that pluralists had generally bypassed questions of rationality; indeed, they had assumed that the goal of dispersing power had meant that irrationality and inefficiency had to be accepted. However, though Lindblom was here arguing with the early pluralists, it could be said that he was constructing a better basis for the pluralist argument than hitherto existed. Thus although Lindblom specifically denied his links with other pluralists, he was reforming pluralist thought rather than rejecting it.

One remarkable feature of the pluralist orientation is that it is reinforced by a separate literature on decision-making, namely, incrementalism. The incremental approach as set out by Lindblom, Braybrooke and Lindblom, and Wildavsky, rested on the notion of multiplicity of participants, each with some distinctive position and some political resources.[23] Therefore, the desirability of a society with dispersed resources was augmented by the claimed virtues of the incrementalist methods, which gave a means to make decisions by learning from experience.

The fragmentation of policy-making to a multiplicity of strategic problem solvers is seen as the key to coordination.

Groups become watchdogs for values they fear will become neglected by other groups . . . It is possible for each decision maker to specialize in this

[22] Ibid. 13.
[23] D. Braybrooke and C. E. Lindblom, *A Strategy of Decision* (New York: Free Press, 1963); A. Wildavsky, *The Politics of the Budgetary Process* (New York: Little, Brown & Co., 1984).

way since . . . none are required to anticipate all the possible failures and
adverse consequences of a decision . . .

In explaining the co-ordination process . . . we have made no reference to
centrally controlled adjustments of decision makers to each other. They
adjust because they are pursuing a partisan purpose.[24]

If we attempt to pull together the elements of a general pluralist
model from these accounts, a common core emerges. First, empirical
studies had confirmed that power was fragmented and decentralized
in western systems. There are dispersed inequalities. Secondly, there
was a consequent assumption that groups with interests that were
being neglected could and would have attention paid to their
objections, although all groups could not be 'winners'. Thirdly, this
dispersion of power was a desirable feature in any system
approaching the status of a democracy. Fourthly, understanding the
practice of a political system has to be based upon observation of the
process of policy development. Fifthly, political outcomes in
different policy sectors will reflect different power holders and the
different processes within these areas. Sixthly, the formal process of
political choice through elections and parliamentary activity was
likely to mislead about the actual distribution of power. Seventhly,
there was an assumption that the interaction of interests would
supply a practical alternative to the 'general will' as the source of
legitimate authority. To this core we can add Miller's point that the
instability of the pluralistic bargaining process helps bind participants to the process,[25] tomorrow may well produce a better
outcome.

Pluralism is the theoretical window-dressing adopted by a
generation of students of the policy process who have found that it
better accords with their findings than does the picture-book
account of policy-making through party manifestos and Parliament.
This may not be respectable methodology but realism must respect
that few of the 'pluralist' investigations are founded on a pre-existing
theory. Still, if one aspect of pluralism is its implication for
understanding the decision process in a particular sector, there is
also the larger question of what conditions within a society advance
the society to democratic status. Pluralism is not simply a model to
understand a particular decision, for Dahl especially it is a means to
understand and thereby support the fragile system of polyarchy.

---

[24] Lindblom, *Intelligence of Democracy*, 156.
[25] N. T. Miller, 'Pluralism and Social Choice', *American Political Science Review*, 77
(1983), cited in F. Bealey, *Democracy in the Contemporary State* (Oxford: Clarendon
Press, 1988).

WHAT THE PLURALISTS DID NOT SAY

Though pluralism is much disputed, the pluralists seem to have anticipated most of the reservations about the normative desirability of the system they outlined. It is a puzzle that there were so many attacks upon pluralism when there was such a poorly articulated 'dominant paradigm'. Dahl has commented that:

Pluralist theory came to designate a strange melange of ideas. In fact, a good deal of 'theory' consisted of interpretations by hostile critics . . . frequently the result was a 'theory' that probably no competent political theorist—pluralist or not—would find plausible.[26]

It is easier to find pluralism described by its critics than by its advocates. Moreover, Dahl is a much better source on the difficulties associated with what was later termed pluralism than he is as an advocate of that pluralism. It seems a commonplace to suggest that Dahl was once a naïve and uncritical pluralist who recanted and began to attack his earlier position. In fact the original material avoided the pitfalls that critics are inclined to read into pluralism. For example, Dahl and Lindblom plainly disliked the notion of the state as ringholder for interests. They noted that there may well be no 'sovereign people':

Many decisions are made by a loose confederacy of giant organizations . . . Under those conditions decisions can be arrived at only through horse trading, bargaining, the negotiation of treaties. Stripped of its glamour, shorn of its magical legalistic incantations, government very often turns out to be simply one of the bargainers . . . government must engage in horse trading with corporations, trade unions, farm organizations, and other groups with control in the society.

In describing this picture, Dahl and Lindblom do *not* accept it as desirable:

there is no guarantee that bargaining among organizations will necessarily produce results that accord with the highly ranked preferences of the greater number; gigantic bargaining organizations can be as much out of touch with 'particularized situations' as the government . . .[27]

They say there is no guarantee that bargaining will produce decisions that even crudely accord with the preferences of the greater number. They say that to secure these kinds of outcomes, the government hierarchy must, at the very minimum, intervene in the bargaining process.

[26] Dahl, 'Polyarchy, Pluralism and Scale'.
[27] Dahl and Lindblom, *Politics, Economics and Welfare*, 498–501.

They criticize the notion that national level bargaining between interest groups will give satisfactory outcomes:

It is one thing to recognize that in plain fact the greater number cannot rule: that faced with the power of gigantic social organizations of enormous control, their representatives in government must sometimes bargain, concede, compromise, and appease in order to avoid the destruction of minimum consensus . . . and perhaps even civil war. But it is quite another to turn this social fact into a prescription of the desirable, and to argue in effect that politicians should not even attempt to exercise 'the last say', but should turn that power over to national organizations bargaining among themselves. For if the goal, and the machinery of approximating political equality, majority rule, and polyarchy are abandoned, then it is difficult to find any criteria within the Western tradition to justify one bargain as against another.[28]

On the notion of equality among groups Dahl and Lindblom said:

this major error might be called the fallacy of *the false equation*; that the arguments for political and subjective equality among individuals can be transferred to groups. But, of course, this is absurd . . . How far can the absurdity go? Should the 'rich' have equal bargaining power with the 'poor'—even if the rich are 1 per cent of the population and the poor are 20 per cent . . . Should both be equal to the middle class?[29]

Dahl's own qualifications to his description of the American system remove the naïve and complacent tone:

To be 'heard' covers a wide range of activities . . . Clearly, it does not mean that every group has an equal control over the outcome. In American politics, as in all other societies, control over decisions is unevenly distributed; neither individuals nor groups are political equals. When I say that a group is heard 'effectively' I mean that one or more officials are not only ready to listen to the noise, but expect to suffer in some significant way if they do not placate the group, its leaders, or its most vociferous members.[30]

Though pluralism has been out of academic fashion in the past decade, its problem is not that it has disintegrated under the stresses of operationalization but it has never gelled into that coherent model at which critics can take ready aim. It is a rather simple idea about the nature of political life, not a sophisticated set of observations, predictions and value positions. Criticism is misdirected if it attacks the pluralist account for a lack of homogeneity which no one has pretended exists.

[28] Dahl and Lindblom, *Politics, Economics and Welfare*, 507.
[29] Ibid. 504.
[30] R. A. Dahl, *A Preface to Democratic Theory* (Chicago, Ill.: Chicago University Press, 1956), 145.

Pluralism is perhaps no more than an anti-theory.[31] What it is rejecting is more important than what it is establishing. The pluralist image of a complex political process with multiple participants and uncertain outcomes is a denial of élite and Marxist accounts. As Cox argued in 1988: 'pluralism as a concept is not an explanation of anything. On the contrary, pluralism is a description of a political form of the state, in which the question of which interests dominate is an open empirical question.'[32]

CORPORATISM OR WHAT SHOULD HAVE HAPPENED IN 1979

If we accept this very weak defence of pluralism we might then better understand the pluralist frustration of the past decade. Schmitter's line is now well known. It was just the sort of thing to appeal to those of a radical cast of mind: in other words, to almost the whole profession. It attacked the 'conceptual torpor and theoretical orthodoxy in the discipline of political science'. He presented the concept of corporatism as, 'a sort of paradigmatic revolution when juxtaposed to the long predominant "pluralist" way of describing and analysing the role of organized interest groups'.[33] The corporatist approach thus stood as a corrective to what was seen as conventional pluralist political science, although it might be noted in passing that few political scientists, explicitly at least, view themselves as pluralists. Schmitter's well-known definition of corporatism saw 'the constituent units . . . organised into a limited number of singular, compulsory, non-competitive, hierarchically ordered and functionally differentiated categories . . .'.[34] Corporatism was then presented not as an ideal type to contrast with western societies but as a summary description of political practice in these societies.

Though Schmitter saw similarities between the models, he was seeking to present a clear alternative to pluralism. In the pluralist model, he suggested, there are a large number of competing groups. In a corporatist system there are a few groups, each in a specially

---

[31] I wish to thank Brendan O'Leary for making this point in very useful comments on an earlier draft of this article. His criticisms have, on the whole, been avoided rather than met.

[32] A. Cox, 'The Old and New Testament of Corporatism: Is it a Political Form or a Method of Policy Making?', *Political Studies*, 36/2 (1988), 303.

[33] P. Schmitter, 'Still the Century of Corporatism?', and 'Introduction', P. Schmitter and G. Lehmbruch (eds.), *Trends Towards Corporatist Intermediation* (London: Sage, 1979); Lehmbruch and Schmitter, *Patterns of Corporatist Policy-Making* (London: Sage, 1982).

[34] Schmitter, 'Still the Century of Corporatism', 13.

privileged relationship with the state. He stressed that the groups have a dual role: both articulating demands on behalf of members and controlling members on behalf of government. Some authors would lay great stress on the fact that in a corporatist system the groups regulate members on behalf of the state but it is difficult to imagine pluralist bargaining if the groups cannot control their members and fulfil their agreements.

However, as well as presenting an alternative to pluralism—which given the scrappy state of pluralist theory seems perfectly legitimate—Schmitter seemed to be inclined to throw out not only the baby and the bathwater but also the bathroom and the whole rambling mansion of pluralism. As Almond complained with his celebrated remark in connection with Berger's *Organizing Interests in Western Europe*,[35] 'The casualness of the search of the earlier literature and the distortion of its contents are serious weaknesses in an otherwise important contribution to the interest group literature.[36] The claim is that the original corporatist assault on pluralism nowhere made a realistic effort to engage in debate with the antecedent arguments.

Almond's message was that corporatism was a variety of pluralism, to be distinguished from a more disaggregated competitive variety at one extreme and from a state-controlled variety at the other. This was not, as some supporters of corporatism assumed, a statement about the superiority of pluralism over corporatism or a determination to concede that nothing was new. It was a testament to the immense confusion that already surrounded pluralism. Almond's point was that pluralism was a label for a very broad set of concerns that included the questions now posed by the corporatists. Almond said:

> Thus, the questions we ask about interest groups ought to be sufficiently versatile to grapple with differing historical contexts. We do not need a new theory whenever things seem to go awry. Perhaps, before we declare them obsolete, we need to know, and to understand a bit better, the theories we have. When Schmitter proclaimed that the century of corporatism was still with us, our knowledge was already such as to suggest that some degree of pluralism was built into modern differentiated societies, whether authoritarian or democratic.[37]

The consequence of presenting corporatism as a radically new paradigm was that it created a debate about its pretensions to

[35] S. D. Berger (ed.), *Organizing Interests in Western Europe: Pluralism, Corporatism and the Transformation of Politics* (Cambridge: Cambridge University Press, 1981).

[36] G. Almond, 'Corporatism, Pluralism and Professional Memory', *World Politics*, 25/2 (1983), 252.

[37] Ibid. 251.

novelty that detracted from the ways in which it was novel. Interest group participation in the running of centralized economic planning was not the concern of the so-called pluralists of the 1950s but it did not invalidate their work. It has not been profitable to spend a decade ignoring the existing literature and starting our discussion of economically sophisticated western democracies from the specialist work of historical and authoritarian corporatism. They deserve attention but not as the foundations of the study of contemporary society.

THE PLURALISMS OF THE 1970S

While Schmitter's idea of pluralism as 'units organized into an unspecified number of multiple, voluntary, competitive, nonhierarchically ordered and self-determined . . . categories'[38] was a crude summary of the pluralism of the 1950s, there is just about a resemblance. However in the 1960s and 1970s decision-making studies suggested quite a different model of interest-group activity was cohabiting under the pluralist label. Schmitter suggested that pluralism was about equal access, competition and lack of governmental control. But a school of interpretation as suggested by Truman's emphasis upon regularized relationships in *The Governmental Process* had clearly emerged. This is most fully described perhaps in Randall Ripley and Grace Franklin's book *Congress: The Bureaucracy and Public Policy*.[39] There they describe the sub-government phenomenon. Even earlier there was work by Lowi, Freeman, Cater, and others.[40] This concerned labels such as 'subgovernment', 'iron triangle', and 'segmented pluralism'. All this work was based on the assumption that there is *not* open competition and that access is denied to groups not in clientelistic relations with departments or agencies. This is so obviously a different idea from the pluralism of *Who Governs* that it is remarkable that the distinction was obscured for so long.

Writing in the US in 1978, Kelso described the first type as *laissez-faire* pluralism. He presents this form of pluralism as involving competition among political élites and bargaining among interest

[38] Schmitter, 'Still the Century of Corporatism', 15.

[39] R. Ripley and G. Franklin, *Congress: The Bureaucracy and Public Policy* (Homewood, Ill.: Dorsey, 1984), 8.

[40] T. Lowri, 'Four Systems of Policy, Politics and Choice', *Public Administration Review*, 32 (1972); J. L. Freeman, *The Political Process* (New York: Random House, 1964); D. Carter, *Power in Washington* (New York: Random House, 1964).

groups. He says that like their *laissez-faire* counterparts in economics, such pluralists view the political arena as a competitive market-place in which any entrepreneur can gain entry to sell his views. However, Kelso also went on to describe quite a different sort of model, the sort used by Cater, Freeman and others. This he called *corporate pluralism*. He presents this second type as follows:

Lowi and McConnell see the fragmentation of the polity into a series of small, autonomous fiefdoms . . . certain groups have been able to acquire controlling power within individual policy areas . . . various parties have been able to isolate their detractors and enjoy the luxury of making decisions without negotiating or bargaining with their competitors. Any self-correcting pressures . . . have been overwhelmed . . .[41]

Separately from Kelso a number of writers in Europe had used the corporate pluralist term. It was probably first used by Stein Rokkan. In a chapter in 1966 he had the famous passage:

The crucial decisions on economic policy are rarely taken in the parties or in Parliament: the central arena is the bargaining table where the Government authorities meet directly with the trade union leaders, the representatives of the farmers, the small holders, and the fishermen, and the delegates of the Employers' Association. These yearly rounds of negotiations have in fact come to mean more in the lives of rank and file citizens than the formal elections.[42]

The idea was taken up by Robert Kvavik, who distinguished between corporate pluralism and *competitive pluralism*.[43] Writing with Martin Heisler in 1974, Kvavik discussed group participation in the decision-making process on a continuing basis. For them access was established and structured. The Heisler–Kvavik discussion of 'structured co-optation' (a recurrent phrase) is manifestly relevant for a discussion of realistic models of modern interest politics and clearly fits a segmented pluralism/sectorized corporatism version of politics. They identify, 'a scheme of sectoral representation akin to neo-corporatism or perhaps more accurately, corporate pluralism'.[44] Schmitter cites this work only to dismiss it. In fact this form of pluralism is very different from competitive or *laissez-faire* pluralism and is difficult to disentangle from corporatism.

[41] W. A. Kelso, *American Democratic Theory* (Westport, Conn.: Greenwood Press, 1978).

[42] S. Rokkan, in R. Dahl (ed.), *Political Opposition in Western Democracies* (New Haven, Conn. and London: Yale University Press, 1966).

[43] R. Kvavik, *Interest Groups in Norwegian Politics* (Princeton, NJ: Princeton University Press, 1964).

[44] M. Heisler and R. Kvavik, 'Patterns of European Politics', in M. Heisler (ed.), *Politics in Europe* (New York: David McKay, 1974).

The idea of corporatism being a post-pluralist paradigm revolution is eroded when one takes into account these variants of pluralism. One of the prominent corporatism scholars, Lehmbruch claimed that it was with the intimate mutual penetration of state bureaux and large interest organizations that the traditional concept of interest representation becomes quite inappropriate for a theoretical understanding of corporatism. But what was the iron triangle literature if it was not about intimate mutual penetration.

This weakness in the corporatist revolution is aggravated when we consider the *societal corporatism* version of corporatism. Its features are more akin to pluralism than the state version allows. Why this is particularly problematic is that it is societal corporatism that is seen as present in post-liberal, advanced capitalist, organized democratic welfare states. In other words it is the ill-distinguished version that we are forced to apply to the cases that particularly interest us. The cost of making the definition more relevant is to make it less distinctive. Martin has concluded that under societal corporatism governments and groups are in a bargaining relationship varying only in degree from pluralist forms.[45]

COMMON GROUND?

There have been a number of restatements by both Schmitter and Lehmbruch. The latter distinguishes between sectoral corporatism and corporatist concertation. Sectoral corporatism he presents as limited to specific sectors of the economy or to specific policy areas. There are strong institutional links between government and organizations. There are regular consultations and group representation on advisory bodies.[46] Schmitter also accepts such a distinction and indeed goes on to point out that 'the net results of "sectoral" or "selective" corporatisms is a pattern of entrenched policy segmentation which renders more difficult . . . efforts at . . . comprehensive concertation . . .'.[47] This sort of distinction removes the problem of a barrier between corporatism and corporate pluralism: the societal corporatism model is clearly a relabelling of the corporate pluralist concept. In this new light it is also clearer exactly what a full

[45] R. Martin, 'Pluralism and the New Corporatism', *Political Studies*, 31/1 (1983), 86.

[46] G. Lehmbruch, 'Concertation and the Structure of Corporatist Networks', in J. Goldthorpe (ed.), *Order and Conflict in Contemporary Capitalism* (Oxford: Oxford University Press, 1984).

[47] P. Schmitter, 'Neo-Corporatism and the State', in W. Grant (ed.), *The Political Economy of Corporatism* (London: Macmillan, 1985), 47.

corporatist system would look like. In essence corporatism is about attempts at macro-level and cross-sectoral political management. The importance of this new distinction in the corporatist literature is perhaps underscored by looking at the case of the US. It is well provided with examples of subgovernments or sectoral corporatism but, compared with European examples, is underdeveloped in terms of centralized corporatist concertation.

Now that corporatism has moved to be an ideal-type rather than summary label, its utility has improved. However, as this common ground of sorts has emerged between the revised corporatists and the qualified pluralists, an extra term has been added to the analytical vocabulary. Dissenting from the comparatively tidy corporate pluralist model—specifically its iron triangle form—in 1978 Hugh Heclo presented his *issue network* proposition.[48] This discussed the erosion and breakdown of subgovernments through the increased number and influence of non-clientelistic groups. It can be argued that the iron triangle epithet exaggerated the tendencies to rigid sectorization implied by the subgovernment writers but Heclo was claiming that the policy process had so changed that such an orderly image as the iron triangle was no longer appropriate. This image of a recontested policy market is echoed in a number of American sources such as Gais, *et al.*[49] There is a very different image of interest-group activity here. Whereas the corporate pluralists saw the closing down of competition in favour of certain established interests, there seems here to be an idea of a competition between interests with different goals and values. This stress on the increase in the number of competing pressure groups brings to mind Wilson's earlier argument that the claim by Dahl and Truman in the 1950s and 1960s of widely dispersed power and numerous interests was *more valid* in the 1970s than it had been earlier. His conclusion was 'Towards Pluralism'. He said the 'interest groups have come closer in short, to playing the role they were always supposed to—but did not—in American politics'.[50]

In summary then, the later work would suggest that western political systems are not slipping gradually towards the order and predictability of anything like corporatism but that the mobilization of more and more groups—often of a consumerist, public interest or environmental nature—demands a less orderly model of the

[48] H. Heclo, 'Issue Networks and the Executive Establishment', in A. King (ed.), *The New American Political System* (Washington, DC: American Enterprise Institute, 1978).

[49] T. H. Gais, M. Peterson, and J. Walker, 'Interest Groups, Iron Triangle and Representative Institutions', *British Journal of Political Science*, 14/2 (1984).

[50] G. Wilson, *Interest Groups in the USA* (Oxford: Clarendon Press, 1981), 145.

process. At least in some policy areas this requires a move back from the corporate pluralism of the 1970s to the competitive pluralism of the 1950s.

It can therefore be seen that the theoretical menu is not an either/or choice between pluralism or corporatism because the original pluralist accounts always had two important strains. Some form of competitive pluralism versus sectoral or mesocorporatism/corporate pluralism look like the options with most relevance for western political systems. But there is a growing range of work that says that our conclusions are likely to be different sector by sector; that we cannot draw conclusions about *the* system as a pattern of sectorally different processes exist. Salisbury, *et al.* claim that there are simply different arrangements in different sectors: 'Domain subsystems have been seen to have relatively stable patterns of interaction, quite sharply ideological and bipolar in the labor policy domain but fragmented, primarily among sets of specialized producer organizations, in the other areas',[51] Laumann and Knoke in *The Organizational State* also suggest that the appropriate unit of analysis for studies of policy formation is not the state understood in the institutional sense but the state as a collection of policy arenas incorporating both governmental and private actors. They define their key concept of the policy domain as a subsystem 'identified by specifying a substantively defined criterion of mutual relevance or common orientation among a set of consequential actors concerned with formulating, advocating, and selecting courses of action (i.e. policy options) that are intended to resolve the delimited substantive problems in question'.[52]

DO WE STILL NEED PLURALISM?

This review has found no well-elaborated pluralist theory that can be rediscovered. Instead there are a multiplicity of ideas about interest groups, loosely tied together by a pluralist tag. Some of the pluralist writing seems to anticipate later non-pluralist accounts; they seem different expressions of the same approach rather than alternatives. It may well be that the pluralist and non-pluralist approaches can coexist. To pursue one sort of approach does not seem to presuppose the inferiority of the other. In finding

[51] R. Salisbury, J. Heinz, E. Laumann, and C. Nelson, 'Who Works with Whom? Interest Group Alliances and Opposition', *American Political Science Review*, 81/4 (1987), 1217–34.
[52] E. O. Laumann and D. Knoke, *The Organizational State* (Madison, Wis.: University of Wisconsin Press, 1987).

weaknesses in the existing statements on pluralism, the implication is not that we need to reject that whole tradition but that we need to build on and improve it. We do not need to replace the pluralist paradigm but belatedly to explore the puzzles and inconsistencies it has engendered.

Though there now is clearly a well-developed tendency to advance by drawing up more elaborate and sectorized models of the political system, we should not discount the pluralist accounts. For one thing, to ignore the past is to court the danger of fashions and fads. For another, developments in China and the USSR have underlined the need for criteria in deciding how to measure developments toward democracy. Thirdly, as we as political scientists look for a more elaborate picture of our own political arrangements, we might make better sense of the untidy heterogeneity in pluralism. The inconsistencies may appear to be a strength and not a weakness. The idea that the pluralist account is not to be an important part of a developed subject contradicts too much empirical work to be probable. There are just too many remarks in the pluralist corpus—about networks, rules of the game, about forms of state/group relationship—that leap out with contemporary relevance for the discipline to imagine that they can be ignored at little cost. Moreover, the current idea of different stories in different policy areas is a central part of pluralist thought. The non-theory of pluralism is not uncomfortable at the notion of such fragmentation and variety. Finally, if we return to *Who Governs* we can in retrospect see the importance of Dahl's emphasis on skill in the *art* of politics. Political outcomes are the result of processes and not simply the consequence of structures.

PART II

PRESSURE GROUPS IN PRACTICE

5

DEMOCRATIZATION AND THE GROWTH OF PRESSURE GROUPS IN SOVIET AND POST-SOVIET POLITICS

TERRY COX

A major aspect of developments in Soviet politics in the late 1980s was the growth of political activity outside the formal channels of the state and the ruling Communist Party. During this period the first steps were taken to set up opposition parties and independent trade unions, and the ties were loosened between the state and the previously incorporated official trade unions, and youth and women's movements. However, the most dramatic and far-reaching change was the expansion of informal interest group activity.

Of course, the question of group influence on Soviet politics is not new. It was also the subject of an academic debate in the 1960s and 1970s which produced a wide range of opinions about the nature, and the extent of influence of group activity in the Soviet political system of that period. Moreover, the findings of this earlier debate are still relevant in that they provide a background for understanding the more recent developments.

THE DEBATE ON SOVIET INTEREST GROUPS

The original debate on the relevance of a group approach to Soviet politics was initiated in the mid-1960s by Gordon Skilling,[1] who argued that although Soviet politics was different from that of Western democracies, a focus on groups would reveal aspects of policy-making obscured by the hitherto predominant totalitarian theory, and, in particular, would highlight the stages before and after the formal making of decisions by the topmost leaders. Adopting the term 'political interest group', Skilling defined it as an

© Terry Cox 1993.

[1] H. G. Skilling, 'Interest Groups and Soviet Politics', *World Politics*, 18/3 (1966).

'aggregate of persons who possess certain common characteristics and share certain attitudes on public issues, and who adopt distinct positions on these issues and make definite claims on those in authority'.[2] It was accepted that groups might often be overlapping and in a state of flux, and that in Soviet conditions, few groups would have any formal organization. Such informal groups would be found especially at lower levels of society, while greater degrees of interaction and organization would be found among interest groups within the élites and state institutions.

Skilling's work prompted several studies, either of particular groups, or of policy areas where group influences could be examined. The whole body of research was the subject of much debate, especially around the issues of the extent to which groups could be clearly identified in the context of Soviet politics, and of the significance of group pressures for the character of the Soviet political system. The studies covered a range of groups, either from within the formal institutions of the state, such as party officials, security police, and the military, or from less powerful professional groups such as industrial managers, economists, creative writers, criminologists, and jurists.[3]

A problem shared by much of the above-mentioned work was the extent to which the evidence clearly established the operation of interest groups. While all the studies found evidence of groups sharing common interests, and of activities by group members aimed at pursuing or defending their interests, it proved more difficult to go beyond this and establish patterns of interaction between group members, or to show the existence of any formal organization of groups. Apart from the studies of particular groups, other researchers examined particular policy issues or reforms as a means of identifying the role of interest groups.[4] Perhaps the policy area providing the clearest example of the influence of pressure group activity on policy outcomes was environmental policy.[5]

[2] H. G. Skilling and F. Griffiths (eds.), *Interest Groups in Soviet Politics* (Princeton, NJ: Princeton University Press, 1971), 24.

[3] See e.g. V. Andrle, *Managerial Power in the Soviet Union* (Farnborough: Lexington Books, 1976); J. Azrael, *Managerial Power and Soviet Politics* (Cambridge, Mass.: Harvard University Press, 1966); Skilling and Griffiths, *Interest Groups*; P. H. Solomon, *Soviet Criminologists and Criminal Policy* (New York: Columbia University Press, 1978).

[4] See T. H. Friedgut, 'Interest Groups in Soviet Policy Making: The MTS Reforms', *Soviet Studies*, 28/4 (1976); J. Schwartz and W. Keech, 'Group Influences and the Policy Process in the Soviet Union', in F. Fleron (ed.), *Communist Studies and the Social Sciences* (Chicago: Rand McNally); P. Stewart, 'Soviet Interest Groups and the Policy Process: The Repeal of Production Education', *World Politics*, 22/1 (1969).

[5] See D. R. Kelley, 'Environmental Policy Making in the USSR', *Soviet Studies*, 28/4 (1976); T. Gustafson, *Reform in Soviet Politics: Lessons of Recent Policies on Land and Water* (Cambridge: Cambridge University Press, 1981).

According to Kelley, in a situation where official bureaucratic interests were split between their industrial management and environmental protection responsibilities, a significant influence was exerted by informal 'opinion groups', especially among writers, journalists, and scientists. Again, however, no formal group organization was identified, and it was unclear how far the opinion groups concerned were actually able to act in concert.[6]

Before 1985 the only clear examples of organized unofficial political groups in Soviet politics were the dissidents, and, ironically, as people who had gone beyond the law, they were the groups with least influence over the formal channels of policy-making. Not all dissident groups were likely to articulate political interests but some, described by Tokes as 'instrumental pragmatists', sought to reform rather than to challenge the system.[7] They shared not only some common ground with representatives of the system, but also similar personal contacts and social background, and these provided potential ways of influencing policy discussions. Unlike the other groups studied, such dissident groups clearly had group consciousness and organization, shared values, and made definitive demands on those in authority. However, at least as far as the Brezhnev years were concerned, they seemed to have even less influence than the more legitimate groups.

By the end of the 1970s, an impressive body of research had been accumulated.[8] It provided a great deal of information about informal processes of Soviet politics and the nature of policy inputs from society at large. However, many questions remained about what exactly the research was able to show about Soviet politics. For some, such as Jerry Hough,[9] the Soviet Union was a form of 'institutionalised pluralism', where, unlike in the West, groups could articulate interests and seek to influence policy only if they operated through official institutions. Since this kind of interest representation seemed to require a higher degree of centralized direction and co-ordination than is usually associated with pluralism, other

[6] Kelley, 'Environmental Policy Making', 589.
[7] R. Tokes, 'Dissent: The Politics for Change in the USSR', in H. W. Morton and R. L. Tokes (eds.), *Soviet Politics and Society in the 1970s* (New York: Free Press, 1974).
[8] For more detailed discussion of studies of Soviet interest groups see J. Lowenhardt, *Decision-Making in Soviet Politics* (London: Macmillan, 1981); H. G. Skilling, 'Interest Groups and Communist Politics Revisited', in S. White and D. Nelson (eds.), *Communist Politics: A Reader* (London: Macmillan, 1986). An extended version of the discussion above can be found in an earlier version of this article, T. Cox 'Pressure Group Development in Soviet Politics', *Strathclyde Papers on Government and Politics*, 77 (1990).
[9] J. F. Hough, *The Soviet Union and Social Science Theory* (Cambridge, Mass.: Harvard University Press, 1977), 547.

writers preferred to characterize the Soviet system as a kind of corporatism. Drawing on the work of Schmitter,[10] Bunce and Echolls argued that the Soviet system, as it had developed in the Brezhnev period, involved the incorporation of key interests into the system of state management.[11]

In contrast to Hough, and Bunce and Echolls, other writers cast doubts on the idea that pressure groups could operate in the Soviet Union with the degree of either independence or organization that the terms pluralism and corporatism imply. For example, in reviewing a wide range of studies, Lowenhardt concluded that 'certain groups or institutions may perhaps be said to behave as interest groups . . . but often the common interests of their members will be quite limited in number and will be overshadowed by their different and conflicting interests'. Instead of interest groups, Lowenhardt suggested it was preferable to discuss interest representation in terms of 'policy coalitions' which emerge around a given issue from time to time, drawing on members of different institutions or opinion groups, but then collapse when the issue is resolved or becomes less important.[12]

Another problem has been raised by Brown,[13] who sees the use of pluralist terminology in the Soviet context as 'conceptual stretching', where relatively insignificant similarities between the Soviet and Western political systems are accentuated, and significant differences are played down. He felt able to accept the existence of what he preferred to describe as 'opinion groupings', and to recognize it may be possible to detect 'elements of pluralism' in Soviet politics, but the key question, he argued, was that of autonomy, and compared with Western political systems, groups in the Soviet Union had very little of it. 'The control which Soviet leaders have over the political agenda, their control over the flow of information, their capacity to make potential issues non-issues, while not complete, are beyond the dreams even of a Richard Nixon.'[14]

In raising such matters as control over the political agenda, and the power to turn issues into non-issues, Brown was extending the discussion into areas which imply fundamental criticisms of the

[10] P. Schmitter, 'Still the Century of Corporatism?' *Review of Politics*, 36 (1974).

[11] V. Bunce and J. M. Echolls, 'Soviet Politics in the Brezhnev Era: "Pluralism" or "Corporatism"?', in D. R. Kelley, *Soviet Politics in the Brezhnev Era* (New York: Praeger, 1980).

[12] Lowenhardt, *Decision-Making in Soviet Politics*, 86–7.

[13] A. H. Brown, 'Pluralism, Power and the Soviet Political System', in S. Solomon (ed.), *Pluralism in the Soviet Union* (London: Macmillan, 1983).

[14] Ibid. 69.

whole methodology of interest group research. The point was made more explicitly by McAuley,[15] who argued that the interest group approach 'tends to concentrate on *what* happens, *how* things are done, rather than asking, in some broader sense, *why* political activities and relationships take the form that they do'. As a result, although the research of the 1960s and 1970s was able to produce a new kind of evidence on the informal processes of Soviet politics, it could only attempt to reveal that which was the result of peoples' positive actions. It did not attempt to investigate moves behind the scenes to control agendas, or power of the kind that went unchallenged because it was unrecognized, or taken for granted. Therefore, following Brown's point, the research could not discern between situations where interest representation could take place with relatively little constraint, and therefore with the potential to influence significantly policy-making, and situations where it was severely constrained by powerful interests that were beyond and immune from the kind of political dialogue the interest group research was able to reveal.

The idea that such overbearing power did exist and constrain the information of informal interest groups was, of course, always accepted in most western work on Soviet politics in the 1960s and 1970s, and indeed, was accepted by Skilling and most other contributors to the debate. Only a minority of scholars were prepared to go as far as Hough in portraying the Soviet political system as a form of pluralism. However, in the light of recent changes in the nature of that system under Gorbachev, it must be asked whether, on the one hand, the reform process itself revealed a greater role for pressure group influence over policy than had been possible before, and on the other hand, whether the reforms created a new situation allowing a greater scope for interest group politics. Each of these will be discussed in turn below.

POLITICAL INTERESTS AND PERESTROIKA

In the late 1970s two different reformist tendencies can be identified in Soviet politics. On the one hand, there were the dissident groups such as those involving civil rights campaigners Andrei Sakharov or Roy Medvedev, while, on the other hand, there were professional groups and liberal reformist academics remaining within the system such as those associated with the sociologist Tat'yana Zaslavskaya, the economist Avel Aganbegyan, or the political scientist Fyodor

[15] M. McAuley, *Politics and the Soviet Union* (Harmondsworth: Penguin, 1977), 163.

Burlatskii. These, of course, are the kind of groupings most closely conforming to the concept of interest group used in the western studies of Soviet politics reviewed above. Although the two groups were separate in so far as they operated within or outside the rules of the system, in many ways they shared common outlooks and experience, having similar social and educational backgrounds, and in some cases, moving in the same social circles.

In retrospect, it can be seen that such groups had some effect on policy change in the 1980s. The more immediate influence was exerted by reformist academics, especially economists and other social scientists. Under Brezhnev, while the Party leadership presented a united front against reform, there was little the reformers could do beyond keeping their ideas alive through academic research. By the early 1980s, however, new political opportunities were emerging. A new group of younger politicians such as Gorbachev, Ryzhkov, Yakovlev, and others showed themselves interested in new ideas to overcome problems such as falling growth rates, poor labour morale, and the growing corruption in society.

Also, more than previous generations of political leaders, they had received higher education and therefore shared similar social and educational backgrounds to the liberal intelligentsia. In the early 1980s a regular dialogue was established between academic reformers and the rising generation of politicians. Informal discussion meetings were held to which academics were invited to present papers outlining criticisms of the existing system and proposals for reform. One such paper was the now famous 'Novosibirsk Report', leaked anonymously to the West at the time, and later revealed to have been the work of Tat'yana Zaslavskaya.[16]

After 1985, with Gorbachev in power, the reformist academics were brought closer to the centre of power as policy advisors. Some took an active part in drafting new legislation and joined in debates behind the scenes.[17] Then, as the policy of glasnost' was implemented, and growing numbers of political prisoners were released, the voices of former dissident reformers such as Sakharov and Timofeev began to be heard in public debates and in the media. Sakharov and other dissidents contributed in turn to the ever-quickening pace of reforms, adding their voices to those pressing for greater freedoms of speech and movement, and reforms of the

[16] After excerpts had appeared in the Western Press, a full translation appeared in *Survey*, 28/1 (1984).

[17] e.g. a number of academics, especially lawyers and economists, were consulted in the drafting of legislation aimed at a growth in private sector economic activity. See T. Cox, 'The Private Sector and Policy Change in the Soviet Union', *Slovo*, 2/2 (1989).

electoral system to allow greater choice of candidates. It became increasingly noticeable that the views of the more liberal Party and government leaders differed little if at all, from those of many former dissidents and reformers.

In the long run therefore, it can be argued, both dissident and academic opinion groups active in the 1970s did have a profound effect on policy in that, eventually, their ideas were largely embodied in the government's reforms in the late 1980s. In a sense, this would seem to be a vindication of the interest group approach to the study of Soviet politics, since its supporters always claimed such influence would be possible. On closer examination, however, the vindication is at best, conditional. Bearing in mind the objections discussed above concerning the limitations on the scope of interest group activity and influence, it is necessary to ask what specific changes took place to remove the severe constraint experienced by reformist interests up to the mid-1980s. In other words, it is necessary to ask questions about changes in the deeper structure of power in Soviet society, 'behind the scenes' from the kind of activities revealed by the interest group research.

An answer to such questions may be found not simply by examining the relations between the Party élite and emerging interest groups, but by examining wider social and economic factors affecting the power of the élite, the extent of their cohesion, and the capacity of non-élite groups to mobilize around particular issues. As long as the top Party leadership had been relatively united in its consensus against the reformers, group pressure had little effect, except in a few exceptional cases where the top policy-makers were undecided themselves. However, by the mid-1980s there had been a breakdown of the conditions supporting the atmosphere of consensus and compromise based on inactivity in policy-making which had typified the Brezhnev years. In the years since the Second World War Soviet society had become more complex and differentiated as a result of increased industrialization and urbanization. The population had become more educated, with higher expectations and more sophisticated demands than in the past. Faced with such a situation, the centralized command economy became less and less able to cope. It proved increasingly difficult for a centralized bureaucracy either to administer a complex industrial economy, or to gather and assess information on an increasingly differentiated population.

The changing social context prompted two important political developments. First, a new generation of politicians were joining the élite and bringing new and more critical ideas with them. Second, and at the same time, Soviet society was increasingly seen by its political leaders to be in crisis.[18] In such circumstances, access to policy-makers became increasingly open for outside pressure groups. Divisions in the leadership, and then outright sponsorship by the faction that was to be victorious, assured unprecedented influence for reformist opinion.

Thus, a brief review of the factors behind the emergence of reformist politics offers partly support, but partly qualification of the earlier interest group approach. On the one hand, the sources of the reformist ideas were groups identified as significant by the interest group research, especially the reformist academics and moderate dissidents. On the other hand, it was only when the old Soviet system entered a crisis that such groups could go beyond articulating an interest and were able to insert it into the policy agenda.

THE EMERGENCE OF GROUP POLITICS

Once in power, awareness of the severity of the crisis was heightened by such factors as the Chernobyl disaster, the worsening situation in the supply of consumer goods, and growing public criticism enabled by the policy of glasnost'. These developments created a new situation for the activities of pressure groups in Soviet politics. In response to each stage in the growth of the crisis, the Gorbachev leadership adopted more and more radical policy solutions. In each case, the inspiration for these can be found in ideas originally put forward by academics or activists from outside the Party leadership. At the same time reformists and other activists gradually found restrictions on their ability to express political ideas and to organize politically were being lifted.

During the years 1987 and 1989 a series of developments took place whose combined effect was radically to change the terms on which politics was conducted in the Soviet Union. These included:

1. the abolition of the office of censor and its replacement by self-censorship by editors;
2. the removal of restrictions on discussion groups and political clubs operating entirely outside the Party or other approved public organizations;
3. a change in official attitudes to political meetings and demonstrations;
4. changes in the electoral system facilitating multi-candidate elections and the nomination of non-Communist candidates;

[18] M. S. Gorbachev, *Perestroika* (London: Fontana, 1988).

5. increased official tolerance of unofficial strikes.

As a result of these developments, a space was created for the emergence of legal, open organization in the pursuit of particular social group interests or with the aim of pressuring government to make particular changes or allocations. The process took place in a number of stages.

Even before Gorbachev came to power some unofficial groups were formed, especially self-help groups of veterans of the war in Afghanistan, and groups of young people concerned with ecological issues. By the mid-1980s, a number of branches of 'Pamyat'' (Memory) had been formed in cities around the country. This began as an organization concerned with the preservation of Russian culture generally, including Russian literature, architecture, and the countryside, but then became a more overtly nationalist, anti-semitic organization.

During 1986 and 1987, as the restrictions were eased on groups forming without official registration, many other groups were formed. They included specific local campaigns to defend or preserve historical buildings, various local voluntary groups offering support and advice to the elderly and the disabled, cultural and hobbies groups, and political discussion groups. Many had a short life-span, an overlapping membership, and little formal organization. However, others survived and grew, became more organized, and sometimes affiliated with like-minded groups around the country. In all, the number of unofficial groups grew dramatically in the late 1980s to an estimated 60,000 by 1989.[19] Their membership was mainly young, with the majority in the 25 to 35 age group, and, with the exception of the trade unions, and possibly the Afghan veterans' groups, mainly drawn from professional and intelligentsia groups.

Many of the new unofficial groups had little or no political role beyond providing a context for people to share and pursue their interests outside the control of the state or the Communist Party. Others, however, began to develop aims and activities typical either of interest groups or of pressure groups in the West. Examples of groups that could be seen as interest groups were the above-mentioned Afghan war veterans' groups, and the 'Miloserdie' (Charity) organization, which offered help to the disabled and elderly people living on their own. Such groups represented more specifically the interests of their members as a distinct section of society, and are best seen as sectional or interest groups.

[19] *Pravda* (10 Feb. 1989).

Also partly belonging to this category, but also taking on more of a pressure group role, were the new independent trade unions. No longer content to be represented by the incorporated official unions, Soviet workers increasingly resorted to the weapon of the unofficial strike, culminating in the miners' strikes of 1989 and 1990. After the end of the strikes, some committees stayed in existence to monitor the implementation of the strike agreements and formed the basis for local unofficial unions such as the Union of Kuzbass Workers. Separate unions also emerged in other industries, and even within the army.[20] Several independent union branches affiliated to new independent federations of unions such as the strongly politically oriented (and pro-Yeltsin) 'Sotsprof' (Federation of Socialist Trade Unions), or the regionally based Moscow Federation of Trade Unions. A recent development is the growth of a separate union, MAKKIP, representing workers in small private and leased businesses.[21]

A distinctive feature of the new unions has been the breadth of their interests. Their aims have been not only to secure improvements in working conditions and wages for their members, but to support market oriented reforms which they have tended to see so far, as in the longer-term interests of their members. During the first half of 1992, despite high rates of inflation, a chronic problem of poor food supplies, and the growing threat of large-scale unemployment, the new governments of the independent republics were not faced with such strong strike action as the Soviet government experienced in its last two years. Nevertheless, the unions have remained active, especially in the debate over privatization, and they are potentially a very strong force if they decide to offer direct opposition to the new governments.[22]

Complementing the development of groups representing labour, other groups have emerged to pursue the interests of various kinds of employers. These include separate organizations for people leasing enterprises from the state, new independent entrepreneurs, co-operative members, managers of state enterprises, and chairmen and directors of public sector farms. As with the new trade unions, the employers' organizations have broad political platforms, with views on a range of general policy issues, as well as a narrower role

[20] M. Galeotti, 'Civil Society in Uniform', *Russia and the World*, 17 (1990).

[21] M. Nagaitsev, 'Trade Unions in Moscow', *Labour Focus on Eastern Europe*, 41 (1992), 17.

[22] For further discussion of the development of the independent trade union movement in Russia and the Soviet Union see e.g. D. Mandel, 'The Re-birth of the Soviet Labour Movement', *Politics and Society*, 18/3 (1990); and id., 'The Struggle for Power in the Soviet Economy', *Socialist Register 1991* (London: Merlin, 1991).

of representing their members' particular interests. They operate mainly by attempting to influence contacts in government and parliament. As yet the employers have not developed clear local or industry-based organizational structures, and there is no regular or established framework for negotiation with government or organized labour. Potentially, however, the influence of such groups is very strong.[23]

Alongside such developments, the period since 1988 has also witnessed the emergence of clearly political pressure groups, seeking to influence policy and change the structure of power in accordance with the attitudes and ideology of their membership. These groups have their origin in the political discussion groups that grew up with glasnost' and perestroika. Various socialist clubs, independent from and critical of the Communist Party, were formed from 1986 onwards, including the 'Perestroika' Club, and the KSI [Club of Social Initiatives in Moscow]. On the initiative of the KSI, a nationwide conference of left clubs was held in August 1987, and out of it emerged a new Federation of Socialist Clubs.[24] Tactically, they saw some possibility of co-operating with the reformist wing of the Communist Party, and took part with them in various popular front organizations. These in turn were particularly active in supporting reformist candidates in elections for the Congress of Peoples' Deputies in early 1989, including Yeltsin's successful campaign in Moscow.[25]

Members of more liberal clubs met later, in May 1988, to form the Democratic Union.[26] These groups were always more entrenched in their opposition to the Communist Party, and could see no hope of co-operation with it. Ideologically, they were opposed to socialism and favoured the full introduction of a capitalist market economy along with a pluralist political system. Tactically, they tended to remain aloof from the Popular Fronts.

Outside the Russian Republic the situation was further compli-cated by the national independence question. At a different pace in each republic, first national identity, and then national independ-ence became major political issues which the reforms brought to a new prominence. Indeed, such concerns were so strong that, although the same diversity of groups emerged in many of the Soviet republics, the national question served to overcome divisions and

[23] For further information on employers' groups see S. Peregudoc, I. Semenko and A. Zudin, *Business Associations in the USSR and After: Their Growth and Political Role*, PAIS Papers n. 110, University of Warwick, 1992.

[24] A. Severukhin, 'The Left Unites', *Labour Focus on Eastern Europe*, 9/3 (1987).

[25] B. Kagarlitsky, *Farewell Perestroika* (London: Verso, 1990).

[26] V. Brovkin, 'Revolution From Below', *Soviet Studies*, 42/2 (1990).

create a more united opposition movement sooner than was possible in Russia. These developments in the non-Russian republics were particularly significant. In the context of perestroika reforms aimed at devolving some decision-making away from the centre, and requiring local governments and enterprises to balance their own accounts, many local republic Communist party leaderships responded to the growing popularity of the popular fronts by breaking into factions, some of which then formed new alliances with popular front groups.[27]

As a result of the 1990 elections, popular front governments came to power, and in varying degrees declared their independence from the Soviet government, not only in the Baltic and Transcaucasian republics, but even in Russia itself with the election of Yeltsin to the presidency and popular front candidates to head Moscow and Leningrad city councils. The elections of 1989 and 1990 also had a number of important effects on the unofficial political groups. First they provided a stimulus for the groups to organize and work together, to project their ideas to the general public in an unprecedented way. Second the prestige of the Communist Party was badly dented and their political programme was found wanting. Third, in several of the Soviet republics, popular front organizations won large majorities, fuelling nationalist sentiments among the local populations, and bringing about significant realignments in the group structures of republic level politics.

In the wake of the electoral victories of various democratic movements and politicians, realignments took place from 1990 based on the emerging parliamentary politics of the new assemblies. In Russia, for example, 'Democratic Russia' became the chief support group for Yeltsin and his policies. However, by the end of 1991, it was beginning to split up into various smaller groups. Meanwhile other attempts have been made to establish political parties, including Christian Democrats, Social Democrats, and a British style Labour Party with links to sections of the new trade union movement. As yet, however, there is no clear-cut distinction between political parties and pressure groups. Parties like those mentioned above have loose and fluctuating structures and member-ships, often have only tenuous links with parliamentary repre-sentatives, and have not yet developed well-organized electoral machines. Others, such as The Party of Free Labour, representing

---

[27] See e.g. P. Goble, 'Ethnic Politics in the USSR', *Problems of Communism* (1989); R. Suny, 'State, Civil Society, and Ethnic Cultural Consolidation in the USSR', in A. Dallin and G. Lapidus (eds.), *The Soviet System in Crisis* (Boulder, Colo.: Westview, 1991).

new entrepreneurs, and the Peasant Party, representing new independent family farmers, are more clearly pressure groups that have adopted a party name.[28]

THE INFLUENCE OF THE NEW GROUPS

In the absence of any detailed research so far on the political influence or role in policy-making of any of the new groups, it is difficult to judge how great their political impact has been. However, there are grounds for thinking the influence of at least some groups has been considerable, and that the new political situation after the break-up of the Soviet Union could be still more favourable for pressure groups.

Among the most influential in the final years of the Soviet Union, were the groups associated with the popular fronts in the Baltic republics. Indeed, since the popular fronts, such as 'Sajudis' in Lithuania, rapidly made the transition from pressure group, to *de facto* opposition party, to governing party, they would seem to have been spectacularly successful. At the level of the Soviet Union as a whole, a case can also be made that the influence of opposition political groups was strong. Most of the increasingly radical reforms introduced by the Party leadership under Gorbachev, including the growth of the private sector of the economy, the reforms of the legislatures and electoral law, and the abolition of the Party's constitutional right to a 'leading role' in society all began as proposals from groups outside official Party or government circles, whether among reformist academic specialists, or among unofficial political groups.[29]

Furthermore, since the break-up of the Soviet Union, the scope for independent voices to exert an influence has clearly grown. The ideas of academics and professionals are as much in evidence in, for example, the current political debates in Russia or the Ukraine, as they were in Soviet politics before. Of course, the names have now changed and on the whole a new younger generation has emerged, such as the sociologist Starovoitova or the economist Yavlinskii. Moreover, more-organized pressure groups, both reformist and conservative, are emerging in pursuit of specific policy objectives.

[28] For further details of the various attempts to set up political groups and parties, see V. Tolz, *The USSR's Emerging Multiparty System* (New York: Praeger, 1990); and J. Aves, P. Duncan and G. Hosking, *The Road to Post-Communism: New Political Movements in the USSR 1985–1991* (London: 1992).

[29] V. Tolz, 'Informal Groups and Soviet Politics in 1989', *Radio Liberty Report on the USSR*, 1/47 (1989).

This has been evident, for example, in recent debates on privatization and land reform, where groups representing a range of interests, from state enterprise managers to new private entrepreneurs, to trade unions, have all tried both to publicize their views and to lobby decision-makers and elected representatives.

There can be little doubt that in the period since 1988 informal groups have played a significant role in Soviet and post-Soviet politics. One interpretation of this is to see it as part of the growth of civil society based on a pluralism of interests. Within the Gorbachev administration there seemed to be a belief that interest groups could be co-opted into a grand pro-perestroika alliance under the leadership of a reformed Communist Party. This strategy rested on an assumption that the Soviet system, as reformed by perestroika, did not present insuperable barriers to interest group activity because there was a basic harmony of interests underlying the Soviet system. Ironically, although the successful opposition to Gorbachev revealed the falsity of such assumptions, there are signs that the new governments in many of the successor states also claim a basic harmony of social group interests, albeit now based on common national interest rather than the nature of the 'socialist system'. This again leads to assumptions that, for example, all social groups can find common cause in privatization, or market reforms, despite their consequences in terms of inflation or unemployment.

Furthermore, the idea that the increased scope for group activity represents a growth of pluralism and civil society is open to the same criticisms as those levelled against pluralist and corporatist interpretations of politics in the Brezhnev period. If, alternatively, group influence is understood in the context of the deeper structure of political power, then the scope of group influence at any particular time can be seen as dependent on factors other than the direct relations between informal groups and government. Also significant are the degree to which power holders can monopolize decision-making power, incorporate various sections of society within the system, or attempt to control policy agendas. Underlying these are questions about the logic of the system as a whole which underlies participants' ideas and behaviour. This raises difficult questions about just who does hold power, and what is the character of the underlying social structure of the new successor states to the Soviet Union.

Independent group activity emerged in Soviet politics under Gorbachev, and has grown in its successor states, at a time when the old structures were crumbling and the power of the old central authorities was being eroded. It is possible that with the eventual establishment of new stable power structures, interest group politics will come to be seen as a feature only of the transitional period between regimes. Only when a new stable order emerges in the successor states will it be possible to assess the prospects for interest group politics. However, such an assessment will also depend on a research agenda that goes beyond the questions addressed by the previous research on group processes in Soviet politics, and also investigates deeper sociological issues about the emerging nature of power in those societies.

6

INTEREST GROUP BEHAVIOUR IN BRITAIN: CONTINUITY AND CHANGE

JEREMY J. RICHARDSON

ORGANIZATIONAL PRACTICE MAKES PERFECT?

Of all the Western democracies, Britain has perhaps the longest-established interest group *system*. Thus, despite the lack of a written constitution, British policy-making has certain well-established procedures—standard operating procedures—which generally accord interest groups a key role in the policy process. Policies are normally formulated by governments only after the so-called 'affected' interests have been consulted. Thus, all government departments have 'consultation lists' which include all of the organized interests who are considered to be central to the successful implementation of policy. Not only is there a strong supposition that this consultation will take place (and that it should not be 'sham' consultation), but, increasingly, the right to be consulted is enshrined in legislation for particular sectors. Moreover, Britain's membership of the European Community provides additional points of access for groups.

Thus, all policy areas exhibit a high degree of group density, in the sense that virtually every interest is now *organized*. Moreover, the tendency is for there to be a high degree of density in terms of membership also, with the result that groups can claim a high degree of legitimacy because of their representativeness. Policy-makers are therefore faced with a complex constellation of groups in each policy area or sub-area, and by interest organizations that are professional and bureaucratized and represent a high proportion of potential members. Although elected governments are able to claim a special degree of legitimacy, groups also claim a degree of legitimacy, both in their own right and because British governments are invariably elected by only a minority of electors, under Britain's 'first past the post' electoral system.

Even apparently 'new' areas—such as environmentalism—in fact have a long tradition of interest group activity in Britain. The focus of that activity may have changed over time, as the portfolio of issues under the general label 'environmental' has changed. Also new groups have been formed and have joined the existing group network. But, as Lowe and Goyder point out, it was the Victorians who formed 'the first nature conservation group, the first building preservation group, the first outdoor pursuit group'.[1] Ashby and Anderson cite the example of one of the earliest pressure groups against air pollution—the Manchester Association for the Prevention of Smoke—which was formed as early as 1843.[2] Most national-level environmental groups were formed at least before the Second World War (for example, the Council for the Protection of Rural England was formed in 1926, and the Natural Society for Clean Air was formed in 1929). Wotton has identified the formation of many groups in the eighteenth century, such as the First Catholic Association (1760) and the Committee for Effecting the Abolition of the Slave Trade.[3]

Patricia Hollis has captured the essential origins of the British pluralist tradition in her description of Victorian politics, as follows:

Forty years before, the existence of such pressure was illegitimate, unnecessary or both; now it was a necessary tool of social reform, a necessary aid to government, evidence of healthy public concern. Pressure from without had both stretched the arena of government and access to government, and in the process had thrown up feminist groups on the rights of prostitutes, evangelicals on the wrongs of prostitutes, public health groups on the diseases of prostitutes, Shaftesbury and Gladstone on refuges for prostitutes, and sabbatarians for no prostitution on Sundays. Victorian life was engagingly pluralist.[4]

So embedded are groups in the political process in Britain that writers have identified the strength of groups as one of the causes of Britain's economic decline. The now classic view of the detrimental effect of groups in Britain has been formulated by Mancur Olson as follows:

Britain has precisely the powerful network of specialised interest organisations that the argument developed here would lead us to expect in a country

---

[1] P. Lowe and J. Goyder, *Environmental Groups in Politics* (London: Allen & Unwin, 1983), 17.

[2] E. Ashby and M. Anderson, *The Politics of Clean Air* (Oxford: Oxford University Press, 1981), 7.

[3] G. Wotton, *Pressure Groups in Britain, 1720–1970: An Essay in Interpretation with Original Documents* (London: Allen Lane, 1975), 10, quoted by M. Rush, 'Pressure Politics', in M. Rush (ed.), *Parliament and Pressure Politics* (Oxford: Clarendon Press, 1990).

[4] P. Hollis, *Pressure From Without in Early Victorian England* (London: Edward Arnold, 1974), 25.

with its record of security and military stability . . . In short, with age British society has acquired so many strong organisations and collusions that it suffers from an institutional sclerosis that slows its adaption to changing circumstances and changing technologies.[5]

The alleged 'institutional sclerosis' is caused not by the mere existence of a highly *organized* society, but by the fact that policy change is made more difficult if governments consider that change must be based upon consensus. In other words, the *style* of governance and the underlying values about the political process itself are very important determinants of group influence in Britain. For much of the period since the early formation of groups in Victorian England, there has been strong emphasis on consensus. Indeed, the test of a 'good' policy has often been its *acceptability* to the affected interests. This has meant that policies are peace treaties between government and the affected interests. Like all peace treaties which have been difficult to negotiate, there is a marked reluctance to renegotiate them once they have been agreed. As a result, there has been much more policy stability and continuity than the commonly accepted 'adversarial' model of British politics would suggest. Under that model it is argued that there is considerable policy *discontinuity* after elections, as there are thought to be major differences between the parties. In practice, key indicators such as public expenditure programmes show a remarkable pattern of continuity, notwithstanding changes of government. This continuity can be explained by the fact that whatever the electorate might decide, a new government is faced with the same intractable problems (e.g. Britain's low productivity) and the same constellation of groups benefiting from existing policies—however damaging to the national interest those policies might be. Sam Brittan, like Olson, has also argued that the sum total of practices and special deals which interest groups negotiate is harmful to the interests of society. Referring to Hayek's work, he notes that the main theme of that work is that 'democracy has degenerated into an unprincipled auction to satisfy rival organised groups who can never in the long run be appeased because their demands are mutually incompatible'.[6] As we shall see in our Conclusion, the period 1979–90 saw Mrs Thatcher's Conservative Government attempt to challenge the power of groups in many policy areas, as she believed that consensus was an alternative word for 'fudging' key issues and for avoiding difficult policy choices. That this approach met with

[5] M. Olson (1982), *The Rise and Decline of Nations* (New Haven, Conn.: Yale University Press, 1982), 78.
[6] S. Brittan, *The Role and Limits of Government* (London: Temple Smith, 1983), 24.

very firm (though not always successful) resistance by groups is itself testimony to the fact that they had become used to their rather privileged position in what could be termed the private management of public policy.

SHOOTING WHERE THE DUCKS ARE

In trying to understand the British interest group system, we need to remember that Britain, unlike most of Western Europe, is a unitary state, with comparatively weak local government. Power is heavily concentrated in London (with the exception of Scottish and Welsh offices in Edinburgh and Cardiff which do attract regional lobbies); there is a fusion of Executive and Legislature, with very strong party discipline; and an electoral system which tends to produce exaggerated majorities for the ruling party in Parliament. Generally, governments can and do *govern*. They can introduce annual legislative programmes which have every expectation of being passed by Parliament. It is extremely rare for a government bill to be defeated or withdrawn, and relatively rare for major amendments to be passed by Parliament against the government's wishes. There is also a tendency for Ministers to be rather dependent upon their civil servants for advice, unless there is a strong party policy based upon ideological considerations. In turn, British civil servants are generalists rather than specialists and they, therefore, are dependent on groups for specialist advice. Finally, Britain has unusually centralized media. Despite the existence of regional television and radio companies, the broadcasting output is London-centred. Moreover, Britain has a genuinely *national* newspaper industry, with several widely read national daily newspapers. This too assists the centralization of power—both in terms of agenda-setting and in terms of policy formulation. Apart from influencing the detailed local implementation of policy (itself valuable to groups, of course) there is little point in national groups lobbying at the local or regional level, as power to decide policy does not reside there.

All of these factors tend to produce a directional bias in the lobbying system, as groups concentrate their main energies and resources on the central Executive—the government. This is not to suggest that Britain is totally lacking in the multiple access points so characteristic of the USA—even the British courts are occasionally used by groups to challenge ministerial decisions (e.g. in education). Also, different issues may be processed in different policy 'arenas'. For example, some issues, such as abortion, tend to be processed in the public and parliamentary arenas, whereas others, such as industrial policy, taxation policy, etc., will be processed in the so-called 'bureaucratic' arena of government departments and groups. Most groups, therefore, do pursue multiple lobbying strategies (increasingly so because of the growing importance of the European Community) and would rarely ignore Parliament or indeed public opinion. (They quite often pay little attention to political parties, however). As Rush suggests, 'The very nature of pressure politics allows, and perceptions often encourage, a multi-faceted approach in seeking to influence public policy, characterised not so much by a step by step process as by simultaneous or near-simultaneous pressure to the point of being haphazard.'[7]

Nevertheless, there is a strong bias in favour of one particular arena of decision-making—namely, the government departments in Whitehall. Britain is essentially a *post-parliamentary democracy*, some-times described as an elected dictatorship, as the government of the day is usually so strong in terms of the balance of power between itself and Parliament.[8] If a group had to choose only one point of access to the decision-making arena, it would invariably choose the bureaucratic arena. Providing the minister can be convinced of the group's case, and providing that she or he can persuade the Cabinet to accept her or his proposals (usually not difficult as other Cabinet ministers are absorbed in their own policy problems and are disinclined to 'interfere' in another minister's portfolio, unless a fight for resources is under way), then the proposal is likely to be accepted by Parliament with only relatively minor amendments. As ministers take only a very small percentage of the decisions for which they are formally responsible, this means that the permanent civil service are extremely important in the policy-formulation process. (Britain does not change the personnel in the civil service on the arrival of a new government.) As one lobbyist put it, it is much better to know the man (*sic*) who drafts the letter than the man who signs it!

In practice, of course, groups do not have to choose just one lobbying technique. The 'pecking order' in terms of lobbying priorities is generally government department, Parliament, public opinion (in descending order), yet most effective groups try to lobby in all three arenas of decision-making, in a 'belt and braces' approach to lobbying. This is especially true in the case of Parliament. As Judge has argued, in a useful qualification to the post-parliamentary thesis, it is important to note the symbolic and legitimating functions of Parliament. In his view,

[7] M. Rush, 'Parliament and Pressure Politics: An Overview', in M. Rush (ed.), *Parliament and Pressure Politics* (Oxford: Clarendon Press, 1990), 32.

[8] Jeremy J. Richardson and A. G. Jordan (eds.), *Governing Under Pressure: The Policy Process in a Post-Parliamentary Democracy* (Oxford: Martin Robertson & Co., 1979), 42.

Parliament may neither be routinely nor actively involved in policy discussions, but it impinges upon this process generally in delimiting the independence of any single policy community, and also in factorising into the closed world of Whitehall a requirement to consider wider partisan/parliamentary/public concerns—even if only in the limited sense of seeking to anticipate or to forestall possible future public criticism in Parliament.[9]

His thesis is that Parliament is an important backdrop to all decision-making activity, including that of interest groups. Civil servants and group leaders may develop a very symbiotic relationship, but they both recognize that there is a formal requirement that the Executive has to answer collectively to Parliament. Thus, civil servants act as 'quasi-politicians' when dealing with interest groups as they know their ministers mind and know that she or he will be held accountable to Parliament in some way or other. Moreover, Judge notes that not only does the parliamentary system constrain the policy-making process between departments and groups, 'parliament can become *directly* involved in the policy process when disruptions occur to bureaucratic accommodation. Indeed, settled patterns of consultation are especially prone to disturbance in the face of governmental intransigence or its rejection of the consensual basis of past agreements.'[10] His data confirm that groups do indeed recognize the power of Parliament, although parliamentary contact does vary according to the type of groups (see Table 6.1).

TABLE 6.1   Contacts with Parliament by Insider/
Outside Status

Type of contact	Insider %	n	Outsider %	n
Regular or frequent contact with MPs	85.8	9	66.7	58
Presented written evidence to a select committee	83.0	88	53.1	78
Regular or frequent contact with peers	64.1	68	54.7	80
Presented oral evidence to a select committee	73.6	78	31.8	46
Contacts with all-party groups	51.9	55	14.5	65
Contacts with party subject committees	54.7	58	30.8	45

Source: D. Judge, 'Parliament and Interest Representation', in M. Rush, *Parliament and Pressure Politics*, 36.

The general public cannot be totally ignored either. Although we do not understand the intricacies of processes of opinion formation,

[9] D. Judge, 'Parliament and Interest Representation', in Rush, *Parliament and Pressure Politics*, 32.
[10] Ibid. 33.

there is no doubt that groups do play a significant role in alerting and mobilizing public opinion via the national media. The very centralization of power and media described earlier also facilitates rapid opinion-formation via élite activity. For certain types of issues, a two-minute slot on the main TV news at nine in the evening can soon create the impression, if not the reality, of a strong 'public opinion' to which policy-makers have to respond. Once given media attention, an issue will then attract the parliamentary 'scavengers' who will then run with the issue by applying parliamentary pressure upon the relevant minister. As the issue rolls forward, it will attract more and more groups, in an extending 'issue network' of interests, all claiming a voice in determining policy outcomes. At this point, of course, outcomes become very unpredictable and no one can guarantee victory. If only for this reason, those groups who have achieved insider status and are, therefore, regularly consulted, are often reluctant to let the issue exit from the bureaucratic arena into the glare of publicity which may exist in the public domain.

A VERY BRITISH POLICY STYLE?

Despite the existence of different policy-making arenas and the fact that issues neither arrive on the agenda nor leave it always in *exactly* the same way, it is still possible to identify some fundamental characteristics of the policy process and the role of groups within it. Writing in 1979, just as Mrs Thatcher was about to 'reform' most British institutions, we suggested that beliefs in parliamentary democracy and the distinction between public and private were outdated in modern Britain. Somewhat earlier, Jack Hayward had described the British policy process as 'humdrum';

Firstly, there are no explicit, over-riding medium or long term objectives. Secondly, unplanned decision-making is incremental. Thirdly, humdrum or unplanned decisions are arrived at by a continuous process of mutual adjustment between a plurality of autonomous policy makers operating in the context of a highly fragmented multiple flow of influence. Not only is plenty of scope offered to interest group spokesmen to shape the outcome by participation in the advocacy process. The aim is to secure through bargaining at least passive acceptance of the decision by the interest affected.[11]

Our own gloss on this analysis was to emphasize both the importance of the sectorization of policy-making and the importance

---

[11] J. E. S. Hayward, 'National Aptitudes for Planning in Britain, France and Italy', *Government & Opposition*, 9/4 (1974), 398–9.

of the close interrelationships between public and private actors in what we termed policy communities of departmental officials and interest group bureaucrats.[12] Thus, our model posited strong boundaries between subject-matters, and indistinct, merged relationships between departments and the relevant groups within individual policy areas. The term 'community' was chosen deliberately to reflect the intimate relationship between groups and departments, the development of common perceptions, and the development of a common language for describing policy problems. As in all genuine *communities* in society, an exchange relationship exists between members of the 'village'. The examples of these policy communities which we gave then do not seem that dated even thirteen years later, after Mrs Thatcher's departure!

One or two of the names of organizations have changed—for example, the rating system was abolished by Mrs Thatcher and replaced by the community charge or poll tax—but there is a remarkable stability in the participation of key actors in each sector. (Even in the case of local government and finance, the basic representational system is the same). Thus, in contrast to the conventional model of parliamentary government and party government, we argued that:

In describing the tendencies for boundaries between government and groups to become less distinct through a whole range of pragmatic developments, we see policies being made (and administered) between a myriad of interconnecting, interpenetrating organisations. It is the relationships involved in committees, the *policy community* of departments and groups, the practices of co-option and the consensual style, that perhaps better account for policy outcomes than do examinations of party stances, of manifestoes or of parliamentary influence. The process we describe is obscure—though not necessarily thereby sinister—and is a long way from the clear-cut and traditional principles of parliamentary and party government.[13]

Although new groups may enter policy sectors, and old groups may occasionally disappear or face a reduction in their power and influence, the basic structure of the system appears to be quite stable. Thus, even under Mrs Thatcher's post-1979 regime (see below), it was generally the relationship between government and groups that was (deliberately) placed under stress, not the actual existence of the groups themselves or their right to be consulted.

The picture is, therefore, not static, even though there are gyroscopic tendencies which work eventually to fit new developments back into traditional patterns of behaviour. Despite external

[12] Richardson and Jordan, *Governing Under Pressure*, 43.
[13] Ibid. 73–4.

factors such as world economic changes, membership of the European Community, and Thatcherism, the system of government/group relations is underpinned by the practical day-to-day need for government departments to relate to their clients. James Christoph's perceptive comment, made in 1975, is still apposite today. Thus, he argued that

The vast majority of Whitehall departments manage policies affecting identifiable clienteles, organized or otherwise. While part of the job of civil servants is to analyse, verify, and cost the claims of such groups, and forward them to higher centres of decision, it would be unnatural if officials did not identify in some way with the interests of their clienteles, and within the overall framework of current government policy advance claims finding favor in the department.[14]

The system has acquired its longevity because of what we have termed the 'logic of negotiation'. This logic was aptly captured by Lord Croham, the former Head of the Civil Service. Writing in 1978, he warned new recruits into the Civil Service that

As regards the way government is conducted, this is always changing without anyone noticing it . . . the more central government seeks to intervene in the economy, the less powerful it will become, because it will have to rely on an ever-increasing number of bodies and individuals to do what it wants. Those people in this situation will bargain and make terms. If you believe that elections should determine policies, that policy choices should be clear cut alternatives, and that there is, or should be a wide range of possible alternatives, you will not enjoy the general situation I have forecast, because it is one which creates the need for consensus politics, interparty deals, and bargains with pressure groups. Without such arrangement, it will be difficult to put central government majorities together, or get the various levels of government to function.[15]

Quite often, the use of the word 'consultation' is inappropriate as the government is regularly engaged in *negotiations* with interests. This happens because of a mutual dependency between government and groups. For example, whatever governments may wish to achieve in the National Health Service (NHS) or in education, it cannot be delivered without the co-operation of doctors and teachers. In the end, everyone realizes that the system cannot work if it is based on continuous conflict. Compromise is, therefore, institutionalized and regularized in, literally, hundreds of advisory committees (some

---

[14] J. B. Christoph, 'High Civil Servants and the Politics of Consensualism in Great Britain', in M. Dogan (ed.), *The Mandarins of Western Europe* (New York: Halsted, 1975), 47.

[15] Lord Croham, 'The Developing Structure of United Kingdom Government', *Management Services in Government*, 33/3 (1978), 105–13.

permanent, some *ad hoc*) surrounding government departments. Although this is not uniquely British, the British have developed the advisory system to a fine art. The incorporation of groups into the policy process had, by 1979 and the election of Mrs Thatcher, reached what may be a unique level in comparative terms.

SOMETHING DIFFERENT?

The year 1979 is seen as a watershed in British politics as Britain then experienced the most determined attempt since the Second World War to change its style of government. Yet the very presence of Mrs Thatcher—so dominant on the political landscape—should not blind us to underlying shifts that were possibly underway prior to her election. Thus in 1973–4 the world oil crisis coincided with one of the most turbulent periods in British history—the 1973/4 miners' strike under the Conservative Government of Mr Heath. The alleged 'confrontational' style of Mr Heath (who later was vociferous in condemning Mrs Thatcher's confrontational style!) helped bring about his defeat in the February 1974 election. The new Labour Government quickly returned to consensus politics (often characterized as 'beer and sandwiches' policies, because of the Labour PM's penchant for meetings with the trade unions over beer and sandwiches). Yet we need to remember that Mrs Thatcher was elected in 1979 largely because of severe 'confrontations' between the Labour Government led by Prime Minister Callaghan and the trade union movement, in the so-called 'winter of discontent'. By 1979, not only was the Labour Government faced with a series of very disruptive public service strikes, it had also adopted (in 1976) the principles of monetarism which were later to be identified as the key component of 'Thatcherism' and which led to a more problematic relationship with groups.[16]

While not wishing to exaggerate the degree of continuity from Labour to Conservatives in 1979, it is important to note that it was certainly not a sharp discontinuity, either in policy content or the style of governing. The explanation of the degree of continuity is quite simple—Britain, by the mid-1970s, was facing a deep economic crisis which, as the world recession deepened, placed intolerable strains on the traditionally symbiotic relationship

[16] Jeremy J. Richardson, 'Britain: Changing Policy Styles and Policy Innovation in Response to Crisis', in E. Damgaard, P. Gerlich, and Jeremy J. Richardson (eds.), *The Politics of Economic Crisis: Lessons from Western Europe* (Avebury: Gower, 1989), 11–13.

between governments and groups. Until 1976, the process of governing Britain had been rather like the Dodo's race in Alice in Wonderland—everyone should win and everyone should get prizes. This explains why the most class-ridden society in Western Europe had also produced consensus politics to a high degree—rising prosperity, albeit rising much more slowly than Britain's competitors—had enabled successive governments to 'buy off' discontent. When it became necessary to control public expenditure, as the economy drifted into deep recession, more conflict was inevitable. As is often said of marriage, when poverty enters the door, love flies out of the window, then so the relatively amiable relationship between groups and government was often broken by the need for financial rectitude, as the Government faced increasing budgetary problems. Once the rate of increase in public expenditure was slowed—and in some cases (though not many) public expenditure cut—then so the hitherto good relationships between policy actors deteriorated. Even so, it would be wrong to see the changed relationships between government and groups post-1979 as solely related to resource constraints (real or imagined). Quite clearly, the new Government—and particularly the Prime Minister—was determined on a new style of governing.

The core of this new style was a belief that the distributional coalitions described by Olson (not that any member of the new Government was likely to have read Olson!) had to be broken so that radical policy change could take place. The sexist jibe that Mrs Thatcher could not look at a British institution (or indeed an EC institution) without hitting it with her handbag was much nearer to the truth than the view, encouraged by the Government, that it was resolute in not making policy U-turns. Very many U-turns took place as tactical retreats were often politically necessary, but the overriding aim of addressing the reform deficit was maintained in a wide range of policy sectors. The irony is that very many observers felt that reforms were long overdue, but some believed that they could be achieved via the traditional consensual approach to policy change. Mrs Thatcher rejected that approach, absolutely, and the 1980s was, therefore, characterized by a whole series of deliberate policy challenges to entrenched groups—e.g. in education, the law, health, and industry—which produced a much more conflictual relationship within the policy process. These challenges were not solely to do with resources. There were attempts to redistribute power and influence within particular policy sectors, often setting one member of the old policy community against another. For example, in the health service the public political debate was about the transfer of national health hospitals from the control of regional health authorities to private trusts (still funded by the state), but the reforms were possibly more significant in terms of the redistribution of power within the existing health policy community. Thus some general practitioners, by early 1992, moderated their opposition to the concept of an internal market in health care when they began to realize that the reforms represented a redistribution of power to them *vis-à-vis* hospital consultants. Indeed, the fundamental principle underlying the reforms—separating providers and purchasers of health care by creating an internal market within the NHS—was essentially a challenge to the existing settlement of health policy which had given producers most of the power. The actors were largely the same as in previous decades, but their relative positions within the policy community had changed, as a result of governmental intervention—itself prompted by a mixture of resource constraints and an ideological belief in market mechanisms as the most effective system for allocating scarce resources. These factors led the Thatcher Government 'to challenge the principle of clinical autonomy, an issue which had hitherto been hived off the policy agenda through a process of non-decision-making'.[17]

The Health sector is, perhaps, the example which best captures the essence of the Thatcher Government's attempt to refashion group/government relations—especially with the professions. As Wistow reminds us, although the NHS has been in turmoil in the 1990s, its basic principle remained intact, despite the Thatcher Government. Yet turmoil there was, simply because the Government had, deliberately, destabilized the policy sector. He quotes a newspaper report, as follows:

Mr Willetts, the closest of the 'outsiders' to the NHS review said he asked a senior civil servant what he would do to the NHS if he were the Minister. The reply was 'I'd leave it entirely alone because it is too politically dangerous. Or I'd destabilise it and see what happened'.[18]

This destabilization of policy communities—evident in such diverse areas as health, education, law reform and the structure of the legal profession, and water policy—was almost invariably followed, however, by a return to the accepted values and norms of the policy process. Thus, once a sector had been 'shaken and stirred', the affected interests were then soothed by being invited back into the inner circle of negotiations with government. The new policy style was to address reform deficits by challenging entrenched groups, to

---

[17] G. Wistow, 'The National Health Service', in D. Marsh and R. A. W. Rhodes (eds.), *Implementing Thatcherite Policies: Audit of an Era* (Buckingham: Open University Press, 1992), 114.
[18] Ibid. 116.

insist that the principles underlying the reforms should be maintained (e.g. that there should be a national curriculum in education and that there should be regular testing of pupils), but literally to negotiate the implementation phase with the affected interests and to make significant concessions in that process.[19]

CONCLUSION: A POST-THATCHERITE CONSENSUS?

The removal of Mrs Thatcher from office in 1990 and the re-election of a new Conservative Government under her successor, John Major, in 1992, seem to herald a return to the more traditionalist style of policy-making in Britain. Cabinet government re-emerged almost immediately on her departure and civil servants remarked that they now felt more able to return to a previous form of intimate dialogue with groups, less fearful of a prime-ministerial dictat. Moreover, many of the Thatcherite reforms were entering the consolidation phase, where fellow professionals settled down to make the new policies work. In this phase, the word 'partnership' was often used by ministers as they realized that addressing reform deficits was both politically costly (especially in the health sector) and was a difficult practical task without the active co-operation of groups. Many of the key reforms, e.g. the national curriculum, were up for negotiation and much 'policy erosion' was already underway, via this process, by the time of the 1992 election. For example, in June 1991, government and family doctors were reported as having declared a truce in the dispute over NHS changes when the government set up a joint committee of the Health Department Officers and General Practitioners' leaders to review the experience both of GP practices that had opted to run their own budgets and negotiate contracts for hospital treatment, and of conventional practices.[20] Similarly, in the field of local government finance, which had been bitterly contested throughout the 1980s, it was reported that the Government and the local authority associations were negotiating revisions of the method by which central government assessed local spending needs. These negotiations were taking place in the Settlement Working Group of the Department of Environment and representatives from the Local Authority Associations.[21]

---

[19] For a detailed case-study of one example of destabilization followed by negotiation, see Jeremy J. Richardson and J. W. Moon, 'Policy-Making with a Difference: The Technical and Vocational Education Initiative', *Public Administration* (1984), 23–33.

[20] *Independent*, 10 June 1991.

[21] *Financial Times*, 14 Sept. 1991.

Two examples of consultation/negotiation in two of the most controversial areas of policy change do not, of course, prove that Britain's policy process was 'business as usual' post-Thatcher. However, there were—and are—dozens of similar cases. This should not surprise us. As Marsh and Rhodes note:

despite the Government's expressed desire to centralize power and authority and particularly to reduce the role of interest groups, it is the continued existence and power of policy networks which has acted as the greatest constraint on the development and implementation of radical policy.[22]

Thus, despite attempts radically to change Britain's policy style during the 1980s, interest groups retained their key role as actors in the policy process.

[22] Marsh and Rhodes, *Implementing Thatcherite Policies*, 185.

7

INTEREST GROUPS IN DENMARK

JACOB A. BUKSTI

INTRODUCTION: INTEREST GROUPS AND THE DILEMMA OF DEMOCRACY

It is well documented that interest groups play a central role in Scandinavian political systems. One might even claim that they are one of the basic elements of the so-called 'Scandinavian polity-model'. In Denmark, interest group participation and political compromise are vital parts of the political culture.

Since the first Danish democratic constitution of 1849, the right to form organizations or associations for any legal purpose has been a fundamental principle of Danish democracy. People have used this right to such an extent that Danish society has developed into one of the most highly organized societies in the world. This generalization is valid for both the number of organized interest groups and the degree of popular participation in these groups.[1]

Often, common action and co-operation have in fact proved to be a useful way of obtaining increased strength and influence, but also for solving mutual problems and establishing individual possibilities for personal creativity. In many policy areas, organized interest groups have had a decisive influence on political, economic, social, and cultural development—both through their own direct influence and regulation, and their role in socializing people to rules of democracy.

Thus, the organized groups are important actors in political life and the democratic process. Interest groups may influence political decisions, but at the same time by doing so they incur some kind of responsibility for implementation of these decisions. Consequently, involvement of interest groups in political decision-making may introduce new political opportunities. It may also, however, limit the scope of political actions to such an extent that political

[1] J. A. Buksti and L. N. Johansen, 'Variations in Organizational Participation in Government: the Case of Denmark', *Scandinavian Political Studies*, NS (1979), 197–220; Buksti, *Organisationernes Folk* (Aarhus: Forlaget Politica), 1984.

initiatives are blocked. This represents the political dilemma of the role of organized groups in the democratic process.[2]

THE DANISH SYSTEM OF INTEREST GROUPS

Interest groups do not emerge in a vacuum. The formation of interest groups may be regarded as a result of a complex interaction between a number of specific social and political conditions, various historical traditions, and as a compromise between different interests at a given time.

In Denmark, the interest group system has been analysed in terms of both structure and patterns of influence. As is typical of Scandinavian democracies, Denmark is a relatively small and homogeneous country and is relatively easy to study. Thus, it was possible to measure the number of organized national interest groups first in 1975 and again in 1980. A comprehensive questionnaire was administered to all such interest groups. The data contained information on group size; finances; technical and administrative resources; organizational structure; type, scope, and frequency of contacts with public authorities; and, inter- and intra-organizational linkages.[3] In 1975, the total number identified was 1,946 and in 1980 was 1,990, of which approximately two-thirds were economic-oriented, e.g. trade unions, organizations for business, agriculture, banking, housing, and consumers.

On the basis of this database, the formation and development of the Danish interest group system as a whole is shown in Fig. 7.1. Although it should be noted that the data are restricted to interest groups existing in 1975, the Figure nevertheless shows a very clear pattern. Generally, the formation of groups increased until 1920; it decreased in the 1920s, increased in the 1930s and 1940s, weakened again in the 1950s, and exploded from the 1960s onwards.

The process prior to 1920 is the period in which the industrialization of Danish society began. Economic growth increased[4] and the structure of society was transformed from a traditional rural society into one with a more differentiated and complex social and economic structure. In addition, active governmental intervention in the economy was instituted during the First World War. More importantly, this intervention was carried out amid continuous consultations with organized interest groups, such as trade unions,

---

[2] R. A. Dahl, *Dilemmas of Pluralist Democracy* (New Haven, Conn.: Yale University Press, 1982).

[3] J. A. Buksti and L. N. Johansen, *Danske Organisationers Hvem-Hvad-Hvor* (Copenhagen: Politikens: Forlag, 1977); Buksti, *Organisationernes Folk*.

[4] A. Stinchcombe, 'Social Structure and Organisations', in J. March (ed.), *Handbook of Organisations* (Chicago: Rand McNally, 1965).

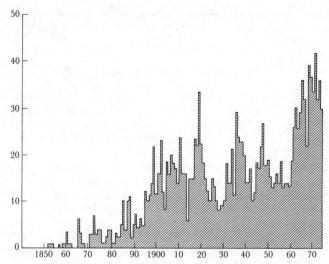

FIGURE 7.1   Annual Growth in the Danish Interest Group System (net growth per year)

employers' associations, agricultural organizations and the Federation of Danish Industries. Thus, it was during this period that the basic structure of the Danish interest group system was formed. As a result of the general economic depression and of increased governmental regulation, this development intensified during the 1930s and the 1940s. Interest groups became deeply integrated in both administration and policy-making. Thus the tradition of intimate co-operation between public bureaucracy and interest groups so typical of Scandinavia was initiated. 'The consulting state' emerged, and a type of 'corporatist' political structure was created.

The 1950s were characterized by unstable economic and political conditions, and by abolition of the regulations established during the Second World War. Economic policy was characterized by a strong 'stop–go' tendency and interest group formation stagnated.

Finally, in the 1960s, the welfare state emerged and public activities expanded enormously both quantitatively and qualitatively. This strongly affected the interest group system as is shown in Fig. 7.1. Public employees and welfare functions were organized, and many of the traditional interest groups were modernized. Over one-third of today's interest groups were established after 1960.

The 1980s have been characterized by many mergers caused by increased external economic and political pressures on interest groups and by the prospects of the emerging European Single

Market. Interest groups have to adapt both their internal structures and political strategies to the changing external conditions.

Thus, the factors which have been crucial to the development of interest groups and to their very influential position in Denmark and elsewhere in Scandinavia, are largely factors which are external to the interest groups themselves. These are the general political, economic, and social developments in society, the expansion of the public sector, and the increasing rate of regulation of the economy.[5] Several systematic studies in other Scandinavian political systems—especially in Norway and Finland—present the same picture.[6]

This trend, however, is not universal for all types of interest groups. It is most evident for economic interest groups which are formed to promote or defend rather specific interests. It is less evident for so-called promotional groups, which are concerned with ideas, values, beliefs, and ideologies.

PATTERNS OF INFLUENCE: THE ROLE AND FUNCTION OF
INTEREST GROUPS

Thus, over time, interest groups in Denmark have become deeply involved in the policy-making process and in the active implementation of the policies. Consequently, it is misleading to see groups as destructive, for example, using strikes, demonstrations, or other actions, in order to force their demands on society. Only a very small part of the total activity of groups is in the public arena. Of much more importance are the semi-private contacts which have been established between the interest groups and the political authorities. It is of course obvious that behind the development of this system of consultation and the establishment of integrated, corporatist structures, lies a latent threat of sanctions if the groups are ignored. On the other hand, the position of interest groups in this system will

---

[5] Buksti and Johansen, 'Variations in Organizational Participation in Government'; Buksti, *Organisationernes Folk.*

[6] A. Hallenstvedt and J. Moren, 'Det organiserte samfunn', in N. R. Ramsøy and M. Vraa (eds.), *Det norske samfunn* (Oslo: Gyldendal, 1975), 323–62; O. Bjerrefjord, 'Fra embetmannstat til embetsmannsstat?', 134–59 in G. Hernes (ed.), *Forhandlingsøkonomi og blandingsadministrasjon* (Oslo: Universitetsforlaget, 1978); M. Egeberg, *Stat og organisasjoner* (Oslo: Universitetsforlaget, 1981); J. P. Olsen, 'The Dilemmas of Organizational Integration in Government', in id., *Organized Democracy* (Oslo: Universitetsforlaget, 1983); V. Helander and R. Lintonen, 1981, 'Relationships between Associations and the Central Administration in Finland', Paper, 6th Nordic Conference of Political Science, Turku, 1981.

have a moderating effect on the groups themselves, because they realize that their political strength is largely dependent on the existing system.

Thus, sanctions by interest groups against policies (or lack of policies) produced by the integrated policy-making system would also constitute a severe threat to the position of the groups themselves. Interest groups prefer political stability and policy-making certainty, and consequently they normally strongly support the existing system and its decisions. Therefore, a close relationship has developed between interest groups and the permanent public bureaucracy, while parliament—the Folketinget—being more unpredictable—is less favoured as a target for group pressure.[7]

There are, however, exceptions to this general characterization of the Danish interest group system. Not all groups are involved in the policy-making process, and, for certain reasons, some groups explicitly want to remain 'outsiders'. These deliberate 'outsiders' are often opposed to the existing policy-making system itself and they seek influence by extra-parliamentary means. One example, as elsewhere in Western Europe, is the Anti-Nuclear Power Movement. Other groups who might be called 'impotent insiders' are involved in policy-making and are consulted in all important matters of their concern, but they lack relevant resources to secure influence on their own, and consequently they merely act as technical consultants to the government. (For example, the Danish fisheries organizations have been impotent insiders in the policy-making process.)

In contrast, the major interest groups, the *real* insiders, are highly integrated into the political process at all levels. They have considerable economic resources and technical expertise, and are able to play a role as permanent participants in the integrated policy-making process so characteristic of the Scandinavian democracies. The most prominent representatives in this category of interest groups are the Danish Confederation of Trade Unions (LO), the Danish Employers' Confederation (DA), the Federation of Danish Industries, the Agricultural Council of Denmark, and the Danish National Association of Local Authorities (KL).

Therefore, although several studies indicate that integrated interest group participation in government in Denmark is not restricted to a small number of interest groups, there are, nevertheless, great variations in the intensity and scope of group involvement in policy-making. These variations can be seen across

---

[7] Buksti, *Organisationernes Folk.*

types of interest groups, resources, and policy areas.[8] Finally, those groups deeply involved in the policy-making process and in the integrated policy-making structures may use different channels and different approaches to secure influence.

Thus, Danish trade unions developed an influential position in the long period from 1924 to 1982 with almost permanent Social Democratic governments. Prior to the election of a bourgeois government in 1982, the trade unions had become very used to having direct political contact with the political leaders. Until recently, they had no need to work closely, on a professional basis, with civil servants in the public bureaucracy. Consequently, their own huge bureaucracies are not highly 'professionalized'. They do, of course, have very close contacts with civil servants, and they are well integrated into the network of public committees and commissions. Yet these integrated, corporatist structures only act as a *supplement* to direct political contacts.[9] Their reliance on the Social Democrats makes trade unions very vulnerable to changes in government and the unions have experienced increasing problems in developing a coherent strategy for exercising political influence, because of lasting bourgeois rule.

Since 1924, the employers' and business organizations have had to realize that they could not rely on the same kind of special relationship with the government, because of the dominance of the Social Democrats. They based their strategy for political influence on professional contact and expertise in relation to civil servants and through the widespread network of public committees and commissions. This makes their influence less vulnerable to political changes, and, at the same time, less visible to the public.

The patterns of influence are different for various interest groups. However, direct contact with, and pressure on, the government attracts more public and mass media attention than the day-to-day relationship between groups and civil servants. Consequently, there may be a false impression that trade unions are the most powerful groups and are the greatest threat to the democratic process.

Notwithstanding sectoral differences and differences between types of groups, interest groups are vital actors in the political process in Denmark and other Scandinavian countries. They participate actively in government both in policy-making and implementation. Several studies show that this participation in the governmental process is certainly not restricted to a small number of

[8] Buksti and Johansen, 'Variations in Organizational Participation in Government'; Buksti, *Organisationernes Folk*.
[9] Buksti, *Organisationernes Folk*.

interest groups. On the contrary, a very large number of groups have some form of contact with the public authorities, although patterns of influence vary greatly from one group to another and across various policy areas.

However, the strong position of interest groups is not necessarily constant but is part of a complex, dynamic, social and political development. Consequently, even strong and powerful organizations have had to adapt to changes in political structures and in their general environment. External changes have differential effects on the various interest groups, and the better the specific group is at adapting its resources and strategy to these changes, the more it will be able to maintain or gain political influence.

CORPORATISM OR SECTORALISM?

The emergence of integrated policy-making structures in vital policy areas of the Danish political system may be seen as a consequence of an interaction between the early process of group formation and the general development of the role of the state.

As shown in Fig. 7.1, the process of organizing interest groups began in the 1880s. At the same time, the role of the state was seen as passive towards the basic economic mechanisms of society. The 'laissez-faire' state would try to support the market mechanisms, but it did not intervene. As a result, a strong market tradition of self-regulation by organized interest groups was established. Specific policy areas, such as the labour market and agriculture, were subject to agreements between the relevant groups without any direct public intervention. Governments and political authorities widely accepted and supported these 'private' agreements and regulations. In fact, governments were active in this process by setting up the institutional framework for making such private agreements, for instance, in the labour market.

During the First World War, and later on during the economic depression of the 1930s, the role of the state vis-à-vis the economy changed. Economic policy with direct public intervention and regulation was established. However, by doing this the government had to intervene in policy areas already regulated by private agreements. As it has always been a strong element in the Danish legal tradition to try to respect private arrangements, this kind of political intervention was not without political and legal difficulties. To avoid, or to minimize, problems, political intervention was made in close co-operation with the social partners and interest groups in particular policy areas. Therefore, interest groups became closely integrated in the policy-making process of public regulation, and corporatist structures emerged.

This development was supported by the historically close links between the trade unions and the Social Democrats, whose domination of government coincided with the establishment of interest group involvement in policy-making. The Social Democrats did not, for obvious reasons, regard interest groups as opponents of political parties or as a threat to the democratic process. On the contrary, for practical political purposes, they saw the possibilities of reducing conflicts in society by integrating potentially antagonistic groups into policy-making. By doing so, the sovereignty of organized interest groups was accepted and their role as political partners in the policy-making process was recognized.

Thus, during the 1930s, strong corporatist structures were established as a means of making policy. Such integrated corporatist structures emerged especially in the labour market and in the agricultural policy sectors. However, these processes were used as the model for numerous other policy areas. In some areas strongly organized interest groups did not exist, and the particular groups had therefore to be given public funding. (For example, the Danish Consumer Council was primarily established to balance the Federation of Danish Industries, in public committees and commissions.)

Undoubtedly, corporatist structures and policy-making traditions are now prominent in most important economic policy areas in the Danish political system. Furthermore, several studies have demonstrated that the existence of autonomous policy sectors, or 'iron triangles', seems crucial to variations in group participation in government.[10] Analysing the political system via policy sectors combines two approaches. First, the policy-sector approach is prompted by the observation that the terms of the political process will depend on the actual policy area concerned.[11] It is obvious that political decisions concerning the labour market are reached by a rather different process from, say, in the field of culture and art. Consequently, the policy area and the policy content can be regarded as the independent variable explaining the characteristics of the specific policy-making process. Secondly, the policy-sector approach departs from the traditional institution-centred analyses of the political system. The focal point of institutional analyses is the

[10] E. Damgaard, 'Politiske sektorer: Jerntrekanter eller løse netvaerk?' *Nordisk Administrativt Tidsskrift*, 2 (1981), 396–411.

[11] L. A. Froman, 'The Categorization of Policy Contents', in A. Ranney (ed.), *Political Science and Public Policy* (Chicago: Markham, 1968).

fact that the main divisions of conflict and co-operation follow the traditional divisions between political institutions, for example, between government and parliament or between political parties and interest groups. In contrast, it has proved more useful to analyse conflict structures and co-operation patterns across different types of institutions.

More precisely, the policy-sector approach claims the existence of separate segments or sectors in the political system. As the actors in these segments may be representatives from various interest groups, MPs, cabinet ministers, civil servants, journalists, and different kinds of experts, the segments cut across the traditional boundaries of political institutions. The participants in these segments form a very tight network with a relatively high degree of communication within the segment and a relatively low level of communication outside it. Moreover, specific norms develop inside the segments, defining central problems, values, and views for the actors concerned. These norms may vary across the segments, and consequently, the way policy issues are handled in the policy-making process may be determined by the way the issues are defined and by whom.

There are considerable points of resemblance between the so-called corporatist model and the policy-sector approach. Both models accept the notion that policy content has a decisive impact on the policy-making process. Thus, integrated corporatist structures are more distinct in some policy areas than in others. Furthermore, both models reflect a concern with the development of common norms in relation to the policy-making process as such and the actual content of the political decisions. Finally, the corporatist model is to a very large extent consistent with the view that the political system empirically consists of a number of closed spheres—segments or sectors—with a high degree of internal communication and a very low level of communication between sectors.

The character and function of the various sectors varies considerably, however, and integrated policy-making structures may be quite evident in one sector, while in another they may be rather embryonic. If a certain sector can be clearly distinguished from other sectors, the sovereignty of the particular sector may be rather high, and such sovereignty tends to facilitate integrated policy-making. For example, until recently, agricultural policy was one of the most well-defined and strongest policy sectors in Denmark.

It also seems obvious that the position of interest groups inside the various sectors may affect the structure of the policy-making process. For instance, organizations in the labour market have many conflicting interests, while in the agricultural sector there seems to be consensus on the basic values of the system. Accordingly, the terms of corporatism may be deeply affected by the existence of conflict or consensus inside the particular sector. In fact, Danish research has found insufficient evidence to support the use of the corporatist model[12] whilst the policy-sector approach has been a successful framework for studying the Danish decision-making process.[13]

Political problems are not usually defined automatically, and as a consequence of the high degree of sectorization of the Danish political system, the government may change the position of interest groups dramatically by intervening in the working of the various policy sectors. Political decision-makers can make interest groups influential, but they can also weaken them.

Furthermore, interest groups cannot exist in a political vacuum. The more exact and specific public policy they have to deal with, the easier it is to legitimate their role to their members and to external actors. Changes in the specific content of public policy or in the specific policy-making process consequently require adaptation of group resources, structures, and activities. In short, interest groups may influence public policy, but changes in public policy and in political and administrative structures will affect the whole basis of policy-making. Thus government and parliament are to a large extent able to determine the role and function of even very strong interest groups.

The Danish case demonstrates quite clearly how the conditions of interest groups have changed recently. First, the Danish policy-making system has been altered by Danish membership of the European Community (EC). Secondly, the role and function of interest groups were put under severe pressure by the change in government in 1982 and by the subsequent Liberal–Conservative bourgeois rule.

INTERNALIZATION OF INTEREST GROUP ACTIVITY

When Denmark joined the EC in 1973, the political and administrative structures in many policy areas were changed. A complex bureaucratic system was established, and new channels of influencing the policy-making process were opened both nationally and

[12] M. Heisler, 'Corporate Pluralism: Where is the Theory?', *Scandinavian Political Studies*, NS, 2/3 (1979).
[13] Buksti, *Organisationernes Folk*.

internationally, especially concerning the EC. The locus of power shifted and new ways of influencing decisions had to be adopted.

Interest groups generally prefer the certainty of the traditional system. Consequently, as elsewhere in the EC, Danish interest groups continued to direct their influence primarily through the traditional policy-making structures at the national level. However, the groups most concerned with EC policy, e.g. the agricultural organizations, immediately established direct contact with the policy-making process.[14] The agricultural organizations are exceptional, however, and until recently the EC activities of Danish interest groups have not been very intense, and were primarily designed to facilitate collection of information on developments at the EC level. It serves, to a considerable degree, as a basis for continued efficient group participation at the *national* level.

But with the approach of the European Single Market (at the end of 1992), many organized interests are directly affected by EC policy. Consequently, prior to the Maastricht referendum, most major Danish interest groups have been quite active at the EC level. Permanent representations have been established, and professional lobbyists have been hired to deal with the specific EC policy-making process.[15]

The core area of interest group activity is no longer restricted to the national policy-making process. Increasingly, policy issues are handled at an international level, especially in the EC. Interest group activity is, therefore, internationalized. At the same time, by acting at the international level interest groups are learning new methods and styles of political influence, which subsequently are used in their activities at the national level. Thus, the traditional formalized integrated structures are frequently being supplemented by informal methods of lobbying.

NEW TRENDS OF INTEREST GROUP INFLUENCE: CHANGES IN ROLE AND STYLE

Danish interest groups have more recently been subject to increasing external pressure because of general problems regarding the functioning of the Danish welfare state, and as a consequence of

---

[14] J. A. Buksti, 'Corporate Structures in Danish EC Policy: Patterns of Organizational Participation and Adaptation', *Journal of Common Market Studies*, 19/2 (1980), 140–59.

[15] Henning Bregnsbo and Nils Chr Sidenius, *Danish Lobbying in Brussels*, Paper presented to the conference 'The Impact of National Traditions on European Public Affairs', 16–17 Jan. 1992, Louvain, Netherlands, 1992.

changes of governmental style after the Liberal–Conservative bourgeois government took office in 1982.

Since 1973, Denmark had faced very serious economic problems and new political challenges. A comprehensive economic crisis policy was implemented. Yet the conditions for political compromise were more complex, and in 1982 the ruling Social Democrats realized that they no longer commanded political support. All political options had failed and they left office without calling an election.[16] A new Liberal–Conservative four-party minority government took over, facing severe economic problems. Furthermore, several elements of the Danish welfare system and of the structure of the public sector in general needed modernization—not just because of the lack of resources, but also as a consequence of changing norms and values in society.

While the Social Democratic strategy had called for 'bargained incomes policy', active government measures against unemployment, and the maintenance of social welfare programmes and public sector employment, the Liberal–Conservative government had a different approach. The new governmental parties rejected the Social Democratic strategy, and instead based their programme on two key elements: to promote the competitiveness of the private business sector through the reduction of interest rates, inflation, and wage increases, and to reduce or limit public spending.[17] As a result, both policy content and policy style changed.

From the beginning, the Liberal–Conservative government deliberately opposed close and permanent integration of interest groups in policy-making. Prominent representatives of the government stated that the reconstruction of the Danish economy was dependent on weakening the power of interest groups. The government was a minority government, but until the general election in 1987 it maintained a stable bourgeois majority in support of its economic policy. Therefore, the most conspicuous change in policy style was the firm determination with which the government tried to impose incomes policies and to limit state and local government spending, despite opposition within and outside parliament. In these respects there were no genuine consultations with important interest groups, or tripartite negotiations as recommended by the Social Democrats.

The overriding goal was to achieve economic recovery after many years of alleged Social Democratic 'mismanagement'. To achieve

[16] E. Damgaard, 'Crisis Politics in Denmark 1974–1987', 7–88 in E. Damgaard, P. Gerlich and Jeremy J. Richardson, *The Politics of Economic Crisis: Lessons from Western Europe* (Aldershot: Avebury, 1989).

[17] Ibid.

this goal, the main strategy was to stay in power. New parliamentary methods and practices were developed in which the government suffered several defeats, and alternative proposals (in opposition to the government) were accepted. In several policy issues it was difficult to distinguish government from opposition.[18] The minority government accepted its weak position and the power of parliament increased.

There was almost total political confusion after the 1987 general election when the government lost its stable majority. Then, after the 1988 general election, the government was changed into a three-party coalition but remained in office. However, in order to cope with unpredictable parliamentary conditions, the government tried to construct alliances with interest groups, especially those dominated by Social Democrats, such as the trade unions.

In conclusion, we might argue that new trends of interest group influence in Denmark are marked by a strong element of political schizophrenia. The role and function of interest groups has changed, and their influence has weakened in some respects and strengthened in others.

On the one hand, the general social, economic, and political development has reduced the strength of traditional integrated policy-making structures. To compensate for this, interest groups have increased informal lobbying and pressure group activities. On the other hand, the government has tried to use interest group influence and support against a politically unpredictable parliament. This approach has increased the scope for political influence by particular interest groups, but has also risked political conflict as a consequence of traditional links between interest groups and specific political parties.

The long-standing influential position of interest groups has become more informal, while the style of lobbying tends to be more flexible and more influenced by the specific situation. The irony is that interest groups are still powerful, as we have come to expect in the Scandinavian democracies, but the dependency of this power on external factors has increased dramatically.

---

[18] E. Damgaard and P. Svensson, 'Who Governs? Parties and Policies in Denmark', *European Journal of Political Research*, 17 (1989), 731–45.

8

INTEREST GROUPS IN ITALY: FROM PRESSURE ACTIVITY TO POLICY NETWORKS

LUCA LANZALACO

INTRODUCTION

Interest groups are conspicuous by their absence from Italian political science literature. LaPalombara[1] noted this lacuna at the beginning of the 1960s and Pasquino[2] spoke of an 'interested veil of silence' which had been lowered on the activity, the role, the relevance, and the risks for democratic regimes of pressure groups. Apart from some relevant theoretical contributions,[3] a quarter of a century passed without any substantial increase in empirical knowledge following LaPalombara's seminal book. This article aims to assess the role of interest groups in Italian politics on the basis of a critical analysis of the scanty and hetrogeneous literature from the 1950s to the present. The debate has been in four main waves, to each of which I will devote a separate section. I shall first provide a broad sketch of the structural characteristics of the interest group system in Italy, while in the final sections the distinctive traits of Italian interest politics will be highlighted.

THE INTEREST GROUP SYSTEM IN ITALY

The Italian interest group system is highly fragmented—a tendency which has become more marked in recent years. The system of

[1] J. LaPalombara, *Interest Groups in Italian Politics* (Princeton, NJ: Princeton University Press, 1964).

[2] G. Pasquino, *Istituzioni, partiti, lobbies* (Bari-Roma: Laterza, 1988).

[3] See D. Fisichella, *Introduzione* to the section 'Partiti politici e gruppi di pressione', in G. Sartori (ed.), *Antologia di scienza politica* (Bologna: il Mulino, 1971); id. (ed.), *Partiti e gruppi di pressione* (Bologna: il Mulino, 1972); G. Pasquino, 'I gruppi di pressione', *Rivista Italiana di scienza politica*, 2 (1972), 161–83; S. Passigli, *Gruppi di pressione*, in A. Negri (ed.), *Scienze Politiche*, i. *Stato e politica* (Milano: Enciclopedia Feltrinelli Fisher, 1970); id., *Introduzione* to the section 'Potere ed elites politiche', in

representation of employers is characterized by the presence of many cross-cutting cleavages, concerning firm size, sector of production, political allegiance, legal status of the employer and, occasionally, functions performed by the association. This produces approximately a dozen peak associations.[4] Thus, Italian employers do not have a unitary representative structure like British, German, Swedish, or Spanish employers but are faced with a range of peak associations often competing with each other.[5]

In addition, the system of labour representation is relatively fragmented, even if in comparative terms it is less distinctive. The deepest cleavage is a political one, between three confederations, each of which has different party allegiances. Recently, an occupational cleavage has emerged following the strengthening of autonomous trade unions, the so-called COBAS or shop-floor committees.[6]

The structure and organization of peak associations provide an insight into the high degree of fragmentation of organized economic interests in Italy. However, a similar sectional structure exists for non-economic pressure groups. Here, both in the field of Catholic associationalism, and in that of other non-economic interests, such as feminism, environmentalism, and consumerism, many associations often compete with each other.[7] With so little integration from an organizational perspective, authors such as LaPalombara[8] have recently begun to speak of a neo-pluralist trend.

This tendency to form associations of various types is deeply rooted in Italian history. It intensified during the Fascist period, increased after the Second World War,[9] and has shown a peculiar growth in recent years.[10] We can therefore agree that 'Italian society

G. Sartori (ed.), *Antologia di scienza politica* (Bologna: il Mulino, 1971); G. Sartori, (1959), 'Gruppi di interesse o gruppi di pressione ?, *il Mulino* (1959), 7–42.

[4] A. Martinelli and T. Treu, *Employers Associations in Italy*, in J. P. Windmuller and A. Gladstone (eds.), *Employers Associations and Industrial Relations: A Comparative Study*, (Oxford: Clarendon Press, 1984), 264–93.

[5] See L. Lanzalaco, *Pininfarina President of the Confederation of Industry and the Problems of Business Interest Associations*, in R. Y. Nanetti and R. Catanzaro (eds.), *Politics in Italy: A Reader*, iv. (London: Pinter, 1990), 102–23; id., *Dall'impresa all'associazione. Le organizzazioni degli imprenditori: la Confindustria in prospettiva comparata* (Milan: Angeli, 1990).

[6] L. Bordogna, 'Archipelago Cobas': Fragmentation of Representation and Labour Conflicts, in R. Y. Nanetti, R. Leonardi, and P. Corbetta (eds.), *Italian Politics: A Review*, iv. (London: Pinter, 1989).

[7] See M. Diani, *Isole nell'arcipelago* (Bologna: il Mulino, 1988); id., *The Italian Ecology Movement: From Radicalism to Moderation*, in W. Rudig (ed.), *Green Politics*, i. (Edinburgh: Edinburgh University Press, 1990).

[8] J. LaPalombara, *Democracy Italian Style* (New Haven, Yale University Press, 1987).

[9] LaPalombara, *Interest Groups*.

[10] A. Mortara (ed.), *Le associazioni italiane*, 2nd edn. (Milan: Ciriec-Angeli, 1983).

has had considerable experience with secondary associations'.[11] And when LaPalombara speaks of the 'weakness of the Italian civil society', he is not referring to the quantitative aspects of associationalism, but to the modes of action of these associations. They tend to be incorporated into the public administration and into the political 'game',[12] which results in a loss of autonomy (especially by political parties), and operate as mere public or quasi-public bodies, so that private associations tend to be highly 'politicized'.[13] This tendency involves not only economic interest associations, but also non-functional groups such as sporting associations, which make up over three-quarters of all associations.[14] The high level of 'partyness' of Italian interest groups[15] may in part be explained by the attempts by political parties to control and shape the process of 'structuration' of the interest group system in the reconstruction of Italian democracy after the demise of the Fascist regime.[16] The structure of the Italian interest group system—namely its extreme fragmentation—and the relevance of political cleavages and allegiances, play a central role in explaining the nature of interest group activity and the peculiar interplay between *interest group* politics and *party* politics in Italy, even if more recently this nexus has been eroded and is becoming more tenuous.

MODES OF INTEREST GROUP ACTIVITY IN THE 1950S AND 1960S

The above-noted structural traits were identified in original research into interest groups in Italy in the late 1950s and early 1960s.[17] The main contribution to this wave of studies was LaPalombara's seminal book *Interest Groups in Italian Politics*. Following a general review of interest groups in Italy, he focused on two of them: Confindustria and Catholic Action. The former represents private industrial employers, while the latter is the main voice of the Catholic Church. He concluded that 'the greatest degree of acknowledged interaction between interest groups and government

[11] LaPalombara, *Interest Groups*, 172.

[12] A. Pizzorno, *I soggetti del pluralismo* (Bologna: il Mulino, 1980), 37–8.

[13] LaPalombara, *Interest Groups*, 143.

[14] Mortara, *Le associazioni italiane*.

[15] P. Allum (1980), 'Les groupes de pression en Italie', in *Revue française de science politique*, 5 (1980), 148–72.

[16] L. Morlino (ed.), *Costruire la democrazia: consolidamento democratico e gruppi di interesse in Italia (1943–1958)* (Bologna: Il Mulino, 1992).

[17] See LaPalombara, *Interest Groups*, Introduction;, O. M. Petracca, 'Gli studi sui gruppi di pressione in Italia', in G. Wootton, *I gruppi di interesse* (Bologna: il Mulino, 1975).

seems to involve the sector of public administration',[18] and that these interactions may assume the form of *clientela* or of *parentela*.

The *clientela* relationship exists when an interest group, for whatever reasons, succeeds in becoming, in the eyes of a given administrative agency, the natural expression and representative of a given social sector which, in turn, constitutes the natural target or reference point for the activity of the administrative agency.[19]

In comparison, the *parentela* relationship,

involves a relatively close and integral relationship between certain associational interest groups, on the one hand, and the politically dominant Christian Democratic Party on the other. . . . Where *parentela* exists, and where certain other related conditions are met, interest groups that enjoy the relationship can exercise considerable influence over a bureaucracy quite apart from any consideration of *clientela*.[20]

Furthermore, political parties also have a crucial role in *clientela* relations, increasing trust and confidence between interest group representatives and public administration representatives.[21] These types of relationships are extremely widespread and they characterize the Italian style of interest politics.

Another diffuse mode of interaction between interest groups and public authorities is lobbying which 'involves a two-sided relationship between, on the one hand, an interest group that makes demands, and, on the other hand, a legislator who is formally in a position to satisfy the demands that are communicated'.[22] The analysis of the patterns of lobbying activities clearly shows that

Italy's interest groups are isolative and essentially non-bargaining. Antagonistic groups that rarely communicate with each other and go in search of legislators of like ideological predispositions are ill-equipped to bargain democratically. The basic divisions that permeate the society are not aggregated but actually exacerbated by the pattern of group interaction with political parties . . . because the fragmented groups find their equivalents in some of the political parties. Indeed, the latter, in order to assure themselves a portion of those who are potential group members, will often contribute directly to the fractionalization of interests. The deep, basic conflicts of the social system are therefore reproduced intact in the legislature.[23]

As we shall see, this analysis of Italian interest politics is still generally accepted.

---

[18] LaPalombara, *Interest Groups*, 252.   [19] Ibid. 262.
[20] Ibid. 306.   [21] Ibid. 290.
[22] Ibid. 21.   [23] Ibid. 249.

Interest Groups in Italian Politics must not be seen as a point of departure for interest group studies in Italy, but as a point of arrival, since it was published at the end of a rich political debate[24] about the role of interest groups in Italian politics. This debate was characterized by two main traits. First, the discovery that actual political processes do not mirror the formal legal norms and procedures. The principle of political equality of all citizens before the state is challenged by interest groups that influence decision-making and implementation. Secondly, the intervention of interest groups is often seen as a *pathological* distortion of the *normal* processes of representation—an *interference* of illegitimate actors in decision-making. For this reason, both the debate about interest groups and the empirical research into their structure and action have been rather critical: interest group activity is not studied and described, it is *denounced* as if it were intrinsically dangerous for democracy.

The 'discovery' of interest groups provoked two different reactions. Some saw interest groups as a pathological phenomenon and proposed a tough regulation of their actions in order to prevent them from wielding pressure on democratic political processes. Others adopted an alternative line suggesting that the phenomenon of interest groups is *physiological* to democratic systems. What makes it pathological in the Italian case is not the strength of the interest groups but the weakness of Italian democratic institutions. This weakness is likely to be due to the fact that 'in Italy the interest groups are not a *consequence* of political democracy, but are actually prior to it, and therefore in a position of extraordinary power vis-à-vis the democratic state'.[25] The manner in which the consolidation of the democratic regime occurred in Italy; the legacy left by this process;[26] the disparity between the strength of interest groups institutionalized during the Fascist regime; and the newness and consequent fragility of the new democratic regime jointly explain the pervasiveness of interest groups in decision-making. From this diagnosis it follows that strong regulation of interest groups was

[24] See 'I gruppi di pressione', ed. CIRD (Centro Italiano Ricerche e Documentazione), in *Tempi moderni* (Apr.–June 1960; July–Sept. 1960; Oct.–Dec. 1960); J. Meynaud and C. Risè, *I gruppi di interesse in Italia e in Francia* (Naples, ESI, 1963).

[25] LaPalombara, *Interest Groups*, 8.

[26] See L. Morlino, 'From Fascism to Weak Democracy: The Change of Regime in Italy (1938–1948)', Paper presented at the Summer School on Comparative European Politics, Florence, European University Institute, June–July 1982; id., *Democratic Consolidation and Non Democratic Legacy in Italy*, Paper presented at the ECPR workshop on 'Prospects and Dilemmas of democratic Consolidation in Latin America', Rimini, Apr. 1988, mimeo; id. (ed.), *Costruire la democrazia. Consolidamento democratico e gruppi di interesse in Italia (1943–1958)* (Bologna: il Mulino, 1992).

unlikely to be effective since it would restrict interest groups without addressing the weakness of the democratic institutions. It is this weakness that is the almost unique feature of the Italian case. Hence, the proposed solution was not to weaken interest groups, but to consider reforming the institutions. The terms of this debate, and the contrast between the two positions, continue to be relevant today in the current debate about the regulation of lobbying.

Between the mid-1950s and mid-1960s, a crucial change occurred in the Italian political system. The assumption by the political class, in particular by the Christian Democratic Party, of a more autonomous position in dealing with private business interests, combined with the entry of the Socialist Party in the coalition government at the beginning of the 1960s, led to significant changes in interest-group strategies. Their direct channels of access to decision-making were now threatened. For example, this change weakened Confindustria, and allowed direct relationships between firms and political parties to develop.[27] More generally, clientelism was both of increased importance yet was also modified.[28] As a result of these changes, scholars in the 1970s shifted their attention from the *internal* structure of interest groups and their relationship with institutional actors to a new issue—namely the complex interplay between interest groups and political parties.

In this period, Alessandro Pizzorno[29] developed an influential analysis, augmented by Farneti,[30] and recently 'revisited' by Pasquino.[31] It involves the operation of the Italian political system based on the transformation of political parties. The reduction of *solidarity areas* and the dominance of *interest systems* and of particularistic demands within political parties are seen as phenomena ingrained in the evolution of party organization and, more generally, of pluralistic systems of representation.[32] From this perspective, it is the *void* left by the disappearance of political collective identities, embedded in political parties, that presents opportunities both for new forms of interest representation and for pressure from specific and particularistic interests. Thus, once the democratic regime was in place, political parties lost their role of aggregating political demands and became mere channels for interest groups.

[27] A. Martinelli, 'Organized Business and Italian Politics: Confindustria and the Christian Democrats in the Postwar Period', in *West European Politics* (1979), 67–87.

[28] L. Graziano, *Clientelismo e sistema politico: Il caso italiano* (Milan: Angeli, 1980).

[29] Pizzorno, *I Soggetti del pluralismo*.

[30] P. Farneti, *I partiti politici e il sistema di potere*, in Valerio Castronovo (ed.), *L'Italia contemporanea 1945–1947* (Turin: Einaudi, 1974).

[31] Pasquino, *Istituzioni, partiti, lobbies*.

[32] A. Pizzorno, 'Interests and Parties in Pluralism', in S. Berger (ed.), *Organizing Interests in Western Europe* (Cambridge: Cambridge University Press, 1981).

Pizzorno's analysis focuses neither on the pathological nature of interest-group action nor on the weakness of institutions. The distinctive characteristics of Italian politics during the late 1950s and 1960s—from the fractionalization of political parties to legislative particularism, from clientelism to *sottogoverno*—are parts of a unique process that is a *natural* and *spontaneous* evolution of all the systems of political representation. If this evolutionary model has acquired peculiar characteristics in Italy, it is due, on the one hand, to the exclusion of the left-wing opposition from government, and on the other hand, to the individual mobilization of the middle classes.[33] Both of these factors led to a rapid decline of political participation, to an increasing electoral focus for political parties, and to the emergence of particularistic demands.

The main merit of Pizzorno's analysis is to challenge the conventional analysis of the relationships between political parties and civil society. He emphasized that the attempted 'colonization' may be in the opposite direction: Not only may political parties 'colonize' interest groups in order to control civil society, but interest groups may penetrate political parties, using them as channels to pursue their particularistic interests. In other words, it is the transformation of mass political parties[34] into catch-all parties[35] that offers huge opportunities for interest groups within political parties. Also, as LaPalombara highlighted, it is only by representing particular interests and specific demands, and not aggregating them into collective interests and general demands, that parties can develop and stabilize their electoral support.

Another influential interpretation of the peculiarities of the Italian political system has been advanced by Giuliano Amato.[36] He suggests that the peculiarity of the Italian case can be captured by the model of *governo spartitorio*, literally 'sharing out government'. In this model, interest groups express distributive and redistributive demands and their representatives match these demands and distribute economic resources without efforts to aggregate them. Metaphorically speaking, we may say that in the 'sharing out' model the activity of government does not assist the development of common long-term objectives, but is intent upon 'dividing the pie'

[33] Id., 'Middle Strata in the Mechanisms of Consensus', in D. Pinto (ed.), *Contemporary Italian Sociology: A Reader* (Cambridge: Cambridge University Press, 1982), 101–22.

[34] M. Duverger, *Les Partis politiques* (Paris: Colin, 1951).

[35] O. Kirchheimer, 'The Transformation of the Western European Party Systems', in J. LaPalombara and M. Weiner (eds.), *Political Parties and Political Development* (Princeton, NJ: Princeton University Press, 1966).

[36] G. Amato, *Economia, politica e istituzioni in Italia* (Bologna: il Mulino, 1976).

into many slices, by means of distributive policies, in order to satisfy in the short term as many particularistic demands as possible in order to develop electoral support.

The roots of this phenomenon are in the lack of a complete industrial revolution, in the relative backwardness of Italian industrial development, and in the consequent absence of any hegemony of the Italian industrial bourgeoisie which has been constrained to negotiate its power position with other pre-capitalistic groups, such as farmers and artisans. The fragmentation of the system of representation of business interests, and the absence of a party specifically representing the Italian industrial bourgeoisie[37] is a good indicator of its weakness and of the absence of its hegemony over other social groups. This absence of hegemony also had consequences for the political strategies of the labour movement in that, instead of adopting a coherent reformistic strategy, it has often resorted to a low-profile strategy of participation in the 'sharing out government'.[38] Therefore, the weakness and fragmentation of the right-wing also had an impact on the pro-labour political forces which have been shifting from radicalism in the industrial relations arena to consociationalism in the political one, and vice versa.[39] Thus, a link exists between the peculiar configuration of the interest group system, the fragmentation of public policies, and the characteristics of the party system. Both Pizzorno's and Amato's contribution were crucial to theoretical and analytical perspectives, as they placed the analysis of and the relationship between the dynamics of the *whole political system* and those of interest politics at the core of the debate.

NEO-CORPORATISM AND NEO-LOCALISM

This link between political parties and interest politics was also relevant to the two approaches which assumed a leading role in the study of interactions between organized interests and public authorities during the 1980s—namely the neo-corporatist and the neo-localist perspectives.

[37] A. Martinelli, A. Chiesi, and N. Dalla Chiesa, *I grandi imprenditori italiani* (Milan: Feltrinelli, 1981).

[38] See Cesos, *Sindacalisti in Parlamento, iii. Le attività non legislative* (Rome: Edizioni Lavoro, 1986); Cesos–Ires, *Sindacalisti in Parlamento, i. Il caso della CISL* (Rome: Ediesse-Edizioni Lavoro, 1982); id., *Sindacalisti in Parlamento, ii. Il caso della CGIL* (Rome: Ediesse-Edizioni Lavoro, 1984).

[39] M. Golden, 'Interest Representation, Party Systems, and the State', *Comparative Politics* (1986), 279–301.

Even though there have been various attempts to involve unions in policy-making[40] the degree of co-operation between unions and the state in shaping and implementing economic policies by means of centralized forms of concertation has substantially failed. What are the reasons for this failure? There are two explanations. First, the absence of a pro-labour party in government reduces the confidence of unions in the state. Secondly, there are deep political cleavages within and between unions, who are allied to different political parties. This weakens the labour movement,[41] and makes union strategies dependent on political game contingencies. The dynamic of the Italian party system had a crucial impact in determining the failure of bi- and tri-lateral forms of policy concertation and hence, in shaping Italian interest politics, moving it away from a neo-corporatist pattern.

Another factor, often neglected, that might explain this phenomenon is the high level of fragmentation of the business interest group system. The absence in Italy of an inclusive peak association that is able to 'internalize' the conflicts among the employers operating in different sectors of the economy, dramatically reduces the capability of business interest associations to deal with intersectoral policies, such as fiscal and labour market policies. In an interest group system characterized by a high level of fragmentation, the associations tend to displace the costs of social pacts on to the other sectors of the economy, and intersectoral policies are therefore doomed to failure. This hypothesis could explain, on the one hand, the reluctant involvement of employers in neo-corporative concertation, and, on the other, the distrust which unions have of business interest associations as political interlocutors.[42] Unions are more likely to enter social pacts in those countries in which there is a strong, inclusive, and, hence, reliable peak association representing all employers.[43]

[40] See M. Regini, *I dilemmi del sindacato* (Bologna: il Mulino, 1981); id., 'Changing Relationship between labour and the State in Italy: Towards a Neo-Corporatist System?' in Lembruch and Schmitter (eds.), *Patterns of Corporatist Policy-Making* (London: Sage, 1982); id., 'Relazioni industriali e sistema politico: l'evoluzione recente e le prospettive degli anni '80', in M. Carrieri and P. Perulli (eds.), *Il teorema sindacale* (Bologna: il Mulino, 1985), 15–40.

[41] Golden, 'Interest Representation, Party Systems, and the State'.

[42] A. Chiesi and A. Martinelli, 'The Representation of Business Interests as a Mechanism of Social Regulation', in P. Lange and M. Regini (eds.), *State and Social Regulation: New Perspectives on the Italian Case* (Cambridge: Cambridge University Press, 1989), 187–269.

[43] W. Coleman and W. Grant, 'The Organizational Cohesion and Political Access of Business: A Study of Comprehensive Associations', *European Journal of Political Research*, 16 (1988), 467–87.

The predominance of the neo-corporatist approach in Italian debate for nearly a decade had the effect of concentrating attention on a phenomenon that in practice is relatively marginal in Italian interest politics and it delayed the development of a better understanding of Italian interest group structures and activity. Of course, the failure of concertation practices does not mean the absence of *any* relationship between organized interests and the state, and so, for almost a decade, the attention of scholars has been focused on analysing, criticizing, and hoping for (or fearing) centralized social pacts. Meanwhile, interest groups (not only industry employers and trade unions, but also artisans, co-operatives, shopkeepers, farmers, etc.) were participating in other (more or less visible or legitimized) forms of policy-making and implementation (from lobbying, to participation in consultative bodies, from corruption to parliamentary action) both at the central and at the local level.

One of these types of interest group activity has been analysed by Marco Cammelli[44] in his study of the consultative bodies within public administration. His research shows that 'administration by committees' is a widespread practice in Italian public administration. These organs, located in central ministries, involve both private and public interests, namely public servants, interest group representatives, and experts. Even if their activity is often concerned with the operation of the public administration system itself, 'the aspect in which the use of committees is more significant is surely the external one, namely as a channel by means of which the reality of social groups and of other public institutions finds a mode and a reason of representation within the administrative organs of the state'.[45] The establishment of committees shows two periods of intense development, 1943–8 and 1963–8, corresponding with phases of dramatic political change. Thus these committees may be seen as important instruments of legitimation of the state during periods of political instability. Furthermore, 'the administration by committees is a very stable organisational pattern that tends to become rigid',[46] both in its operation and in its composition. It also tends towards an increasing *fragmentation* (functional and sectoral committees prevail over multifunctional and intersectoral ones) and *decentralization* at the regional level.

These tendencies have an important impact on interest politics. The increasing rigidity of the composition of these consultative

[44] M. Cammelli, *L'amministrazione per collegi* (Bologna: il Mulino, 1980).
[45] Ibid. 258.   [46] Ibid. 261.

bodies reduces the channels of access of new interest groups and, hence, the degree of competition of the interest group system. Also, the functional fragmentation of these bodies rewards specific interests and penalizes the most general ones.[47] Another characteristic of the 'administration by committees' is its *impermeability* to political parties, due to the central role which civil servants have in its operation and their relative autonomy from the politicians officially in charge of the Ministries. In contrast, the administrative committees present a high degree of openness to economic interests. The presence of employers' representatives is very conspicuous in all the committees dealing with economic matters, and unions are seldom present in those in which employers are absent. Cammelli concludes that 'the theses recently advanced that a tri-partite (unions, employers associations and *public administration*)' management of specific economic policies is still operating seem, on the results of the research, to be fully confirmed'.[48]

Cammelli analyses what we may call the bureaucratic 'alternative' to neo-corporatism. Other scholars have done the same at the local and regional levels. First, the existence of a high degree of involvement of interest groups, in particular unions,[49] in consultative bodies at the local and regional levels[50] was identified, confirming at the sub-national level those tendencies which Cammelli[51] had found at the national level.

These pervasive interactions between peripheral (local and regional) public authorities and interest groups—that may also assume the form of pressure, of lobbying, or of concertation,[52] and of participation in implementation[53]—are often cemented by the presence of *territorial subcultures*. For example, there is often a regional dominance by specific political parties (the ex-Communist Party in central regions of Italy and the Christian Democratic Party in north-eastern regions) and a weak link between functional (interest

[47] Ibid. 266–8 and 275.
[48] Ibid. 274 (my emphasis).
[49] I. Regalia, 'Non più apprendisti stregoni? Sindacati ed istituzioni in periferia', in Stato e mercato (1987); id., 'Sindacati e governi periferici' in *Democrazia e diritto* (1985).
[50] See T. Treu, M. Roccella, and G. Ferrari, *Sindacalisti nelle istituzioni* (Rome: Edizioni Lavoro, 1979); IRSI, *Il sindacato nello stato* (Rome: Edizioni Lavoro, 1981).
[51] Cammelli, *L'amministrazione per collegi.*
[52] See M. Morisi (ed.), *Rappresentanza politica e regioni: Questioni e materiali di ricerca sui consigli regionali* (Milan: Angeli, 1987); L. Lanzalaco, 'Parlamenti regionali e gruppi di interesse in Italia: Il caso della Lombardia', in *Rivista Trimestrale di Scienza dell'Amministrazione*, 1/2 (1989).
[53] M. Regini, 'I rapporti tra amministrazione e sindacati nell'implementazione delle politiche pubbliche', Introduzione, in ISAP, *I rapporti tra pubblica amministrazione e sindacati* (Milan: Giuffrè, 1987).

groups) and territorial (political parties) representation[54] and political participation. Territorial subcultures are present in the so-called Third Italy that includes those regions with a concentration of small-sized firms.

Where a territorial subculture is present there is a diffuse overlapping membership, and a political contiguity between political parties and interest groups. Hence, strong coalitions emerge *at the local and regional levels* among politicians, public authorities, and interest group (both trade unions and employers' associations) representatives of the same political 'colour'. These coalitions operate as a type of lobby directed at the *central organs of the state*. The mix between functional and territorial sub-units can be found in the organization of both business associations[55] and trade unions.[56]

The main thesis of the neo-localist approach is that the presence of these territorial subcultures operates as an efficient mechanism of political integration and consensus-building in those polities polarized around a class cleavage in which neo-corporatist trends have failed. In fact, in some polities, such as Italy and France, the integration of conflicts cannot occur at the centre but shifts to the periphery. The *horizontal* conflict between capital and labour is translated into a *vertical* conflict between local coalitions (between trade unions, employers' assocations, and local authorities) and central government. Neo-localism may operate as a functional equivalent of neo-corporatism that requires the integration of conflicts at the *centre* of the political system,[57] and neo-localist trends may explain the peculiarity of the Italian case of neo-corporatist failure, in contrast to the trends of other European countries.

The conclusion that can be drawn at the end of the 1980s, after a decade devoted to the debate about neo-corporatism, is that empirical evidence shows a quite curious tendency. In Italy, economic interest groups, namely unions and business interest associations, have been actually involved in voluntary and co-operative forms of conflict regulation and decision-making, but these

[54] C. Trigilia, 'Struttura di classe e sistema politico: Neocorporativismo o neo-localismo?' *Inchiesta*, 47/47 (1980), 37–59; id., *Grandi partiti e piccole imprese* (Bologna: il Mulino, 1986); M. Fedele (ed.), *Il sistema politico locale* (Bari: De Donato, 1983).

[55] See M. Maraffi, 'Business Interest Organizations, Regional Governments and Industrial Policies in Italy', Paper presented at the workshop on 'Political Adjustment to Economic Problems at the Local Level in Britain and Italy', European University Institute, Florence, May 1985. P. Schmitter and L. Lanzalaco, *Regions and the Organization of Business Interests*, in W. Coleman and H. Jacek (eds.), *Regionalism, Business Interests and Public Policy* (London: Sage, 1990).

[56] F. Ferraresi and A. Milanaccio, 'Organizzazione dei sindacati', in ISAP, *La regionalizzazione* (Milano: Giuffrè, 1983), ii. (1983), 823–61.

[57] Trigilia, *Struttura di classe e sistema politico*.

concertation arrangements occurred involving *institutional actors* (public administration instead of executives) and *levels of governance* (local and regional organs instead of national ones) that are significantly *different* from those forecasted by the neo-corporatist approach.

TOWARDS THE NINETIES: LOBBIES AND POLICY NETWORKS

At the end of the 1980s Italian political scientists returned to the issue of interest group activity at the national level, *outside* neo-corporatist arrangements. As might have been predicted, they discovered that a network of relationships, scarcely visible and not institutionalized, exists between interest groups, political parties, and decisional processes both at the national and at the peripheral levels. The channels of this increasingly fragmented interest group 'offensive' are twofold. There is the conventional intervention of lobbies, trying to influence policy-making, and there is the ambitious attempt by *policy networks*—involving experts, operators, public servants, politicians—to remove decision-making processes from democratically controlled arenas, displacing institutional actors. The emergence of lobbies and policy networks may be interpreted as the joint effect of (*a*) the decline of the representativeness of political parties and the fading of traditional collective identities linked to them, and (*b*) the increasing 'vulnerability' and 'permeability' of institutions in the face of organized interests.[58]

Thus there are essentially two elements on which the debate is currently focused. The first concerns the lobbying activity (its forms, its legitimacy, its regulation), and especially involves political debate.[59] The second element is the operation of policy networks and their relationship with party politics.

There are two different perspectives on lobbying. The first views the legal regulation of the lobbies as the solution to the problems of interest group activity. The logic underlying this position is that lobbies do actually exist and so the only sensible thing is to regulate their activity by means of a 'register of lobbyists' and to specify some norms of 'correct' behaviour. The second approach sees these measures as of little use and proposes institutional reforms—for example, to shift from a pure proportional system to a majoritarian

---

[58] Pasquino, *Istituzioni, partiti, lobbies.*
[59] See A. Maccanico, Intervista, 'Lobbisti per legge', by Renzo Rosati, *L'Europeo*, 47/1988 (18 Nov. 1988); G. Pasquino, 'A che servirebbe l'albo dei lobbisti?', *La Repubblica* (22 Nov. 1988); P. Trupia, 'Lobby: al di là del moralismo', *Impresa & stato* (Oct. 1988).

one, and the abolition of the preference vote, reducing the incentives for candidates and deputies to establish privileged relationships with lobbies.

More scientifically (and less politically) oriented is the interest in networks. The 'discovery' of policy networks[60] in the recent scientific debate (widely influenced by the recent Italian interest in policy analysis) focuses once again on the role of political parties. Some observers argue that policy networks form around, and depend upon, party loyalties.[61] Other researchers[62] suggest that policy network coalitions form around issue-oriented alliances that cut across traditional party allegiances. From this perspective, the emergence of policy networks should have the effect of restraining the tendency of Italian interest politics to be dependent on party politics. This is an important point because, in LaPalombara's opinion, the *clientela* relationship, even if it is a bureaucratic intervention, is partially subservient to party logic. In contrast, Cammelli[63] argues that public administration seems to be partially impermeable to party influence. It appears that in the decades from LaPalombara's to Cammelli's research and up to the present, there has been an increasing autonomy of public administration–interest group interactions from party politics. Hence, a crucial point for future research is to discover whether the direct interactions with the public administration system may represent an increasingly important way for interest groups to escape from party control and to analyse the effect that these interactions have on relations between civil servants and political leaders.[64]

The study of interest group activity in Italy now needs to go beyond both the pressure and the corporatist paradigms. In fact, the former is too rigid in assuming the distinction between those who take decisions and those who try to influence them, while empirical evidence has also shown that non-institutional and private actors may play the role of decision-makers. The latter has emphasized this point but in its analysis there is a bias towards modes of interaction

---

[60] See P. Lange and M. Regini (eds.), *State, Market and Social Regulation: New Perspectives on Italy* (Cambridge: Cambridge University Press, 1989); Pasquino, *Istituzioni, partiti, lobbies.*

[61] G. Pasquino, *Unregulated Regulators: Parties and Party Government*, in Lange and Regini, *State and Social Regulation*, 29–50.

[62] B. Dente and G. Regonini (1989), *Politics and Policies in Italy*, in P. Lange and M. Regini (eds.), (1989), 51–80; Lange and Regini, Introduction: 'Interests and Institutions: Forms of Social Regulation and Public Policy-Making' and 'Conclusions: The Italian Case between Continuity and Change', *State and Social Regulation*, 1–28 and 249–72.

[63] Cammelli, *L'amministrazione per collegi.*

[64] ISAP, *I rapporti tra partiti politici e pubblica amministrazione* (Milan: Giuffrè, 1989).

that involve in a visible way central executive bodies and highly inclusive interest associations. Meanwhile, empirical evidence has shown that the most widespread modes of interaction consist of scarcely visible relationships within policy networks in which experts, politicians, civil servants, and representatives of very fragmented interests are present. It is not surprising that the policy analysis approach is having an effect on Italian scholars, to the extent that it can provide analytical tools for the interpretation of this complex reality.

INTEREST GROUPS, POLITICAL PARTIES, AND PUBLIC POLICY IN ITALY: A CASE OF OLIGOPOLISTIC PLURALISM?

To conclude, a high degree of continuity seems to exist in Italian interest politics, and the results of LaPalombara's early research are still substantially valid today. Only three really new elements have emerged in the past twenty-five years. The first is the relevance of the structure of interest groups and their relationships with policy-making at the local and regional levels. The policy networks and communities that are present in territorial subcultures, and the clientelistic relationships between local interest groups and national politicians[65] have an important role not only in explaining what happens at the *sub*national level but at the *national* level as well. The local and regional levels of governance provide interest groups, at least in Italy, with an alternative channel of access to policy-making and implementation that strengthen their position *vis-à-vis* the national organs. The second new element is that the relationship between interest groups and public administration seems to have gradually reached a greater degree of autonomy from political parties. But as we have seen, it is not clear the extent to which interest politics is actually independent from party politics. The third element is the emergence of new political actors that develop their actions outside both political parties and interest groups. These phenomena, noticed mainly at the local level,[66] show that the crisis of traditional forms of representation has involved not only political parties but also traditional interest groups. The concept of

---

[65] Graziano, *Clientelismo e sistema politico.*

[66] See Censis, 'Le nuove rappresentanze urbane', Progetto biennale di ricerca e confronto, *Interessi e rappresentanze* (Rome: Censis, 1989); M. Diani and L. Lanzalaco, *I nuovi associazionismi economici e civili a Milano* (Milan: Istituto Superiore di Sociologia, 1990); P. Fareri, 'La progettazione del governo di Milano: nuovi attori per la metropoli matura', in B. Dente, P. Fareri, and M. Morisi, *Metropoli per progetti* (Bologna: il Mulino, 1990).

'interest group' changes its empirical connotations, referring to a huge and heterogeneous range of actors not confined to the traditional forms of interest associations.

Nevertheless, these are slight modifications and trends, which do not *radically* alter the structural characteristics of Italian interest politics, namely its high level of fragmentation and of dependence on party politics with the subsequent fragmentation of economic and welfare policies.[67] It is precisely from the relationship between the elements of this fragmentation—party system, interest group system, and public policies—that it is possible to draw some general conclusions about the Italian case.

The first point concerns the relationship between political parties and interest groups. Until the end of the 1960s, political parties had been viewed as 'colonizing' interest groups.[68] Lately, the opposite seems to be the case. Such an analysis is adequate only for the analysis of *conjunctural* cycles, not for explaining *structural* traits of this relationship. The inadequacy of this superficial one-sided causal relation (emphasizing sometimes the leading role of political parties and sometimes that of interest groups) is due to the fact that it is based on a vision of political parties and interest groups as *two distinct types of actors* eventually influencing each other. In contrast, it is better to see interest groups and political parties as two aspects of the same system of political representation, developed through a unique and unitary historical process. This analytical perspective is also supported by the fact that the fragmentation of the interest group system is paralleled by a high degree of fragmentation of the Italian party system, defined by Sartori[69] as a case of polarized pluralism.

Secondly, a political system characterized by a high level of fragmentation of its interest groups and political parties producing particularistic public policies, is subject to high demands for access to decisional processes. It requires rigid mechanisms of exclusion and selection of interests in order to regulate the flow of demands. In fact, Italian interest politics is highly fragmented, yet widespread forms of exclusion of interests from decisional arenas exist—for example, as suggested earlier, public administration committees are not open to new interests, and in the policy communities at the

---

[67] See Amato, *Economia, politica e istituzioni in Italia*: M. Paci, *La struttura sociale italiana* (Bologna: il Mulino, 1982); U. Ascoli (ed.), *Welfare state all'italiana* (Rome and Bari: Laterza, 1984); M. Ferrera, *Il welfare state in Italia* (Bologna: il Mulino, 1984); id., *Politics, Institutional Features and the Government of Industry*, in Lange and Regini, *State and Social Regulation*, 111–28.

[68] A. Manoukian, *La presenza sociale del PCI e della DC* (Bologna, il Mulino, 1968).

[69] G. Sartori, *Teoria dei partiti e caso italiano* (Milan: Sugarco, 1982).

territorial level only interest groups of the political 'colour' of the governing party are admitted. Finally, policy networks tend, by definition, to be closed from external influences. Paradoxically, while Italian politics may be defined as *pluralistic* if we look at the *civil society* arena, this definition no longer holds true if we look at the *institutional* arena where the decisional processes do not seem to be open to all pressures, but only to some privileged ones. Italian politics may therefore be defined as a case of *oligopolistic pluralism*—even if this may seem a contradiction in terms, since pluralism should involve open competition between interest groups.[70] A pluralistic and fragmented network of interest groups and associations at the level of civil society is confronted by relatively high 'entry barriers' to decisional processes at the institutional level, both at the national and at the local/regional levels. In some cases these 'entry barriers' seem to be (or to have been) controlled by political parties in order to have 'friendly' interlocutors, in others by public administration officials in order to stabilize their interactions and to rationalize their activity, and in others they are controlled by the same interest groups in order to strengthen their monopolistic or oligopolistic position towards their actual and potential membership. When the excluded interests are (politically) strong they have the power to displace decisional processes from institutional arenas. When they are weak they remain unheeded.

Here we reach the crucial issue, namely, the presumed 'peculiarity' of Italian interest politics. In which sense are Italian interest politics different from other Western democracies? What is it that so much concerns Italian scholars? Is it the *mode* in which interest groups operate or is it the *type* of interest groups operating?

If Italian interest politics may be seen as a case of *oligopolistic pluralism* (a mix of pluralism at the societal level and exclusion at the institutional level), the critical attitude of Italian scholars towards interest groups is not due to Italian interest group activity that is 'normal', as it would be impossible to insulate decision-making from interest pressures, but it emerges from the observation that *only some interests* have access to decision-making arenas. Others—namely associations representing diffuse, weak, emerging, and public interests—are systematically excluded from decision-making processes. If this is so, what is needed is not to pursue the unrealizable objective of reducing the access of interest groups to decision-making processes but, on the contrary, to open up the

---

[70] P. Schmitter, 'Still the Century of Corporatism?', *Review of Politics* (1974), 85–131.

decision-making arenas to *new* and hitherto excluded interests, providing them with equal opportunities of representation, adopting a more universalistic pattern of interaction with public authorities, and reducing the degree of oligopoly of certain interests. This would in turn cause a shift towards a system of real *competitive pluralism* among interest groups and, thence, towards a mature pluralistic democracy in Italy.

9

AMERICAN INTEREST GROUPS

GRAHAM K. WILSON

WHAT DO AMERICAN INTEREST GROUPS DO?

In view of the considerable fluctuations which have taken place in the importance attached to interest groups in the USA, it is particularly important to understand the nature of their operations.

In the first place, interest groups are increasingly involved in electoral politics. Perhaps the first interest group to be involved in electoral politics was business; Mark Hanna, relying on business executives' fear of the populists, raised millions of dollars for the Republicans in the 1896 election. But interest group involvement in elections is not limited to giving money. Interest groups can provide volunteers to work in election campaigns who are sometimes interest group officials on paid leave, equipment such as phone banks to contact and mobilize supporters, propoganda, and endorsements. Propoganda and equipment need not be counted as a campaign contribution if they are used to 'communicate' with members of the interest group and their families

The first interest to become *methodically* involved in electoral politics was labour. By the late 1950s, the AFL-CIO had an important organization, the Committee on Political Education (COPE), raising campaign contributions and systematically distributing them to its political friends . . . In a sense, the history of interest group involvement in electoral politics in the last thirty years is a history of the gradual dispersion of COPE's techniques amongst both economic and non-economic interest groups. Today, most interest groups copy COPE in grading the votes of legislators. Negative as well as positive endorsements are now common; thus, environmental groups have singled out the 'Dirty Dozen' legislators with the worst environmental records.

Perhaps no reform increased the opportunities for interest group activity more than campaign finance reform. Reforms in campaign finance, such as the 1974 Campaign Finance Act as interpreted by the Federal Elections Commission, allowed interest groups to form

Reprinted in abridged form from Graham K. Wilson, *Interest Groups* (Oxford: Basil Blackwell, 1991), 39–75, by permission of Blackwell Publishers.

Political Action Committees which could contribute up to $10,000 to each candidate per election (with up to $5,000 in both the primary and general elections). PACs linked to economic groups, such as corporations or unions, were particularly advantaged by Federal Election Commission rulings which allowed them to pay the often considerable expenses of operating their PACs.

Aided by the 1974 Campaign Finance Act, there has been a tremendous growth in the proportion of economic interest groups with PACs; nearly all unions and trade associations as well as most large corporations today raise money to distribute through PACs to candidates for office. Contributions are limited to $5,000 per election, but clearly 100 interest groups acting in concert can have a substantial impact. There is evidence that certain PACs such the AFL-CIO's COPE or BIPAC (the Business Industry Political Action Committee) trigger contributions from allied PACs when they support a candidate.

LOBBYING

It is significant that most studies of lobbying in the United States focus on the relationship between interest groups and the legislature, not, as would be the case in many other systems, on relations between interest groups and the executive which will be discussed shortly. Though this preoccupation with interest groups and the Congress is in part a defect in the political science literature on American interest groups, it also reflects the enormous attention that interest groups give Congress. A recent study found that practically no interest groups focus exclusively on the executive branch.[1] While the largest section of interest group representatives claimed to focus equally on the legislature and executive, a large minority focused exclusively on Congress. Labour unions in particular were overwhelmingly concerned with lobbying Congress, perhaps because of the poor relations between them and the Reagan administration. In my own study of the political activities of large companies, their Washington representatives attached more impor-tance by far to lobbing Congress than to any other form of action.

Congress is more readily approachable for interest groups for several reasons. We have already discussed one—PAC contribu-

---

[1] Robert Salisbury, John P. Heinz, Edward O. Laumann, and Robert L. Nelson, 'Who Works with Whom? Patterns of Interest Group Alliance and Opposition', Paper presented to the Annual Meeting of the American Political Science Association, Washington DC, 1986; Edward O. Laumann, John P. Heinz, Robert L. Nelson, and Robert Salisbury, 'Organizations in Political Action: Representing Interests in National Policymaking', Paper presented at the Annual Meeting of the American Sociological Convention, New York, 1986.

tions. Senators and Representatives may well also come from an area where an interest group, though a small proportion of the national population, accounts for a substantial proportion of the electorates; farmers are an obvious example. It is probable that as the American electorate has become more volatile, legislators are more attentive to smaller and smaller groups in their constituencies. Moreover, it is customary in Congress for legislators to seek out assignments to committees which will enable them to provide useful services to constituents. Thus the agriculture committees are always dominated by legislators from rural America and the Armed Services committees contain legislators with numerous defence contractors or military bases in their districts or states. Finally, legislators generally feel that they have a duty, as well as an interest in terms of re-election, in helping interests important to their constituents. . . .

INTEREST GROUPS AND THE EXECUTIVE BRANCH

As in all western democracies, the expansion of the size and scope of government over the last century has inevitably led to the devolution to the executive branch of a wide range of responsibilities. Although the Congress has protected its prerogatives better than most legislatures, it is no more possible for Congress than for any other legislature to settle through legislation all the details which might arise in implementing its Acts. Details—even crucial details—must be left to executive branch agencies to determine. Interest groups therefore have great need to influence the way in which bureaucrats interpret the mandate they have been given by Congress.[2]

There is no doubt that, as in all political systems, much of the interchange between bureaucrats and interest group officials is concerned with the exchange of technical information and is so technical in nature that it would not be seen by participants as a political relationship. Bureaucrats seek guidance and assistance in implementing policy; interest group officials seek to avoid what they would consider to be ill-informed policy implementation.

The relationship between bureaucrats and interest groups in the United States is unusually suffused with politics, however. The reason for this is that the bureaucracy in the United States is forced

[2] On this see John Chubb, *Interest Groups and the Bureaucracy* (Stanford, Calif.: Stanford University Press, 1983); Herbert Kaufman, *The Administrative Behavior of Federal Bureau Chiefs*, Washington DC: Brookings Institution, 1981; Harold Seidman, *Politics, Position and Power* (New York: New York University Press, 1986); Joel Aberbach, Robert Putman, and Bert A. Rockman, *Bureaucrats and Politicians in Western Democracies* (Cambridge, Mass.: Harvard University Press, 1981).

by the nature of the American political system to make constant political calculations in its day-to-day work. American bureaucracy, apart from having at least as strong inclinations to go its own way as any other bureaucracy, is the servant of at least two, and sometimes three, masters. These are the president, the Congress, and the courts. The familiarity of the president's title, chief executive, suggests little more need be said about the ability of the president to issue orders to the bureaucracy. Less familiar is the fact that the committees of Congress which oversee government agencies have substantial power over those agencies because of their ability to reduce or deny agency requests for funds or legislation. . . . Many agency leaders find that the relevant congressional committees are a more vivid presence in their lives than is the presidency, which has little time to devote to overseeing the numerous relatively mundane agencies of government. In turn, congressional committees are frequently composed of legislators who come from areas vitally affected by the work of the relevant government agency.

INTEREST GROUPS AND THE COURTS

A further distinctive feature of American interest groups is the frequency with which they turn to the law. Interest groups reach the courts in a variety of ways. First, interest groups may be direct parties to a civil suit. Unions, for example, may seek an order of *mandamus* ordering an agency to implement an act of Congress concerning occupational safety and health which the agency has failed to implement. Second, interest groups may encourage an individual, who may or may not be a member, to bring a test case, the expenses of which will be borne by the interest group. Third, an interest group may be able, under the legislation creating a regulatory agency, to challenge its decisions in the Appeals Courts. OSHA's regulations may be challenged by any affected interest either on the grounds that its regulation has been made following incomplete or improper procedures or on the grounds that the agency's decisions were not supported by adequate justification on the record. Finally, interest groups may intervene in cases which, in their view, raise crucial issues even if they are not directly a party to the dispute. An example would be the numerous briefs filed *amicus curiae* (the requirement that federal agencies or federally funded agencies take steps to see that their contractors, students, etc. have the same proportion of racial minorities or women as the qualified population). Such *amicus* briefs can be seen as a form of lobbying the judiciary. In general, the courts have proved ever readier to provide a forum for interest groups. . . . The spirit of judicial activism which gained ground in the United States from the 1950s onwards has made judges happier than ever to resolve major issues. The fact that the courts have been the policy-making institutions on such contentious issues as abortion is well known. It is less widely appreciated that, as Martin Shapiro notes, courts are in practice heavily involved in *economic* issues such as regulation, and have proved ever readier to overturn the determinations of expert regulatory agencies on what constitutes good public policy.[3]

Something of a tradition has developed of regarding use of the courts by interest groups as being particularly advantageous for groups which are incapable of prevailing in other parts of the political system, particularly those groups representing the comparatively weak or powerless. The tradition has arisen because of the fame of cases such as *Brown* v. *The Board of Education of Topeka*, which declared racial segregation unconstitutional, and because of declarations by the court (e.g. in *NAACP* v. *Button*)[4] that the courts have a particular responsibility to listen to the weak. Yet it would be quite incorrect to assume that the courts are used only by civil rights groups. . . . Studies suggest that all interest groups involved in conflict over public policy use the courts, whatever the character of the group. Moreover, like all other forms of political action, use of the courts requires resources and is more readily available to those groups with the necessary resources at their command. American corporations have never been short of lawyers, though public interest and civil rights groups are rarely so fortunate.

None the less, interest groups which might otherwise have failed have been able to succeed through legal action. Courts have played an important role in expanding the interest group system both through supporting requests from groups which at the time could not command a majority in Congress or support from the president (e.g. the NAACP (National Association for the Advancement of Colored People) in 1954) while the courts' preoccupation with procedural due process in administration has allowed more groups more opportunity to comment on policy proposals. Yet the involvement of the courts in so many areas important to interest groups has also had its costs. In particular, it can be argued that frequent court cases, inherently adversarial in character, have failed to promote compromise. On the contrary, rather than compromise

---

[3] Martin Shapiro, 'The Supreme Court's "Return" to Economic Regulation', *Studies in American Political Development*, i. (New Haven, Conn.: and London, Yale University Press, 1986), 97–123.

[4] *NAACP* v. *Button*, 371 US 415, 1963.

with each other or relevant government agencies, interest groups may well be obdurate, hoping to gain in court what they might fail to gain in negotiation. The frequency of recourse to the courts does something to explain the highly adversarial character of the American interest group system.

OTHER FORMS OF INTEREST REPRESENTATION

It is vital to recognize the importance in interest group representation in the United States of people who are not full-time employees of interest groups. Of particular significance are Washington lawyers and contract lobbyists to whom we referred earlier. Washington law firms, such as Arnold and Porter, are not merely legal practitioners but are also in effect lobbyists. The size of the Washington bar expanded rapidly in the 1970s, not because of a growth in litigation but because affluent interests (e.g. corporations) hired lawyers more often to represent them. Similarly, contract, or, as they are humorously termed, 'hired gun', lobbyists are available—such as Charls [sic] Walker—to represent interests (usually corporations) on a specific issue.

GENERAL CHARACTERISTICS OF THE INTEREST GROUP SYSTEM

So far, we have been concerned with the tactics used by interest groups and their effectiveness. How, though, might we characterize not the tactics of individual interest groups but the nature of the entire interest group system? . . . Interest groups in the United States are today, as Tocqueville found in the 1830s, involved in almost every issue of the day. . . . Yet, interest group activity is not synonymous with interest group influence. There are indeed several aspects of the American interest group system which might limit its significance.

First, the American interest group system is fragmented. That is to say, not only do interest groups in different fields compete with each other for influence, but there is also usually competition by interest groups for members from the same sector of society. There is rarely a single interest group which speak for a sector of society but rather several groups compete for the title. Thus the National Association of Manufacturers (NAM), Chamber of Commerce, and Business Roundtable all make some claims to speak for the business community. The American Farm Bureau Federation (AFBF), National Farmers' Union (NFU), the Grange, and the American

Agriculture Movement all make claims to be the voice of the collective interests of American farmers, even though the NFU and AFBF have radically different, conflicting views of what those interests are. Labour is somewhat more united, even though powerful unions such as the United Auto Workers (UAW), United Mineworkers and the Teamsters have spent long periods outside the umbrella organization for labour, the American Federation of Labor-Congress of Industrial Organizations (AFL-CIO), and rejoined in part because of the dramatic decline in the power of organized labour in the USA.

Second, the degree of integration achieved within each interest group sector is limited. The ties between different types of business organization are limited. Trade associations, representing specific industries, are not clearly integrated into the structure of general business organizations representing the collective interests of business as they are in many other systems. Instead, individual corporations affiliate separately to trade associations and business umbrella organizations which may, or may not, co-operate. Similarly, there are dozens of interest groups representing farmers producing individual commodities such as wheat, milk, or beef. These commodity organizations have only informal contracts with general agriculture organizations such as the AFBF or NFU. The AFL-CIO has only the most tenuous hold over affiliated unions which reject claims by the organization to influence their industrial or political behaviour. Indeed, the cumbersome title of the organization is itself a reminder of the deep conflict between generally liberal industrial unions (such as the UAW) and conservative craft unions (such as the Carpenters).

Third, American economic interest groups have generally achieved a low density of membership. That is to say, the percentages of farmers joining the farm interest groups or the proportion of workers joining unions is far below the percentages achieved in most other democracies. It is ironic, and important, that, though the United States has been celebrated by many writers as the country whose citizens are the most likely to join interest groups, participation in those groups which would be thought the most obvious groups to join in many other countries, the economic interest groups, are much less successful in recruiting members than their counterparts in other countries. To the extent that the notion that Americans have an unusually high propensity to join interest groups can be sustained at all, it must be sustained with reference to non-economic groups concerned with political or social causes.

Fourth, American interest groups are highly geared to political action rather than more technical activity. Activities such as gathering and distributing campaign contributions, lobbying legislators, and, for this too is a political strategy, bringing court cases dominate the work of the American interest groups. Technocrats—economists, scientists, accountants—are employed by American interest groups but the overall atmosphere of American interest groups is more political than in most other political systems. Indeed, it is common to find that economic interest groups advocate policies which seem far removed from their areas of expertise. Thus the AFL-CIO has been the bedrock of liberal coalitions on issues such as civil rights legislation or moves towards national health insurance. The American Farm Bureau Federation has campaigned for issues as far removed from its obvious areas of interest as expelling the United Nations from American soil. The American Medical Association has been accused of forming coalitions with conservative groups such as tobacco interests which are generally associated with products injurious to health. Permanent though informal coalitions or networks link liberal or conservative groups on a wide variety of issues. Clearly, a tricky calculation is required by interest groups. Coalitions have great advantages, broadening the range and number of politicians to whom appeals can be made for support, and transforming what might otherwise seem a selfish interest into something broader and nobler. Yet coalitions can also damage the standing of an interest group by dragging it into commitments which are damaging to its interests or credibility. When the Consumers' Federation was obliged to support protectionist legislation by the United Auto Workers, which had done much to maintain and support the organization in the past, not only the interests of consumers but the credibility of the organization was damaged. The American interest group sometimes seems more like a political party than a highly technocratic, tightly focused lobby for a particular interest. The range of issues on which the AFL-CIO and the American Farm Bureau Federation express themselves is truly extraordinary. The AFBF's commitment for many years to expelling the United Nations from American territory was not exactly closely related to agricultural policy concerns.

Fifth, the interest group system has to compete with a variety of rivals for the title of representing interests in society. Corporations frequently act independently of trade associations or business umbrella organizations, functioning as interest groups in their own right with PACs, Washington offices and lobbyists of their own. Wealthy interests such as corporations frequently turn for help with a problem they have with government to Washington law firms or political consultants, not to interest groups. Most important of all, representatives and senators are expected to help interests in their districts and states in need of help, be they defence contractors, universities, or farmers. Frequently, as in the case of the Farm Bureau's claims that farmers prefer a free market to government subsidies, legislators make a judgement of what their constituents want which conflicts with the interest group's judgement. Politicians around the world pay some attention to representing their constituents, regardless of ideology. American legislators, operating in the context of a weak party system, pay unusually great, and possibly increasing, attention to representing constituents' interests. Few American politicians would accept without question claims that a national interest group necessarily represents the views of their constituents for whom it claims to speak. It is by no means unusual for an American legislator to tell an interest group spokesperson that he or she is not speaking for the legislator's constituents.

Sixth, though in practice it is often easy to predict which political party an interest group will favour, ties with political parties are rarely formalized. Thus, though the AFL-CIO has been the most important single source of support for liberal Democratic candidates for Congress, it has no institutionalized place within the party. The AFL-CIO still claims to be non-partisan and the Democratic Party has never set aside any seats at its Convention or on its National Committee for representatives of labour. Indeed, most interest groups, including business, make some effort to avoid being linked too closely to a political party, even while they accept being called liberal or conservative. Indeed, much to the dismay of conservatives, business has given large campaign contributions to those liberal Democrats in Congress who occupy key positions and are certain to be re-elected.

Finally we should re-emphasize the ubiquity and strength of those mass membership interest groups not representing producers. There is no other country in which women's interests are represented by an interest group to match the organizational quality of the National Organization for Women. No other country has produced a 'good government' interest group to match Common Cause. The American environmentalist groups have been rivalled in very few countries (e.g. West Germany). American economic interest groups are unimpressive by international standards. But in no other country do non-economic groups show greater vitality.

In short, the American interest group system, like many other aspects of the American political system, is untidy, competitive, often noisy and very varied. American interest groups play a more obvious role in politics than their counterparts in other countries. It is not clear, however, that their greater visibility is matched by

greater importance. In the next section we turn to explaining those
influences which have shaped the American interest group system.

EXPLAINING THE AMERICAN INTEREST GROUP SYSTEM

As is always the case, the American interest group system is a
product of the state, society, and the historical experience within
which the system has developed.

The structure of the American state helps to explain many of the
features of the interest group system which we have noted. Most
obviously, the fragmented American state, designed as a system of
separate institutions sharing power and since more fragmented by
custom and politics within each institution, provides multiple points
of access for interest groups. Interest groups, often each finding a
part of government which is attentive, have less need to unite than in
more unitary systems of government where points of access to
decision-making may be limited. Moreover, government, itself
divided, cannot enforce tidiness or unity on the interest group
system. It has been possible for British governments to require
interest groups to merge or to maintain the dominance of a single
interest group in its field. The formation of the employers' group the
Confederation of British Industry (CBI) and the continuing
dominance of the National Farmers' Union are obvious examples.
The advantages to government of having a single interest group
rather than competing groups will be discussed later. Our concern
at present is to emphasize the impossibility of the state creating a
less competitive, more integrated interest group system. For even if
the White House announced that it would accept only one group as
the legitimate representative of farmers, for example, the House, the
Senate and the courts may all take a different attitude. Indeed,
different departments, or different congressional committees, may
respond with differing enthusiasm or hostility to the competing
interest groups. The fragmented American state is inherently
incapable of promoting a more united, tidier interest group system.

That is not to say that the American state has had no impact on
interest groups. Though the prevalent doctrine asserts the autonomy
of interest groups so that the Supreme Court has strongly attacked
arguments that the state is entitled to alter the balance between
competing groups (e.g. by trying to prevent domination of a
referendum campaign by the wealthier interests), in reality, the state
has often intervened to promote particular groups. The Farm
Bureau, the National Rifle Association, and the Chamber of
Commerce all received useful assistance from government in their

early days. It can be argued that industrial unions could not have developed in the USA in the face of determined and often violent employer resistance without the protection of the National Labor Relations Board established during the New Deal. It can also be argued that the decline of unions to their present miserable state has been caused in part by features of labour law adopted in the 1940s. An unintended consequence of the American anti-trust laws has been to inhibit the development of trade associations, so much less important in the United States than in many western democracies. Thus, it is not that the American state has ever lived up to the theory of leaving interest groups totally autonomous with their development guided only by an invisible hand of competition; state influences on interest groups have been too common for that. However, the inability of the American state to promote a hierarchical system of monopolistic interest groups on the neo-corporatist model has always been evident. State involvement has never been sufficiently unified itself to achieve such an objective.

The American interest group system has also been profoundly influenced by the weakness of class consciousness and conflict in the USA. Although American unions once represented 35 per cent of the work-force, the period of union strength was brief (about 1941 to 1961) and was the product of such passing influences as government assistance, wartime labour shortages and the economic dominance of the United States which reduced the competitive forces operating on American employers. The weakness of organized labour in the United States in turn obviated the need for employers to form strong interest groups. The comparative weakness of trade associations and business umbrella groups in the United States reflects the fact that strong challenges to the collective interests of business are rare. When such challenges have emerged (e.g. from unions in the 1930s or from public interest groups in the early 1970s), a rapid strengthening of employers' organizations has been evident. . . . However, serious challenges to business have been few. Because of the weakness of unions and employers' organizations, other economic interests—such as farmers—have not been faced with a situation in which it appears that unless they organize, they will be surrounded by better organized interests. In consequence, their interest groups, too, have remained somewhat underdeveloped.

Yet if economic interests have remained weak and divided, non-economic interests have been encouraged by aspects of the American system. The Constitution (in the Bill of Rights) gave interest groups certain clear rights (e.g. to assemble and to petition government). Ever since, the political culture has emphasized the value of participation in non-economic interest groups (while remaining ambivalent about economic, sometimes called *special* interest groups). The ambivalent feelings of Americans about political parties clearly advantage interest groups. The upsurge of interest in political participation amongst more educated Americans in the 1960s and 1970s coincided with a period of particular distrust of political parties. The public interest groups were beneficiaries of an increased interest in participation which was not directed towards the parties. The comparative weakness of political parties in America has made the money, organization and occasionally the votes which interest groups might offer the more attractive. It is instructive to contrast the political fear which the National Rifle Association instils in the United States with the limited impact of such groups in Great Britain. Interest groups concerned with such foreign policy questions as aid to Israel, support for Greece (against Turkey) and sanctions against South Africa have achieved an importance unmatched in any other democracy. American politicians respond more readily than most to interest group pressures particularly when—as in the case of the foreign policy groups and unlike the situation for business or labour—there is no organized opposition.

CONCLUSIONS: CONSEQUENCES OF THE INTEREST GROUP SYSTEM

We have argued that the American interest group system is unusually competitive, fragmented and, in the case of economic groups, surprisingly weak. Yet many Americans remain concerned that their system of government is too frequently dominated by special interests at the expense of the public interest. Can these fears be reconciled with evidence that American interest groups are often surprisingly weak?

In fact, they can. In the first place, as we have noted, interests are often represented through institutions other than interest groups. Agricultural subsidies, for example, may be maintained more by the activities of the strategically placed rural legislators on the agriculture committees than by the strength of agricultural interest groups. Similarly, the reluctance of most American politicians to enact more sensible gun control laws may be due more to their fear of losing the votes of the many millions of Americans who like to own guns than to the activities of the National Rifle Association. Support for Israel may be due more to the fear of losing Jewish-American votes in elections in key states than to the activities of the pro-Israel interest groups. American politicians often pursue blocks of voters without any prompting by interest groups. Nor need such behaviour be unprincipled. As we have seen, representatives and senators in the United States often see it as part of their job to advance the interests of interest groups in their districts or states.

Yet, the structure of the interest group system itself may promote irresponsibility. As Olson, amongst others, has noted,[5] interest groups with a wide range of members (e.g. representing nearly all the work-force) can take a more statesmanlike view of things than can less encompassing interest groups (e.g. independent unions representing fragments of the work-force). For the all-encompassing interest group has less need to worry about both losing members to a competitor through showing moderation and seeing its members lose ground if it alone shows moderation while other groups press home their advantage. In brief, when there are numerous competing groups, each group cannot escape the 'prisoners' dilemma' in which though all would benefit from co-operation, none can guarantee that co-operation will occur. It is therefore rational for interest groups to press home their concerns and to forget about making sacrifices to the common good, for they cannot assume that their sacrifices will be matched by others. Moreover, numerous competing interest groups cannot provide the help in governance that more monopolistic groups can. Competing groups cannot aggregate demands or interests for presentation to government as can monopolistic groups. Neither can they as readily provide assistance in the administration of programmes as groups which are clearly recognized as the sole representatives of their interests. In brief, competitive interest group systems are less likely to assist in promoting good government than more monopolistic systems. The very weakness of competitive interest groups is a root of the problem.

Yet competitive interest group systems can always claim one advantage. The competitive interest group system by definition allows a greater variety of interests to be expressed. A more monopolistic interest group system would almost certainly result in a narrower range of views being articulated with, for example, pro-subsidy farmers suppressing those who wish for a freer market in a single farmers' organization. The American political culture has often placed greater value on representation than effectiveness in government. Perhaps these values are also represented in the interest group system.

Whether or not interest groups in the United States enjoy too much leverage depends not only on them, but on the rest of the

[5] Mancur Olson, *The Rise and Decline of Nations* (New Haven, Conn.: Yale University Press, 1982).

political system. As we noted above, the capacity of the American state to absorb or deflect pressure is not constant. Many of the reforms of the 1970s unconsciously reduced the capacity of the American state to withstand pressure from organized interests. It is possible that in the 1980s this capacity has recovered somewhat. Congress proved capable of enacting large scale budget cuts in 1981 and tax 'reform' in 1986 in the face of strong opposition from many interests. Yet any such recovery should not be exaggerated. The budget cuts of 1981 were shaped in such a way as to impose the greatest burdens on those, such as the poor, with the least political power and to avoid interests, such as the elderly or aircraft manufacturers, with strong interest groups. The budget cuts, as David Stockman complained,[6] were crafted to make sufficient concessions to powerful interests to ensure their passage but at enormous cost to the Treasury. Similarly, tax 'reform' in 1986 was a pill sugared by tax concessions to the wealthy and corporations which had not gained much from the old system. In a sense, the large federal budget deficit is a reminder of how important interest groups have become in the 1970s and 1980s. Whether the United States can continue to afford to allow such success to fragmented, selfish interest groups remains to be seen.

[6] David Stockman, *The Triumph of Politics, The Inside Story of the Reagan Revolution* (New York: Avon Books, 1987).

10

CANADIAN PRESSURE GROUPS: TALKING CHAMELEONS

A. PAUL PROSS

STRUCTURE AND BEHAVIOUR

The functions that pressure groups perform have much to do with both the organizational form they take and the way they behave. We might be tempted to claim that their form follows their function, were it not for the fact that structure is also greatly influenced by such things as the kind of resources made available by the group's members, their determination to promote their common interest through exerting influence and, always, the characteristics of the political system itself. We shall return to these influences after we have looked at the more fundamental aspects of pressure group structure and behaviour.

Earlier, we defined pressure groups as 'organizations whose members act together to influence public policy in order to promote their common interest'. The fact that they are *organizations* is crucial. In political life there are many interests and over time a considerable number exert influence in the policy process, but unless they have access to more resources than most individuals and the majority of companies, they lack the ability to sustain their influence. Unaggregated demand, as political scientists call the political demands of individual persons and corporations, tends to occur sporadically and on a piecemeal basis. Often it is sufficient to achieve or avert specific decisions, such as a spot rezoning in a city plan, but it rarely influences public policy. This is because the process of policy formation is extremely complex, involving many participants, taking place over a long period of time, and usually consisting of innumerable decisions. For most of those who want to take part in this process the only feasible way to do so is to band together, to share costs, to deploy at appropriate times the different

Reprinted in abridged form from A. Paul Pross, 'Canadian Pressure Groups: Talking Chameleons', in Michael S. Whittington and Glen Williams, *Canadian Politics in the 1990s* (Scarborough, Ont.: Nelson Canada, 1989), permission requested.

talents that participation requires, even simply to maintain continuity as the process unfolds—in other words, to organize.

Not all pressure groups organize in the same way or to the same extent. Much depends on what they want to achieve by engaging in the policy process, on the resources they can put into lobbying, and on their understanding of the mechanics of policy-making. Since the way in which all these factors come together has a lot to do with the policy consequences of the work of pressure groups, it is important to try to understand the relationship between the levels of organization pressure groups attain and their behaviour in the policy process.

Our goal here is not simply to understand the behaviour of pressure groups; the way in which they behave can also tell us a great deal about policy-making in specific political systems and even about the political system itself. For example, studies of Canadian pressure group behaviour have led some students to conclude that administrators in Canadian governments have a far greater influence in policy-making than our earlier work on political parties, parliamentary institutions, and legal frameworks had led us to believe.

To understand these aspects of pressure group life we must arrange what we know about them in meaningful patterns. There are various ways to do this. One that is used by many scholars is to classify all groups according to the *kinds of causes* they promote. This usually results in two broadly defined lists: in one, the groups that pursue the self-interest of their members; in the other, the groups that pursue more general, public interests. Some important insights have come from using this approach. For example, as a result of the debate triggered by studies such as *The Logic of Collective Action*,[1] which argues that interest groups only survive if they can offer their members advantages (selective inducements) that can be obtained nowhere else, we now know a great deal about the internal forces that motivate pressure group behaviour and we appreciate more than we ever have before the problems that beset public interest groups. A practical consequence of this improved understanding has been the trend in several countries toward giving public interest groups special assistance in arguing for the public interest before regulatory and policy-making bodies.[2]

Useful though this approach is, it has serious weaknesses. In the first place, the classification system itself is 'messy', for there are far

[1] Mancur Olson, *The Logic of Collective Action* (Cambridge, Mass.: Harvard University Press, 1965).

[2] See Peter H. Schuck, 'Public Interest Groups and the Policy Process', *Public Administration Review*, 37/2 (1972), 132–40.

too many groups that work simultaneously for both selective benefits and the public interest, and it is often difficult to categorize them, there is often a very fine line between self-interest and public interest.[3] More important, however, this method takes a one-sided view of the relationship between pressure groups and governments. Although it admits that pressure group activity is often triggered by government action, such as the creation of a new programme or the ending or and old one, it tends to explain the subsequent behaviour of such groups either in terms of competition between rival groups or in terms of what one writer has called their 'interior life'. In other words, the approach focuses on the effort group members are willing and able to make to convince policy-makers of the rightness of their cause. This concern is very necessary, but it has to be put in perspective. The other partner in the relationship—government— affects pressure group behaviour just as much as does membership commitment, organizational sophistication, and so on. In fact, most pressure groups are *chameleons*: those that take their lobbying role seriously adapt their internal organizations and structure to suit the policy system in which they happen to operate. That is why pressure groups working only at the provincial level in Canada are often quite different from those that concentrate their efforts at the federal level, and why both differ dramatically from their counterparts in Eastern Europe, the Third World, and even the United States.[4]

Several years ago this writer developed a conceptual framework that does try to look at pressure groups from the perspective of the *influence of government* as well as from that of the internal dynamics of groups. This approach starts with the assumption that pressure groups have functions to perform that are as necessary to the development of government policy as those performed by political parties, bureaucracies, executives, and courts. However, the way in which they perform those functions is as much determined by the shape of the policy system as it is by the knowledge, the enthusiasm, the financial capacity, and the other internal characteristics of individual groups.[5] For example, a policy system like Canada's, in which legislatures do not have a large say in policy development, will encourage pressure groups to develop quite differently from those that emerge in a system such as found in the United States, with its emphasis on congressional power.

---

[3] Terry M. Moe, *The Organization of Interests* (Chicago: University of Chicago Press, 1980).

[4] Suzanne D. Berger (ed.), *Organizing Interests in Western Europe* (Cambridge: Cambridge University Press, 1981).

[5] A similar view is put forward by Henry W. Ehrmann in id. (ed.), *Interest Groups on Four Continents* (Pittsburgh, Pa.: University of Pittsburgh Press, 1958).

Institutionalization, this approach argues, gives us the key to understanding pressure group behaviour. If we can come to understand how it is that some groups survive in a political system and become influential and organizationally sophisticated, while others quickly disappear, then we can learn a great deal about their interior life and about their particular policy environment.

An institution is a sophisticated entity, one that not only works to achieve the goals laid down for it, as any organization should, but that actually embodies the values it is built around. Like any organization, it begins life as a collection of individuals gathered to achieve certain objectives. Sometimes such groupings have organizational shape—the members have structured relationships with one another that permit them to carry out specialized tasks—but often they are simply a group of people who want to accomplish something. Gradually, if they stay together, they elaborate an organizational structure, and if they are successful their organization develops into an institution, 'a responsive, adaptive organism' that, to its members and many of those it deals with, has a philosophy, a code of behaviour, and sense of unity related to the values it has come to embody. The Greenpeace Foundation is a good example of such an organization. It is not only sophisticated as an organization with an international structure, but it stands very firmly for certain beliefs and acts accordingly. As a pressure group it is highly institutionalized, even though it is not popular with governments.

When we apply the concept of institutionalization to pressure group analysis we must be very aware of a point made by an early student of institutions, Philip Selznick. 'As institutionalization progresses,' he maintains, 'the enterprise . . . becomes peculiarly competent to do a particular kind of work.'[6] In the case of pressure groups this means that they must become 'peculiarly competent' to carry out the four functions we have already discussed, especially the function of communication. The institutionalized group knows what government is thinking about, what it needs to know, and how to get that information to it at the right time, in the right place, and in the most acceptable form. This means a great deal more than simply button-holing politicians at cocktail parties. It means the group must have an expert staff—or a helpful, well-informed membership—able to communicate with government officials at bureaucratic as well as elected levels, on a continuing basis. The need for this particular competence has led this writer to claim that

---

[6] Philip Selznick, *Leadership in Administration* (New York: Harper & Row, 1957), 139.

one of the defining characteristics of institutionalized pressure groups is 'an extensive knowledge of those sectors of government that affect them and their clients'. In its entirety that definition describes institutional pressure groups as:

groups that possess organizational continuity and cohesion, commensurate human and financial resources, extensive knowledge of those sectors of government that affect them and their clients, a stable membership, concrete and immediate operational objectives associated with philosophies that are broad enough to permit [them] to bargain with government over the application of specific legislation or the achievement of particular concessions, and a willingness to put organizational imperatives ahead of any particular policy concern.[7]

We cannot explain this definition completely here, but we should note several things about it. First, it is very unlikely that any real group could be described in these particular terms. It is an idealized version of a certain kind of group; it is a model with which to compare the various types of groups we come across. Second, because the idea of institutionalization suggests a progression and because this particular model can be used as a bench mark against which other groups can be compared, it becomes possible to think of pressure groups as falling along a continuum. At one extreme we can place institutional groups like those in our model, and at the other we can put those groups that have the opposite characteristics. These, we would argue:

are governed by their orientation toward specific issues . . . and have limited organizational continuity and cohesion, minimal and often naive knowledge of government, fluid membership, a tendency to encounter difficulty in formulating and adhering to short-range objectives, a generally low regard for the organizational mechanisms they have developed for carrying out their goals, and, most important, a narrowly defined purpose, usually the resolution of one or two issues or problems, that inhibits the development of 'selective inducements' designed to broaden the group's membership base.[8]

We call these 'issue-oriented' groups and can readily identify them. They spring up at a moment's notice, usually in reaction to some government action or a private sector activity that only government can change. (They are often seen in city politics confronting developers, highway builders, and planners.) Usually, they disband when their goals are either won or convincingly lost, but occasionally they keep on playing a part in politics and slowly

---

[7] A. Paul Pross, 'Canadian Pressure Groups in the 1970s: Their Role and their Relations with the Public Service', *Canadian Public Administration*, 18/1 (1975), 124.
[8] Ibid.

become recognized voices in policy-making. In order to do this, they have to become more highly organized, developing their 'peculiar competence' to communicate their policy views to government. Since the early 1970s, a number of environmental groups have done this, in effect engaging in the process of institutionalization. They do not, of course, become institutional groups overnight. In fact, very few achieve that status, and most we could describe as either fledgeling or mature, depending on how closely they seem to conform to the models at either end of our continuum.

. . . The organizational development of each kind of group helps define its relationship to the policy process. For example, the issue-orientated group with its supporters participating out of concern for a particular issue usually has a small membership that tries to make up in devotion to the cause what it lacks in resources or staff. Lack of staff is this type of group's most serious deficiency, at least in the Canadian setting, because it generally means that the group does not have expert knowledge about what government is doing or thinking about the issue of concern. Its members tend, therefore, to work in an information vacuum. Not only do they not know what government is thinking, they tend not to know who in government thinks about their particular issue. Their reactions, therefore, tend to be gut reactions directed at the most likely figure in sight, usually a politician, and expressed vociferously in the media.

In the long run these methods do not work. A specific decision may be turned around, but to change policy—which is a mosaic of many decisions—groups need to be close to government thinking, able to overcome the barriers created by administrative secrecy, and knowledgeable about where and when to intervene. In Canada, particularly, where public information legislation was until recently quite antiquated and group participation in policy-making has been considered a privilege, not a right, government officials have in the past been able to undermine any groups too inclined to publicly attack policy simply by withholding vital information. It may be that recent changes in the policy process, particularly in the diffusion of power that has become the norm in Ottawa, is altering this condition. Nevertheless, for many years the authority of information control made government agencies the dominant partner in their relations with pressure groups and forced those issue-orientated groups that did survive to follow a pattern of institutionalization that took them very rapidly from the placard-carrying stage to the collegial and consultative relationship favoured by government.

Yet, though confrontation has been, and perhaps still is, dysfunctional for groups in the long run, in their early life it can be very important, sometimes essential. Since they generally emerge in response to a policy issue, new groups cannot, by definition, have participated in the deliberations that led to the decision they are concerned about. Thus, they enter the policy process at a stage when events are moving beyond their ability to stop them, and only the most drastic measures will have any effect. In these circumstances, confrontation may be the best available strategy, as it makes use of the media's ability to influence the only decision-makers who may still be able to change the course of events—the politicians.

The group that outlives this early 'placard-carrying' stage generally has done so by changing its relationship to its members and by adapting to the policy system. One of the first steps in this adaptation is that the organization must stop being concerned with only one issue and instead take up several causes. Many environmental groups took this route, starting up to prevent the destruction of a particular nature amenity, then switching their concern to large issues. With a broader range of interest the group attracts a wider membership. While the new members may lack the fervent sense of commitment of the group's founders, and may be less inclined to sound a strident ideological note when the group tries to communicate with government, a wider membership base usually broadens the group's financial resources, bringing stability and a strengthened capacity to engage in the information game. Here again group-oriented and policy-oriented developments may take place in tandem. With a steady budget the group may take on a modest staff, a move that usually ensures that finances are better managed and that the members are served more consistently. Financial capacity usually also means that the group can afford to hire professionals—lawyers, public policy experts, public relations specialists—who can help it acquire the information it needs to participate in the policy process. These are the first steps in institutionalization. From this point on, the nature of the organization does not change a great deal. It simply becomes more complex, more capable of adapting to changes in the policy system, and to the disappointment of founding members, more remote and professional, guided increasingly by its paid staff.

Once started on the road to institutionalization the pressure group more readily wins the attention of government officials and, at the same time, is more apt to adapt to meet shifts in government policy process. This largely follows from the decision to hire professionals. Because they are familiar with the way in which policy is made, these people guide the group away from some lines of action and encourage others. In Canada and most European countries this generally means that groups become more and more intimate with the details of bureaucratic decision-making and less and less inclined to use the media except when formal hearings necessitate the presentation of rather general briefs that are intended to create an image rather than promote a specific policy. In the United States, on the other hand, lobbyists can expect to have to argue both in public and in private. With these differences in strategy go differences in organizational structure.

As these comments suggest, the processes of pressure group institutionalization offer us a particularly useful way of discovering the differences between policy systems and even tracing the evolution of our systems over time. In Canada, for example, because we have pressure groups, we often mistakenly think they behave in the same way as American pressure groups. This sometimes leads to the notion that our policy system is becoming more like that of the United States. It is quite true in some respects, particularly when issue-oriented groups exploit the media, that there is more than a superficial resemblance between Canadian and American pressure group behaviour. As soon as we look at the behaviour of more established groups in both countries, however, we see major differences. For example, even well-established American groups readily take part in public debates over policy, while their counterparts in Canada see an appeal to public opinion as a last resort.[9]

Why the difference? In the American system congressional politics plays a large part in policy development, with policy tending to be formed by the congressional committees responsible for a particular field, the administrative agencies carrying out policy, and the interest groups affected by it. Much policy discussion is conducted in private, but there is also an important public element involving committee hearings where rival demands are vigorously presented and where even the most secure, discreet, and established lobby must put its case to the general public as well as to the policy makers.[10]

Canada has had no such public forum. Debate in Parliament has been tightly controlled by the government, and even committee hearings have offered few opportunities for airing grievances, much

[9] For a fuller discussion of this point see W. T. Stanbury, *Business–Government Relations in Canada* (Toronto: Methuen, 1986), ch. 7.

[10] See Randall B. Ripley and Grace A. Franklin, *Congress, the Bureaucracy and Public Policy* (Homewood, Ill.: Dorsey Press, 1976); Robert Presthus's two-volume comparative study on Canada and the United States, *Élite Accommodation in Canadian Politics* (Toronto: Macmillan, 1973) and *Élites in the Policy Process* (Cambridge: Cambridge University Press, 1974); and Mildred A. Schwartz, *The Environment for Policy-Making in Canada and the United States* (Montreal: C. D. Howe Institute, 1981).

less changing policy. The basic form of public policy has been worked out between the political executive and senior administrators. Consequently, lobbyists and others wishing to influence public policy have chosen to do so by approaching and persuading civil servants and Cabinet ministers rather than parliamentarians. There are innumerable consequences to this, some affecting pressure groups, others the policy process itself, most of which we cannot discuss here. Suffice it to say that the end effect of this system is that 'legitimate, wealthy, coherent interests, having multiple access to the legislative process, would tend to be more influential than less legitimate, poor, diffuse interests, having few sources of access to the legislative process'.[11]

It may be that changes in parliamentary procedure, in the structure of policy-making, in the availability of government information, and in our constitutional framework are causing important modifications in this system of pressure group politics, making groups less dependent on bureaucracy and more capable of engaging in open and public debate. At the moment, we have only a few hints that this is the case and no very clear idea as to what the future may bring. However, probably we can assume that a tendency for pressure groups to become more numerous and more publicly active will continue to grow.

PRESSURE GROUPS IN THE POLICY PROCESS: THE ROLE OF POLICY COMMUNITIES

We sometimes think of pressure groups in the singular, acting alone to bring off a policy coup or to thwart some scheme cooking in the 'policy shops', as government policy analysis units are often called. At other times they are described *en masse*: collaborating, competing, and generally rampaging across the policy stage. In general, however, their participation in the policy system is continuous, discreet, and multifaceted.

The first responsibility of any pressure group is to attend to the immediate needs of its clients. This usually means dealing with quite routine problems: alleviating the too stringent application of regulations, negotiating a minor shift in policy, bringing about the slight extension of a service. Such minor irritations along the public sector–private sector interface bring pressure group representatives

[11] Fred Thompson and W. T. Stanbury, 'The Political Economy of Interest Groups in the Legislative Process in Canada', Montreal: Institute for Research on Public Policy, Occasional Paper No. 9, p. viii.

into daily contact with government officials and, while not inspiring in themselves, familiarize them with the subtle changes in administrative routine and attitude that eventually crystallize into a change in policy.[12] When formal policy discussions begin, the understanding developed through these routine contacts is of immense value.

The policy process itself is hard to define: the origins of policy are often obscure and the roles of those who take part are seldom exactly the same from debate to debate. Even so, we do have some general notions as to how the key policy actors—politicians, bureaucrats, and lobbyists—relate to one another, and this helps us develop a rough picture of the part pressure groups play in the process.

The first point that we must bear in mind is that the entire political community is almost never involved in a specific policy discussion. Specialization occurs throughout the policy system. The existence of pressure groups gives us the most obvious evidence of this, but specialization occurs elsewhere as well. Government departments, however large and multifaceted they may appear to be, are confined to a precisely defined territory. Even the political executive finds that only the really big issues are discussed by the entire Cabinet. All the rest are handled by individual Cabinet ministers or by specialized Cabinet committees. Richard Crossman, once a member of the British Cabinet, remarked in his diary that 'we come briefed by our departments to fight for our departmental budgets, not as Cabinet ministers with a Cabinet view'.[13] Only prime ministers and presidents play roles that encourage them to consider policy in the round, and they live with such tight schedules that only the most urgent and significant issues come to their attention.

Out of specialization come what we call 'policy communities'—groupings of government agencies, pressure groups, media people, and individuals, including academics, who for various reasons have an interest in a particular policy field and attempt to influence it. Most policy communities consist of two segments: the subgovernment and the attentive public. To all intents and purposes the subgovernment is the policy-making body in the field. It processes most routine policy issues and when doing so is seldom successfully challenged by interlopers. The subgovernment is what

---

[12] There are useful descriptions of these relationships in Kwavnick, *Organized Labour and Pressure Politics* (Montreal: McGill-Queen's University Press, 1972).

[13] Quoted in Jeremy J. Richardson and A. G. Jordan, *Governing Under Pressure: The Policy Process in a Post-Parliamentary Democracy* (Oxford: Martin Robertson & Co., 1979), 26.

has been called 'the durable core of any policy arena'.[14] It consists of the government agencies most directly engaged in setting policy and regulating the field and a small group of interests—generally associations but occasionally major corporations—whose power guarantees them the right to be consulted on virtually a daily basis. Their power wins them a place at the policy table, but government also needs their expert knowledge of the technical aspects of policy.

The power of the inner circle is used to limit the participation of others in policy debate. Those who are excluded congregate in the 'attentive public'. This outer circle includes those who are interested in policy issues but do not participate in policy-making on a frequent, regular basis. The academic community often plays this role, as do journalists working for specialized publications and, of course, a range of organizations and associations whose interest is keen but not acute enough to warrant breaking into the inner circle.

The attentive public lacks the power of the subgovernment, but it still plays a vital part in policy development. Conferences and study sessions organized by professional and interest associations offer opportunities for officials at various levels to converse with the grass roots of their constituency and with journalists and academics who have been studying public policy. Most have views on government performance and are quick to put them forward. Though most are heard sceptically, sometimes patronizingly, they contribute to the process through which government and people gradually amend, extend, and generally adapt policies and programs to the changing needs of the community. Similarly, the newsletters, professional journals, and trade magazines that circulate through the policy community give both the subgovernment and the attentive public plenty of opportunity to shore up, demolish, and generally transmogrify the existing policy edifice. In this turmoil of theories and interests, officialdom—which is almost never monolithic, nearly always pluralistic, and seldom at peace with itself—discerns the policy changes government must make if it is to keep nearly abreast of circumstance. The main function of the attentive public, then, is to maintain a perpetual policy review process. . . .

Pressure groups, along with individual members of the attentive public, are the most mobile members of the policy community. With their annual meetings, their newsletters, their regional organizations, and above all, their informal networks, they have an ability to

[14] John E. Chubb, *Interest Groups and the Bureaucracy: The Politics of Energy* (Stanford, Calif.: Stanford University Press, 1983), 8–10, quoted in William D. Coleman, *Business and Politics: A Study of Collective Action* (Montreal: McGill-Queen's University Press, 1988), 277.

cross organizational lines denied other more formal actors, such as government departments. They can, therefore, act as go-betweens, provide opportunities for quiet meetings between warring agencies, and keep the policy process in motion. These services, together with their ability to evaluate policy and develop opinion, make pressure groups integral members of the policy community.

Before we conclude our comments on the policy community, we have to remember that the most prominent of its members are not primarily interested in making or reformulating policy. Rather, for them, the policy community is a protective device, limiting rather than expanding the opportunities for the public at large to achieve major policy changes. Thus, it is the goal of the subgovernment to keep policy-making at the routine or technical level. If it achieves this, the subgovernment can keep interference to a minimum. Often, however, circumstances outside its control—economic changes, the development of new technologies, changing public concerns—are more than the subgovernment can handle through its system of formal communications and informal networks. Controversy develops, new issues emerge, and more and more interests want to take part in policy-making. Policy debate broadens as levels of conflict rise, so that eventually central issues are taken out of the hands of the subgovernment and policy community and resolved at the highest political levels—by Cabinet and by the First Ministers' Conference. When this occurs, the policy community, as well as policy, is often vastly altered.

PRESSURE GROUPS AND DEMOCRACY

Many people feel that pressure groups are a threat to democratic government. They distrust 'special-interest groups', arguing that their special pleading circumvents the legitimate authority of elected representatives and unfairly competes with the average citizen who approaches government as an individual. They fear that the special-interest state is more easily corruptible than one that debates and settles policy in the open forum of Parliament . . .

With the legitimacy of government rooted in a spatial orientation to political communication, and its effectiveness depending on sectoral organization, the modern democratic state contains a tension that is the most fascinating, most disturbing feature of modern political life. Out of it has come the decline, but certainly not the demise, of the political party and the rise of the pressure group, the ideal instrument for sectoral, specialized communication. With the rise of pressure groups has come a tendency for

institutionalized groups—the majority representing business interests—to dominate debate within policy communities. As William
Coleman has pointed out, because policy-making has become so
diffuse, it is difficult to compel these interests to consider the general
welfare or to be accountable to the public. Equally, it is extremely
difficult for other interests to participate effectively—let alone on
equal terms with business—in public debate.[15] Public interest
groups are especially disadvantaged by this imbalance. Such
developments threaten democratic discourse, as recent concern over
lobbying and over business-interest participation in the free trade
debate demonstrates.[16]

During the 1990s, we will hear increased public discussion of
these issues. Some reform proposals have already been put forward.
In 1987, for example, a parliamentary committee recommended the
registration of lobbyists, and in 1988 a weak registration law was
passed.[17] In another publication I have argued for lobbyist
registration, for strengthening the capacity of parliamentary committees to use and encourage interest group discussion of policy, and
for providing more resources to public interest groups.[18] Most
recently Coleman has made a similar plea for parliamentary reform
and has suggested that Canada follow the lead of small European
states and restructure business interests so that the entire spectrum
of business can be represented by 'a very few organizations that can
give voice to the diversity of interests resulting from territorial and
sectoral factors'.[19] He also argues that labour groups should be
strengthened so that they will acquire both a capacity to speak to
general concerns and an acknowledged responsibility to do so.

Some of these changes are in progress. Parliament, in particular,
has used procedural reforms to encourage more open and vigorous
policy debate. We can expect the regulation of lobbying to take
firmer hold during the 1990s. We may even see greater government
support for public interest groups. There is less likelihood that
business interests will be reorganized in the fashion that Coleman
recommends. Despite similarities between Canada and small
European states, Canada is physically a very large and regionally

[15] Coleman, *Business and Politics*, 261–5.

[16] See e.g. John Sawatsky, *The Insiders: Government Business and the Lobbyists*
(Toronto: McClelland and Stewart, 1987), and Hyman Solomon, 'Business Got its
Feet Wet in Public Policy', *Financial Post* (5 Dec. 1988).

[17] I have given an account of this in 'The Business Card Bill: The Debate over
Lobbyist Registration in Canada', in Grant Jordan (ed.), *Commercial Lobbying*
(forthcoming).

[18] Pross, *Group Politics and Public Policy* (Toronto: Oxford University Press, 1986),
261–72.

[19] Coleman, *Business and Politics*, 169.

diverse country. It is, therefore, doubtful whether even a highly democratic organizational structure for business interests can offset the pull of regional tensions within interest communities. Similarly, it is unlikely that the most prominent public interest groups—such as environmentalists, consumer activists, and women's groups— would be willing to voice their concerns solely through the labour movement. In other words, public supervision of pressure group activity will proceed incrementally in Canada during the decade. Whether it will be either sufficient or appropriate is not clear.

I I

PLURALISM AND PRESSURE POLITICS IN FRANCE

PETER A. HALL

Between the state and society in every industrialized nation stands a network of interest organizations, established to express the views of various social or economic groups to the governing authorities. Along with political parties, this network of organized interests is one of the principal features of the political system whereby the interests of social groups are defined, represented, and pressed upon the government. In most countries, this system of interest intermediation is a widely accepted and well-understood component of the political system. In France, however, the operation of organized interests has always been the subject of suspicion and controversy. It is closely bound up with major debates about the capacities of the French state and the character of French politics as a whole.

Our contemporary understanding of the role of organized interests in France is still derived, in large measure, from studies of French politics that concentrated on the Fourth Republic (1946–58) and the years when Charles de Gaulle and his followers dominated the Fifth Republic (1958–74). Two influential images emerged from these studies. The first portrayed France as a nation with a weak associational life. The French were said to be reluctant to join organizations and the few existing organizations were believed to have weak ties to their rank and file. The second saw France as a nation with a strong state. If other governments made policy in response to pressure from organized interests, the French state was portrayed as a strategic actor, capable of imposing its own preferences on society, even in the face of resistance from organized interests.

Both of these images are rooted in the Jacobin ideology associated with the French Revolution of 1789. In reaction to the many corporate bodies that seemed bastions of privilege under the *ancien régime*, the revolutionaries agreed with Jean-Jacques Rousseau that 'if

Reprinted from Peter A. Hall, Jack Hayward, and Howard Machin, *Developments in French Politics* (London: Macmillan, 1990), 77–92, permission requested.

the general will is to be able to express itself, it is essential that there should be no partial society within the State and that each citizen should think only his own thoughts'. Accordingly, they outlawed secondary associations and proclaimed that the state alone was the legitimate interpreter of the public interest. Even today, this aspect of Jacobin doctrine continues to have an impact on French political discourse. Pressure from organized interest groups, which has generally been seen as a legitimate part of public policy-making in Britain and the USA, is still viewed by many in France as a source of bias, injustice, and inefficiency.[1] Negotiations may occur among organized interests and the state, but state intervention is often seen as the ultimate means for resolving such conflicts. Many French officials relish their position as guardians of the public interest.

Together with the residual impact of Jacobin ideals on political discourse and behaviour in France, a number of factors lent credence to this image of French politics in the 1950s and 1960s. An administrative élite pushed the boundaries of state intervention forward during these decades, in pursuit of socio-economic modernization. Armed with increasing presidential powers and a growing Gaullist party, Charles de Gaulle seemed to rise above even the most powerful of sectarian interests. In comparative terms, it was possible to see France as a special case, marked by the presence of a strong state presiding over a weakly-organized society.

Today, however, this image no longer fits the contours of contemporary French politics. A series of developments, which began in the 1950s and 1960s but were often hidden behind the façade of Gaullist hegemony only to gain increasing momentum in the 1970s and 1980s, have undermined many of our conventional views of French politics. On the one hand, they reveal that France is quite similar to other nations in a variety of unexpected respects. On the other, they suggest that we must recast our understanding of what is distinctive about the politics or organized interests in France.

To begin with, it now seems apparent that associational life in France is alive and well. By 1977, over half of all French men and women belonged to at least one voluntary association, and over 45,000 new associations of one sort or another were being created each year.[2] Most of these groups are non-political; they range from cycling clubs to tenants' associations, from charitable organizations to housing co-operatives, but their growing numbers suggest that French society is highly organized rather than purely individualistic.

---

[1] François de Closets, *Tous Ensemble* (Paris: Seuil, 1985).

[2] See Conseil National de la Vie Associative, *Bilan de la Vie Associative* (Paris: La Documentation française, 1987), and Frank Wilson, *Interest Group Politics in France* (Cambridge: Cambridge University Press, 1987), 14.

To be sure, there are sectors in which French organizations seem less robust than their foreign counterparts. French trade unions, for instance, still have a relatively tenuous relationship to their rank and file. The proportion of the work-force that belongs to a union has fallen from a peak of about 24 per cent in 1975 to around 13 per cent by an optimistic estimate in 1989, partly in response to rising levels of unemployment. In crucial sectors like education, health care and small business, however, French providers are more fully organized than their counterparts in many nations; and such catch-all parties as the RPR and the PS have built up a respectable mass membership. There seem to be few grounds for arguing that the French are less organized, in social or political terms, than the population of most European nations.

Similarly, the strength of the French state *vis-à-vis* organized interests looks considerably different now compared with 20 years ago. One distinctive feature of these relations remains the same: French interest groups are unusually dependent on the state for financial support and official recognition. All formal organizations are required to register with the authorities in France and the government grants some of them official recognition which brings with it membership on a range of consultative bodies. Moreover, the state subsidies roughly half to three-quarters of the operating budget of many organized interest groups; as many as 4,000 public employees may be seconded to such groups as the trade unions.[3] For instance, it is estimated that, in 1979, the national agricultural association, received almost as much in public subsidies (8.6 million francs) as it did from membership dues, its youth wing receiving another 13.3 million francs.[4]

These are substantial sums in comparison to the negligible levels of support provided in Britain or the USA. It is tempting to assume that they give public officials considerable leverage over the activities of organized interests. However, there is little evidence to support this. France's largest trade union, the CGT, was granted state subsidies only after it helped to quell the social disturbances of May 1968, but their receipt seems to have had no discernible effect on the CGTs subsequent behaviour. Conversely, many beneficiaries of state subsidies have entered into bitter conflicts with the state. Over time, state subsidies seem to have done more to sustain such groups than to tame them.

In addition, the Jacobin image of public officials making policy in relative isolation from organized social interests has been belied by

---

[3] See Wilson, *Interest Group Politics*, 136 and *L'Express* (2 Sept. 1988), 19.

[4] John T. S. Keeler, *The Politics of Neo-Corporatism in France* (New York: Oxford University Press, 1987), 233.

the proliferation of consultative bodies associated with policy-making. As public policy stretched into more and more spheres of social life and became increasingly complex, French officials found that they needed information, advice, and at least tacit agreement from the affected social groups in order to design and implement their policies effectively. This is a universal problem in the contemporary world. The French have coped with it by subsidizing organized interests and establishing an extensive network of consultative organs designed to elicit advice and acquiescence from those interests.

The notion of consultation was embodied in the early moderniza-tion commissions of the economic plan and later built into the constitution of the Fifth Republic in the form of the Economic and Social Council which was powerless but positioned, like a latter-day Estates General, to bring the views of social and economic groups to bear on legislation. Moreover, there are a range of representative organizations in many spheres of the French economy, associated particularly with the administration of social policy. Representation on these bodies brings resources and influence to many interest organizations. Regular elections for such representatives provide a benchmark of support among the rank and file and a focal point for much organizational activity. This is another distinctive feature of interest group politics in France. In recent decades, however, the number of consultative bodies has grown steadily. By 1971, there were over 500 such councils, 1,200 committees, and 3,000 commis-sions attached to the French state. The 1970s saw another wave of expansion, as successive governments sought consensual solutions to the intractable fiscal problems posed by slower rates of growth and an expanding welfare state.[5] By 1987, for instance, the peak family association in France, UNAF (National Union of Family Associa-tions), sat on 92 national-level committees alone.

However, many of these consultative bodies exist primarily for show, and French policy-making now reflects a rather uneasy compromise between Jacobin ideals and pluralist politics. Before many major policy initiatives, elaborate soundings are now taken, involving the establishment of new commissions, reports from distinguished groups of experts, and canvassing of the relevant organized interests. Precise policy proposals are then frequently formulated quite independently by public officials and unveiled, only to meet a new chorus of complaints from the affected interests. Depending on the strength of that chorus, the proposals may be

[5] See Henry W. Ehrmann, *Politics in France*, 2nd edn. (Boston: Little, 1971); and *L'Express* (3 July 1987).

changed at the last minute or even withdrawn; but there is often a radical disjunction between the vague consultation that precedes a policy announcement and the hard politicking that follows it. Hence, French interest organizations rarely feel fully involved in policy-making, despite the proliferation of consultative organs. There is still an element of fiat in the behaviour of the public authorities and a great deal of public posturing on the part of organized interests. If France no longer has a state that is above society, this process of policy-making by consultation-fiat-revision is still some distance away from one based on intensive and ongoing negotiation with social groups.

Moreover, there are two distinctive aspects of organized interests in France that tend to militate against the kind of intimate negotiations which often mark relations between the state and organized interests in nations like West Germany or the USA. The first is the divided, and relatively politicized, character of French interest groups themselves; the second is the continuing salience of a tradition of direct protest.

Organized interests in France are often much more factionalized internally than their counterparts in other nations. These internal divisions run along lines of partisan political allegiance as well as functional sub-interests. The labour movement, for example, has never been united under one umbrella organization, such as the British TUC or the West German DGB. Instead, it is divided among competing confederations, many of whom have well-known affinities for particular political parties. Even individual unions, like the FEN, are themselves divided into subsidiary unions along partisan lines, and these subsidiaries, in turn, contain a variety of factions that support one political tendency or another within the major political parties. Farm and business associations are typically less divided along partisan lines but, even here, multiple organizations compete for support. As a result, when public officials seek a body with which to negotiate, it is difficult to find one that can speak for an entire constituency of related interests, and many interest-group conflicts take on a partisan tone.

For the most part, French interest groups operate as their counterparts do in all the industrial democracies. They disseminate their views in pamphlets and the press, lobby legislators when the outcome of any bill is in doubt, and maintain regular contacts with bureaucrats in the relevant ministries. However, pressure politics in France has always moved readily from the corridors of power to the streets. As a result of precedents set in the 1789 Revolution, the events of July 1830, the days of June 1848 and the Paris Commune of 1871, mass demonstrations have become a potent and oft-utilized weapon in the tactical repertoire of organized interests in France. They are used to reinforce rank-and-file solidarity within the organization itself at the same time as they pose a threat to public order which the regime has difficulty ignoring. Out of one sample of interest group leaders, fully a third reported that they used demonstrations, strikes or other forms of direct action to get their views across with at least some frequency, 18 per cent expressing the view that this sort of power struggle was their most effective means of action.[6] As a result, mass demonstrations, often accompanied by some form of public disruption, are a regular feature of pluralist politics in France.

In short, French society is now more organized than ever before, and the French state seems less strong or aloof from societal interests than it was once thought to be. Indeed, through a system of public subsidies and a network of consultative bodies, it helped to create the matrix of organized interests with which it now has to deal. Most of those organizations behave much as their counterparts do elsewhere, yet at times their highly factionalized character and propensity for direct action can render them particularly intractable intermediaries.

PLURALIST POLITICS IN THE 1980s

These observations are confirmed by the course of interest group politics in the 1980s. The election of a Socialist president in 1981 followed by a solid Socialist majority in the legislature was an event of major significance for post-war France. The new government set out to change the balance of power among organized interests in France, away from big business, the large farmers and conservative groups that had been privileged during the years of Gaullist rule, and towards the trade unions, small farmers and Left-leaning organizations in the polity. Here was a natural experiment. Could a new administration use the power of the state to reorganize societal interests in France? The results are apparent in each of the major realms of interest politics.

Agriculture

The French agricultural sector has long been dominated by the FNSEA, a powerful confederal organization that, with the help of Gaullist allies, had been taken over by a modernizing leadership in

---

[6] Wilson, *Interest Group Politics*, 150–3.

the early 1960s and given a powerful position as the privileged intermediary between French farmers and the state. By according the FNSEA representation and influence on the network of local committees that administered agricultural subsidies and land policies crucial to the fate of local farmers, French officials handed the organization a set of selective incentives with which to consolidate its support in the countryside. In return, the FNSEA and its affiliates, like the *Centre National des Jeunes Agriculteurs* (National Organization of Young Farmers), lent support to the modernizing policies of successive conservative governments which were designed to increase the size of land holdings and promote agricultural business in France. Both sides gained. Indeed, relations between the state and the FNSEA began to approach a system of interest intermediation known as neo-corporatist collaboration, in which a single-interest organization is accorded responsibility not only for representing the views of its constituency to the state, but for implementing a variety of public policies as well. Although common in nations like Sweden and Austria, this sort of relationship is relatively rare in France.

The 1981 Mitterrand Government set out to break up this cosy relationship between the state and the FNSEA and give more support to the small farmer. In her first speech, the new Minister of Agriculture declared that: 'it is necessary to end the confusion between the role of professional organizations and that of the state. The former must negotiate and contest if they feel necessary; the state must make the decisions.'[7] In this spirit, she promptly accorded privileged status to three organizations competing with the FNSEA: one dominated by the Communists, another on the far Right, and a hastily-formed amalgam of six Socialist-leaning farmers unions. Most important, the network of committees administering local agricultural policy was to be restructured so as to reduce the influence of the FNSEA and increase that of the Left.

If the French state were as powerful as some suppose, this might have worked, but the FNSEA fought back. After many years of holding back peasant protests against the Gaullists, it gave open support to practices of confrontation that became known as the 'peasant revolt'. Week after week, in 1981–2, groups of peasants demonstrated in Paris and the countryside with the acquiescence of the FNSEA. In Perpignan, they ripped up half a mile of railway track and carried it to the steps of the local *préfecture*. In Calvados, they bombarded the Minister of Agriculture with eggs until she was

---

[7] Keeler, *The Politics of Neo-Corporatism in France*, 219.

forced to an emergency airlift; on 23 March 1982, they filled the streets of Paris with 100,000 angry farmers demonstrating against the new regime.

The Socialists looked in vain for some way to stem the rising tide of agricultural protest. However, the new organizations they hoped would challenge the FNSEA were still too small to exert much influence over farmers. In the prevailing climate, even they saw advantages in attacking the government. In many regions, the authorities had to reappoint FNSEA supporters to local agricultural committees because their competitors had no mass base there and could not agree about whom to appoint to the few positions available. By 1983, the FNSEA still took almost 70 per cent of the vote in elections to the important Chambers of Agriculture. Long-standing organizational relations could not be replaced overnight.

Accordingly, Mitterrand was forced to come to some accommodation with the FNSEA. His next Minister of Agriculture was a conciliator who toned down the proposals for reform and restored collaboration with the FNSEA. Following the 1986 legislative elections, his successor was none other than the former President of the FNSEA himself. In a sphere where local discontent was endemic, the FNSEA had made itself so indispensable as a guarantor of social order and conduit for information and advice that the government could hardly do without it.

Industry

Relations between the state and organized interests in the industrial sphere have been more chaotic but no less significant. In this case, the state has to deal with both employers and labour. Moreover, each of these is represented by a large number of organizations that stretch from plant and firm level to sectoral and peak-level associations.

There are active organizations representing small and medium-sized businesses in France as well as local chambers of commerce and trade associations in most sectors of the economy. Some can be very powerful. In steel, for instance, a powerful trade association became the conduit through which the state channelled billions of francs in successive efforts to rationalize the industry. At the peak level, French employers are grouped together under a general confederation, the CNPF. But collaboration at this level has always been limited by the decentralized nature of the CNPF itself: it is an umbrella organization representing about 800 separate trade associations. With widely disparate interests, these associations have been reluctant to concede real negotiating power to the CNPF;

and, while it makes frequent representations to the government, it only occasionally makes concrete bargains on behalf of industrialists.

When issues of industrial rationalization are at stake, public officials have found it more useful to deal with sectoral organizations or large firms directly. Each ministry generally develops a *tutelle*, or supervisory relationship, with the industries in which it is most interested, whereby the industry responds to the suggestions of the ministry in return for the latter's support inside the government itself. In addition, there is a much more extensive flow of personnel from the senior Civil Service to leading managerial positions in the private sector in France than in Britain or the USA, relations between industry and the state gaining cohesion from this network of personal relations.

Relations between the state and the trade unions are more difficult, for several reasons. First, France has no single or unified union confederation. Only about 13 per cent of the work-force belongs to a union, and five separate confederations compete with each other at plant and national levels: the CGT (supported by about 18 per cent of those eligible to vote in enterprise committee elections), the CFDT (with 11 per cent support), the FO (10 per cent support), the CFTC (4 per cent support), and the CGC (5 per cent support). Second, most of these organizations have weak organizational ties to the rank and file. They can bring thousands of workers into the streets for a 24-hour strike, but their capacity to enforce collective bargains or even collect dues from their membership is limited. Third, many of the French unions are highly politicized; the CGT has close ties to the PCF and the CFDT is known for its Socialist sympathies. Although favoured by the RPR, the FO has tried to maintain an apolitical profile. These factors make co-operation among the unions themselves difficult. As a result, although the French state accords the unions an official role on the agencies that supervise health insurance, old-age pensions and unemployment insurance, it has rarely been able to bargain with them effectively about national economic or incomes policies.

The election of a Socialist Government in 1981 was a watershed for French business, and the CNPF in particular. It had gradually come to support the relatively interventionist policies of the Gaullists in the interest of economic modernization. It continued to do so even in the face of slower rates of growth, a rising tax burden, and stiff regulations regarding lay-offs during the 1970s in order to stave off any challenge from the Left. Once the Socialists were elected and embarked on policies of nationalization, reduced working hours and work-place reform, however, the CNPF became ambivalent about maintaining close ties to the government. Instead, under a new leader, it retreated to a more aggressive rhetorical stance, based on neo-liberal demands for deregulation, lower taxes, and denationalization. This was to have a significant impact on French political discourse. Entrepreneuralism, flexibility and the market became the watchwords of the day.

The Mitterrand Government countered by according *de facto* recognition to a traditional rival of the CNPF, the SNPMI (National Union of Small Industry). Once again, it hoped to break the privileged position of organized interests that had long been sympathetic to the Right, but once again its strategy backfired. The SNPMI gained support rapidly and began to mount demonstrations against both the CNPF and the government. Not to be outdone, its own rivals for the support of small business, the CGPME (Confederation of Small Business) and CID-UNATI (National Artisans Organization), took to the streets as well on three successive days in May 1983.[8] The government was ultimately forced to disown the SNPMI and respond to the neo-liberal climate of opinion that the CNPF had helped foster. After 1986, the CNPF softened its stance somewhat under a new leader, but the Chirac Government took up the neo-liberal rhetoric with enthusiasm.

Relations between the Mitterrand Government and the trade unions were more positive but less straightforward. Mitterrand hoped to strengthen the position of the trade unions *vis-à-vis* business and the state; but he hesitated to go too far in this direction because the most powerful trade union was the Communist-dominated CGT, and Mitterrand did not want to enhance its power in relation to the government or the other unions. Accordingly, some trade unionists were brought into ministerial offices; frequent consultations were held with the unions; and the Auroux laws, designed to strengthen union representation at the plant level, were passed. However, neither the unions nor the government wanted to be seen as the prisoner of the other. Accordingly, consultation was only rarely followed by substantive negotiations; as a result, relations gradually cooled between the government and the unions.

Even worse, rising levels of unemployment were sapping union membership, which fell dramatically during the 1980s. When the Socialist Government turned toward austerity policies after 1982, the unions most closely associated with the government, like the CFDT and CGT, began to lose support among the work-force to

[8] Suzanne Berger, 'The Socialists and the Patronat: The Dilemmas of Co-Existence in a Mixed Economy', in H. Machin and V. Wright (eds.), *Economic Policy and Policy-Making under the Mitterrand Presidency* (London: Printer, 1985).

such organizations at the FO and CGC, which forswore politics in favour of a focus on material benefits and collective bargaining. Hence, even with the Auroux laws, the unions were barely able to strengthen their hand at the plant and firm levels. Meanwhile, the PS did little to build a lasting base for co-operation with the unions at the local level and, when the government left office, labour organizations were even weaker than usual. In yet another sphere, those at the helm of the state had been unable to reorder the underlying patterns of interest organization in society.

Armed with the neo-liberalism that had become popular in business circles, the 1986–8 conservative government continued to reduce industrial subsidies and remove regulations governing lay-offs, despite union opposition. The trade unions were left struggling for members and relatively demoralized in the face of a revival of market rhetoric to which even the Socialists seemed to subscribe. In many cases, employers used these conditions to turn the Auroux laws to their advantage, and industrial relations became considerably quieter in the private sector as the focus turned to collective bargaining and issues of workplace flexibility.

The most important developments at the end of the 1980s, however, were an escalating series of strikes in the public sector, led in this case not by the unions but by *ad hoc* coalitions of militants drawing on widespread rank-and-file discontent with five years of wage austerity. Informal co-ordinating committees of workers took the initiative away from the trade unions and led industrial action by railway workers in 1986, nurses and transport workers in 1988, and prison guards in 1989, often in defiance of statutes forbidding strikes in such sectors. This posed a potentially serious problem for the unions: were they losing their influence over the rank and file? The CGT quickly tried to lend support to these efforts, but the others rushed to keep up. These strikes were also a major problem for the Rocard Government. As economic growth revived, so did the long-standing militancy of the French working class. As new leaders took office in several of the major union confederations, they were faced with the problem of defining new lines of action capable of tapping this discontent.

Individual Issue Areas

There are organized interests operating in most spheres of French policy-making. By and large, they are of two sorts. In areas that have been the subject of policy for many decades, such as education and health care, there are dense networks of organized interests with deeply entrenched positions. In spheres that have become the object of intense concern only more recently, such as those of environmental policy, immigration, and women's issues, many of the relevant interests tend to be grouped into much more loosely organized social movements.

Education policy, for instance, has been a highly controversial subject in France since the 1790s when advocates of secular schooling were first aligned against the supporters of Catholic education. Today, policy-makers confront a powerful set of teacher's associations grouped together into the FEN. Representing two-thirds of all school personnel, the FEN is a virtual empire, linked to 53 service agencies, including savings banks, insurance companies, publishing firms, tourist agencies and old-age homes, worth at least ten billion francs.[9] In addition to the many factions inside the FEN and their Catholic equivalents, policy-makers must also deal with a miscellaneous set of national student organizations and powerful parent–teacher federations, divided between the *Fédération des Conseils de Parents d'Elèves, Nationale des Associations de Parents d'Elèves de l'Enseignement Libre,* representing 860,000 families associated with the Catholic schools.

Although there is no single organization as powerful as the FEN in the sphere of health care, policy-makers there must also deal with a bewildering network of agencies and consultative committees on which health-care providers are strongly represented. The doctors belong to a public organ, the *Ordre des Médecins,* and a variety of unions like the conservative CSMF, linked with others under an umbrella organization, the *Centre National des Professions de Santé* (National Organization of Health Workers). Nurses, medical students, hospital administrators, and others are likewise organized into a variety of associations. Each has a different set of vested interests to defend. Many other traditional policy spheres display a similar pattern.

Any attempt to reform one of these spheres, therefore, is likely to meet stiff opposition from some or all of such groups. The classic case is that of education, where reform has often seemed necessary and notoriously difficult. The experience of the Mitterrand Government provides a typical example of the policy process in such spheres. Alain Savary, the Socialist Minister of Education, made a determined effort at educational reform, including implementation of the traditional Socialist concern to bring private education under state supervision. After his initial proposals met serious opposition from Catholic educators and parents, Savary spent two years

---

[9] John S. Ambler, 'Neo-Corporatism and the Politics of French Education', *West European Politics* (1985), 26.

negotiating a compromise measure with the affected interests. At the last moment, however, the FEN and *Comité National de l'Action Laïque* (National Committee for Secular Action) persuaded the Socialist deputies to amend the proposals again in favour of secularism; and, in response, the Catholic forces brought a million protesters on to the streets of Paris. Savary resigned with only a few of his reforms in place, and Mitterrand gave up the secularization plan altogether. Measures designed to render specialized medical training more selective met a similar fate, as protesting medical students and teachers filled the parking meters of Paris with plaster, and agreement on an appropriate set of reforms eluded the government.

The Socialist Government under Michel Rocard which took office in 1988 fared little better. Although Rocard made educational reform one of his priorities, mandated substantial new funds for the field and appointed a senior figure as the new Minister of Education, his early initiatives led to widespread protests from the teachers' unions and had to be revised in 1989. Rocard himself concluded that French 'society is so rigid, sclerotic, full of corporatisms that even to measure the difficulties to be encountered is impossible, since they are so numerous'.[10]

If the organizations of professional defence in these traditional spheres of policy have served largely as veto groups, the new social movements associated with women's issues, the environment, and immigration function more as ginger groups, bringing new issues on to the political agenda and mobilizing support for specific actions. These groups are generally weak coalitions of activists, often led by intellectuals, with a shifting base of popular support that makes it difficult for them to veto specific policies but which gives them the opportunity to form at least transitory alliances with major political figures and parties. The feminist movement that emerged from the events of May 1968 grouped around the intellectual circles of *Politique et Psychanalyse* in Paris and a loose association known as the *Mouvement de la Libération des Femmes* (Women's Liberation Movement) had notable success securing passage of a liberal abortion law in 1974 and the appointment of a minister for the status of women when the Giscardians saw that it might be advantageous to woo this constituency.

SOS-racisme, created to counter the rising tide of anti-immigrant sentiment in the 1980s, gained sufficient strength as a result of recognition and financial support received from the Mitterrand Government to enable it to build broader support for ethnic tolerance as well as resistance to the racism of the FN. In yet another

[10] *L'Expansion* (9 Sept. 1988), 23.

sphere, French ecologists are represented by about 250 national and 900 regional associations dedicated to preserving the environment; but they have been notably less successful at securing mass support or influence over policy than their counterparts in West Germany or Britain. Despite isolated protests, the government proceeded with an ambitious programme for constructing nuclear reactors in the 1970s; and the relatively weak agencies for environmental protection of the French state have rarely been a match for the well-organized industrial interests they confront. In frustration, the ecologists finally formed their own political party.

RETROSPECT AND PROSPECT

Two hundred years after the French Revolution supposedly wiped out the bastions of privilege in the *ancien régime*, French society again contains a wide variety of organized interests. Indeed, many of these organizations owe a portion of their resources or privileges to the French state itself. Once in place, however, these organizations often take on a life of their own. Most now have independent bases of power, and as Ezra Suleiman[11] and others have pointed out, the French state is not nearly as strong *vis-à-vis* these organizations as was once believed. Three features of the administrative practices of the French state are especially relevant here.

First, most ministries exercise a quasi-official *tutelle* over various groups. As noted above, this entails supervision of the activities of a group but also defence of the interests of that group within the counsels of state. Hence, there is an element of clientelism built into the relations that many groups have with particular ministries or agencies. The two sides exchange favours in such a way as to give some outside organizations a privileged position regarding the state.

Second, although the French state is relatively centralized compared with, say, the American state, there are still many competing agencies and organs within it that can themselves be semi-independent sources of pressure for particular lines of policy and certain kinds of privilege. Notable in this regard are the *grands corps*, specific bodies of experts that undertake a range of tasks and distribute their members widely throughout the administration. Established in many cases during the nineteenth century, many of these *corps* have been able to extend their purview to newly created fields in recent years. Policy-makers contemplating administrative

---

[11] Ezra Suleiman, *Private Power and Centralization in France: The Notaires and the State* (Princeton, NJ: Princeton University Press, 1987).

reorganization, regional decentralization or major engineering projects have often had to cope with their demands as well as those coming from outside groups. The presence of semi-independent organizations inside the state itself further enhances the pluralistic tone of contemporary French politics.

Finally, despite its centralization, there are still many divisions within the French state that interest groups can exploit to secure their objectives. Inside the bureaucracy, they can often play one ministry off against another. The French notaries, for instance, were able to block the Mitterrand Government's attempt to reform their profession by exploiting divisions between the Ministries of Justice and Finance as well as their dependence on the notaries themselves for accurate information about the state of the profession. Similarly, there are times when organized interests can play the legislature off against the Executive. Although the Executive is especially powerful, control over it is divided between the president and prime minister.

In recent years, these divisions have become particularly important. From 1986 to 1988, a Socialist president faced a conservative majority in the legislature led by a Gaullist prime minister. In the face of such *cohabitation*, groups which failed to secure support from the government could in many cases appeal to the president for redress. Moreover, as Gaullist hegemony has waned, factions have opened up in many political parties and the balance of power within the legislature has been much more evenly divided. This offers new opportunities for outside interest. Just as the focus of interest group activity shifted toward the Executive in the early years of the Fifth Republic, we can now expect some attention to shift back to the legislature, as organized interests seek to apply leverage to the fragile alliances there.[12]

However, the principal challenge that interest organizations now face comes not from within France, but from the growing influence of the EC. The policies of the EC became vital to French agriculture but Community initiatives in coal and steel, telecommunications and aerospace have also had a significant impact on French business. As the attempt to secure a unified European market in 1992 proceeds, a growing portion of the regulations affecting French society will be promulgated from Brussels. Following the lead of the farmers and major industrialists, many organized interests can be expected to devote an increasing share of their resources and attention to the European Commission. In some cases, this will entail closer alliances between interest groups and French officials

[12] Berger, 'The Socialists and the Patronat'.

aimed at common opponents in Brussels; in others, it will mean greater participation in European-wide organizations designed to co-ordinate lobbying there.

In sum, a number of convergent trends have enhanced the pluralism of French politics in recent years and shifted some political emphasis away from the state towards civil society. Over the course of the Fifth Republic, interest organizations have become an increasingly important feature of society. The passing of Gaullist hegemony in the 1970s and 1980s has distributed power more broadly among a variety of political parties and undercut the seemingly monolithic character of the state. The gradual internationalization of French business and the growing influence of the EC has moved the axes of influence over social and economic policy away from Paris while the recent surge of interest in market solutions to socio-economic problems has enhanced the role of private sector actors in many economic and cultural spheres. Policymakers will have to come to grips with all these developments during the coming years.

PRESSURE GROUP POLITICS IN WEST GERMANY

LEWIS J. EDINGER

THE ORGANIZATIONAL IMPERATIVE

The processes of interest articulation and accommodation conform closely to the highly formalized patterns of mass representation and élite interaction that generally prevail in West German politics.[1] The Basic Law designates the political parties as the principal non-governmental agents for the co-ordinated flow of domestic policy demands into the governmental system. Interest associations provide a complementary organizational link between state and society.

The Basic Law does not explicitly recognize interest associations, but it grants all citizens the right to form and join such groups, provided they are not in conflict with the criminal code or 'directed against the concept of international understanding'. Pressure group politics designed to promote or prevent decisions by authorities of the state are shaped by several factors. First, access to the 'right' people is restricted by the sheer size and complexity of the political system and the multiplicity of competing demands for authoritative action or inaction. In this respect, West German conditions for interest articulation are not very different from those in similarly constituted advanced industrial countries. Second, the organizational framework and operative rules of the present regime favour access through carefully regulated legal procedures. These funnel multiple policy demands through screening agents before they get to authoritative decision makers. Third, there are the prevailing political norms, which identify legitimate interest articulation with law-abiding behaviour. . . .

West German interest associations are more inclusive, more tightly organized, and occupy a more privileged position in public policy processes than their American counterparts. In certain respects their activities are more closely regulated than in the United States; in others, less so. In fact, if not in name, some of the

[1] This article was published before the unification of Germany.

most important associations antedate the present regime; they are elements of socio-economic and cultural continuity in a country that has been marked by sharp political discontinuities. Lingering identifications with religious, status, and occupational groups— dating back to the Industrial Revolution and beyond—still affect the policy objectives and pressure group activities of the churches and such associations as the League of German Artisans. At the same time, the effect of more recent changes in West German society and politics is reflected in the pre-eminently material and pragmatic perspectives of most interest group leaders and members and in the style of collective bargaining in contemporary pressure group politics. . . .

The extent of the influence of interest group representatives in the councils of government may be based on their personal prestige and connections, on the status of their office, on evidence of mass support for their demands, and on legal and normative criteria endorsing the 'proper' representation of elements considered important in West German society—or on any combination of these. Some pressure group leaders may thus gain attention, if not results, as the presumed spokesmen for persons they only nominally represent and who may not even belong to their organizations. Compulsory membership in interest groups or a high degree of solidarity in voluntary associations may allow others to claim solid backing from their constituents.

In federal, as in state and local politics, interest associations endeavour to influence public policies principally by the following methods: (a) assuring themselves of ready access to key points in authoritative decision-making bodies through the recruitment, placement, and sponsorship of public officials sympathetic to their claims: (b) allocating effective authority to those political positions which are most accessible to them: and (c) having their goals and methods accepted by influential veto groups and, less frequently, by the general public.

How these methods are specifically employed may vary a good deal from group to group and issue to issue. In some cases such activities will be carefully shielded from public view, in others interest group leaders will openly seek to mobilize mass opinion in order to bring pressure to bear on public officials or to replace them. Depending on what they want, when, and from whom, various pressure groups will direct their efforts to different issues and decision-makers. For instance, a business organization may concentrate on economic matters subject to federal legislation and seek to influence relevant federal ministries and parliamentary committees; a pressure group associated with the Roman Catholic church, on the other hand, may be primarily interested in educational policies under the jurisdiction of the states and pursue its objectives at the local and regional level. . . .

Compulsory and Voluntary Organizations

Some West German interest associations are specifically established by law in accordance with corporatist principles going back to the Middle Ages, to represent the different concern of various social and economic groups. Prime examples are the occupational 'chambers' (*Kammern*), which have their roots in the corporate guilds of former times. Unlike the American chambers of commerce, these are quasi-governmental organizations of public law, which exercise compulsory jurisdiction over their members and are supposed to link key sectors of the economy to the state. Most private producers engaged in agriculture, commerce, and manufacturing, as well as members of the so-called free professions—such as self-employed physicians and lawyers—must belong to appropriate local chambers, which determine and enforce rules of occupational standards and conduct. The leading functionaries of these chambers not only represent their members in pressure group politics, but exercise derivative governmental authority over them.

These multiple economic and political functions give considerable weight to policy demands put forward on behalf of the chambers since their quasi-constitutional status makes them one of the most important associational structures providing for an orderly relationship between the economic and the political systems. To co-ordinate and articulate common interests, the local chambers in most of the West German states form regional groupings; their national federations in turn are supposed to defend and promote the interests of the constituent chambers at the federal level of government.

Other associations involved in politics are not based on compulsory membership. These include traditional institutional groups explicitly endorsed and supported by public authorities, particularly the major churches, as well as a host of voluntary organizations for the promotion of symbolic causes and material interests. Some are comprehensive associations performing various tasks and pursuing numerous goals, others have a single main purpose. Religious associations, for example, minister not only to the spiritual needs of their members, but engage in educational and social welfare activities regulated by public authorities. Major business and labour organizations are concerned not only with economic problems, but with social and cultural policy matters. On the other hand, many smaller interest associations—such as the Pensioners' League and the League of War Victims—promote the explicit and exclusive political demands of highly particularistic clienteles.

Although such voluntary associations lack the quasi-governmental authority of the occupational chambers, they are also not as tightly controlled by agencies of the state. At the same time, they are less closely associated with the political parties than interest organizations under former German regimes and in other European countries. Under the present regime these interest associations consequently enjoy quite a bit of political autonomy and flexibility as ostensibly non-partisan pressure groups.

Sometimes a relatively insignificant pressure group may score a success thanks to an intensive publicity campaign, an exceptionally fortuitous combination of circumstances, or a temporary alliance with politically more powerful forces. A touch-and-go electoral battle, for example, may afford the leaders of a small, but tightly organized and united group unusual opportunities to trade their support for desired commitments from party candidates. On the whole, however, the greatest political influence rests with the official and unofficial spokesmen of the large national organizations. Formal and informal inter-élite channels permit them to exert direct pressure on leading party and governmental functionaries: at the same time, the major interest group élites command substantial resources for applying indirect pressure through influential opinion leaders and expressions of mass support for their demands.

Influence through Functional Representation

Whereas American public officials may pay attention to the demands of interest group spokesmen if they wish, West German officials are legally bound to do so. As in most European countries, institutionalized rules for the functional representation of pluralist interests allow pressure groups to bypass the political parties and inject themselves directly into policy-making.

Numerous law and administrative regulations give formal sanction and encouragement to the long-established practice of direct contacts between interest associations and agencies of the state. Thus, in all of the states of the Federal Republic various consultative bodies attached to governmental organs transmit interest group wishes to public officials. In Baden-Württemberg, for example, representatives of the principal economic organizations are regular members of the regional planning council. The same is true in the public media: spokesmen for all of the major interest groups sit on the supervisory boards of the states' radio and television networks along with representatives of the principal political parties.

Similar arrangements exist at the federal level of government. The administrative procedures of the various ministries require that when they draft a bill for submission to the legislature—and most laws originate that way—they must consult the official representatives of the appropriate peak interest organizations (*Spitzenverbände*) and consider their wishes. Effective associational interest articulation through such formal channels is further facilitated by numerous ministerial advisory councils of non-governmental experts connected with interest groups. For example, the West German Council of Economic Experts (Sachverständigenrat) is not a governmental body, in contrast to the American President's Council of Economic Advisers. However, its influence on public policy is more far-reaching since its official task is to provide for the authoritative co-ordination of public and private economic activities at all levels of government.

Functional representation also provides for the co-ordinated articulation of non-partisan sectional and local interests in national pressure group politics. Various subnational governmental units are represented by their respective peak associations. The League of German Cities (Deutscher Städtetag) thus represents the particular interests of large urban municipalities, and the Federation of German Towns and Communities (Deutscher Städte-und Germeindebund) those of smaller municipalities.

These legal arrangements have two chief consequences. First, they encourage behind-the-scenes inter-élite bargaining and accommodation among pressure group spokesmen and key public officials. Such institutionalized practices are favoured by both sides on the grounds that direct negotiations among functional policy specialists facilitate the orderly processing of interest group demands outside the public arena of partisan controversy and party strife.

Second, these procedures induce the rank-and-file members of interest associations to depend on their formal representatives to obtain satisfaction for their policy demands and compel the constituent organizations of federal peak associations to rely on top interest group élites who have direct access to national policy-makers. Here, too, the formal justification for such organizational arrangements is that they provide for the efficient and stable transmission of policy inputs from a pluralist society to the state. The intended object is to prevent the inundation of federal agencies by amorphous individual and group demands and to allow interests to be aggregated and adapted before and while they are considered by executive, legislative, or judicial organs of the Federal Government. From a comparative perspective, as a perceptive observer has noted, West German arrangements for the national representation of functional interests constitute 'an especially clear instance in which entirely formal considerations can increase the power of federated groups and their key functionaries and thus have a major effect on the structure of organized interests'.[2]

Influence through Political Representation

Structures for the functional representation of organized interests, as well as the judicial system, permit West German pressure groups to bypass party and governmental channels of political representation. However, these means also limit their opportunities for influencing the formulation of public policies, and most pressure group leaders therefore try to keep other means available. Experience has taught them that competing interest groups may neutralize each other, especially if they pursue conflicting demands by way of the governmental bureaucracy or the judiciary alone: they have learned that civil servants and the courts may decide that acceding to pressure group demands would not be in the public interest or would violate legitimate principles of law and justice. Moreover, the formal routes of access leading through the major peak associations frequently compel the constituent organizations to subordinate their particular demands to those of the larger federations and generally place smaller interest associations at a disadvantage.

For these reasons pressure group leaders endeavour to develop and maintain close relationships with the manifest political leaders who are recruited by and from the major parties. And here the degree of mutual interdependence, of agreement on basic political principles, and of reciprocity in the exchange of benefits is all-important. Party government leads interest group élites to seek influence over the composition and actions of the political élites while these, for their part, compete for the allegiances of diverse elements in a pluralist society. The power of interest group élites in the political arena will accordingly be enhanced if they can demonstrate their ability to promote or frustrate the objectives of particular political leaders, parties, and factions; these, in turn, will be most accommodating to the demands of those pressure group leaders they consider most effective.

The specific methods employed by interest association leaders to influence authoritative policies through political channels vary a good deal with particular pressure groups, parties, and circumstances, and are frequently obscure. The general public has

---

[2] Reinhard Bendix, *Nation Building and Citizenship* (New York: Wiley, 1964), 133.

been rather critical and suspicious of such activities—even when they are legal; on several occasions, pressure group politics in election campaigns have backfired, harming the parties as well as interest organizations involved. Elected officials and people who want their jobs therefore try to avoid the political stigma of close identification with special interests and to conceal their obligations to pressure groups. At the same time, as we have seen, the major parties—and especially the CDU/CSU—provide for the representation of special interests in their organizations and on their electoral tickets and endeavour to accommodate pressure group demands in their programmes.

In general, there are four methods through which pressure groups seek to influence party leaders in government and parliament: (a) attempts to obtain direct representation in the major party organizations, particularly among their leaders; (b) attempts to gain access to governing party élites through formal and informal, direct and indirect party contacts; (c) attempts to use party contacts to provide both governing and opposition party leaders with selective information and interpretations on particular policy issues (for example, articles in élite publications and 'expert' testimony and memoranda supporting interest group objectives); and (d) offers of electoral assistance to friendly politicians and threats of mobilizing a pressure group's members and financial resources against those who oppose its policy demands.

Electoral pressure group politics today carry less weight than in the early years of the Federal Republic. First of all, interest associations can apparently no longer persuade politicians to quite the same extent that they can deliver the votes of their own members. Second, even the largest and politically most active pressure groups have evidently been unable to induce significant sections of the electorate in general to support their friends and punish their enemies; their publicity campaigns on behalf of particular parties and candidates have thus proven to be rather ineffective. Third, new laws providing public funds for campaign expenses and restricting private contributions have reduced the importance of financial support from pressure groups. Political leaders have consequently been less ready than formerly to accede to the demands of special interests at election time and to compete for their support with pre-election legislative gifts.

As these means have lost effectiveness, other means for exerting influence on political leaders have become more important to West German pressure groups. On national issues these involve principally the effective representation of their policy interests by members of the federal government, by the delegations of the state governments in the Federal Council, and by deputies in the Federal Diet. In this respect traditional patterns of functional representation that bypass political parties have been complemented by the marked increase in collaborative inter-élite relations between manifest and latent political leaders.

The major interest associations have been particularly successful in placing their spokesmen in authoritative decision-making bodies. Key officials in federal ministries have frequently been recruited from corresponding interest groups and sometimes returned to them after leaving office. For instance, the heads and leading members of the Ministry of Labour usually come from the trade unions and those of the Ministry of Agriculture from the farmers' organizations. Even when the bonds are not so close, federal ministers and their principal subordinates tend to act as the spokesmen of their respective interest group clients in formulating public policies.

Such relationships are considered to be mutually advantageous, and West German government leaders welcome and encourage them for more than narrow partisan reasons. They are thought to furnish the political leaders of the state with expert advice and special information not available through other sources, such as on the secret flow of foreign funds into and out of the private economic sector and on the well-guarded investment plans of West German bankers. These contacts are also believed to provide governmental policy-makers with exceptional opportunities for hearing and considering interest group demands and complaints out of the public view. For instance, they are said to be most helpful for weighing the pros and cons of contemplated fiscal measures designed to influence the patterns of wages, prices, and profits. Finally, the representation of private interests in the executive branch of the government is thought to be particularly useful for facilitating inter-élite negotiations prior to a policy decision and for obtaining the co-operation of the affected interest groups in its implementation.

Lobbying is at least as prevalent in West Germany as it is in the United States. Several hundred national organizations maintain offices in the capital city of Bonn to provide them with close contacts between their headquarters and government and party agencies. In West Germany, professional lobbyists are not required to list their names and sponsors in public registers, but they are likely to have better access to federal ministries and legislative bodies if they do. For example, only those interest group spokesmen who are registered with the Federal Diet will normally be allowed to voice their views at public hearings of its committees or be asked to submit written statements. When this regulation was instituted some years ago, all sorts of associations entered their names in the register, from the very largest to some with as few as eight formal members.

On the whole, legislative lobbyists may be less closely controlled than in the United States, but they also have a less significant role in policy-making. In the first place, negotiations on issues involving the major interest associations almost always reach into the top echelons of the peak organizations and the government and focus on direct contacts among corresponding élites. Second, national and subnational legislative organs are less important targets for pressure group politics than in the American federal system, though more so than in such unitary and parliamentary systems as the British. In West Germany, interest group leaders concentrate especially on the executive branch because it is the source of crucial administration regulations and most legislation. Bills introduced by the executive normally become law, whereas bills that originate in the legislature and legislative amendments opposed by the government usually do not.

Interest group representation in West German legislatures is more conspicuous than in the United States. Under the rules of the Diet its members are required to reveal their affiliations with organized pressure groups and on this evidence alone the groups appear to be well represented. Functionaries of business, agricultural, and religious associations are to be found especially among deputies of the CDU/CSU and FDP, whereas trade union officials are likely to be deputies of the SPD. However, the official listings do not mention more covert links to pressure groups, such as those of deputies who may have temporarily severed formal connections but continue to maintain informal interest group ties.

Whether overtly or covertly, such legislative representation of vested interests is particularly pronounced in the committees of the Diet, where most of its policy actions take shape. Through committee assignments, party leaders have enabled various pressure groups to be especially well represented in committees that deal with matters touching on their interests. Most of the legislative manœuvring and bargaining among pressure group spokesmen occurs in the private sessions of these committees and of the corresponding 'study groups' (*Arbeitskreise*) of the different parties.

All of this should not lead us to overestimate the effect of pressure group politics in the Diet. West German interest associations must contend not only with the fact that the Federal government normally exercises tighter party control over the Federal Diet than the American executive does over the Congress, but with constitutional provisions that impose tighter limits on the policy-making powers of the Federal parliament. For instance, neither of its two chambers can compel the government to increase its budgetary proposals. Under these conditions interest groups normally turn to parliament only if they cannot receive satisfaction from the executive branch, and then usually to get desired changes in governmental bills rather than entirely different legislation. The significance of legislative pressure group politics is thus measured not so much by the number of interest group representatives in the Diet as by the amendments that become law through its actions. In this respect interest associations have generally been more effective as veto groups than as promotional groups, and they have achieved more minor than major changes in governmental bills.

THE BIG FOUR

As we have said, economic values and, to a diminishing degree, religious values are basic sources of subcultural group identification in the Federal republic. In pressure group politics these values take the form of organized interests that focus on socio-economic and socio-cultural issues (*Wirtschaftspolitik* and *Kulturpolitik*) and are reflected in the pre-eminence of four major associational constellations: the national producers associations of agriculture, business, and labour, and the religious organizations of the Roman Catholic and Protestant churches.

The effective leaders of these associations constitute a large part of what we have called the latent political élites. They exert pressure on the manifest political élites when public policies seem likely to affect their group. Governmental, administrative, and party leaders are usually very attentive to their demands, but especially so if they believe that policy implementation could be stymied by the major interest group élites. In the case of the principal economic associations, effective interest articulation depends largely—though not entirely—on the strength of the shared material objectives of their respective members and on their leaders' commitment to an instrumental, pragmatic view of the state's socio-economic functions in a dynamic policy environment. In the case of the religious association, effective articulation rests primarily on the persistence and legitimacy of traditional norms that have allowed the religious élites of the two major churches to claim a special role in state and society as the guardians of ethical standards and public morality.

CONVENTIONAL AND UNCONVENTIONAL PRESSURE GROUP
POLITICS

In the Federal Republic, as in other countries, pressure group politics are both sources and products of authoritative public policies. Governmental actions may reflect interest group demands, they may give rise to such demands, and they may curb pressure on public policies. In West Germany this reciprocal relationship between pressure group inputs and governmental outputs is conditioned by the dynamics of a particular policy environment and by particular patterns of interaction among the general public, specific interest groups, the major parties, and agencies of the state.

As we have seen in this chapter, the legitimate expression of regular pressure group demands is tightly structured in accordance with the representative principles of the present regime. Explicit legal provisions for the functional representation of organized interests connect the principal pressure groups directly to executive agencies of the state; more indirect and informal arrangements provide for the political representation of organized interests in elective bodies through their ties to the major parties.

As we have also noted, regular West German pressure group politics have been marked by the corporatist vestiges of a pre-industrial society. Present patterns reflect progressive and mutual adaptation between the pressure group subsystem and other components of the ongoing political system, a development that has been particularly pronounced in economic policy-making. Though traditional forms of functional interest articulation continue to have some importance, pressure group politics have by and large come to conform to socio-economic, cultural, and political circumstances that are very different from those of previous German regimes.

On the whole, interest organizations are today less closely controlled by the state, less intimately associated with political parties, and more flexible in their pressure group strategies and tactics than formerly. Most are no longer identified with sharply segmented subcultures, and interest group differences normally tend to involve particular policy issues rather than more profound doctrinal disputes. For example, the failure of an emphatically 'Christian' trade union movement testifies to the detachment of organized labour from clerical as well as anti-clerical ideologies. And as the encapsulated ideological camps of the past have gradually dissolved, tenuous and transitory pressure group coalitions on specific policy issues have become far more common.

The more heterogeneous the membership of an ordinary interest association, the more difficult it is to achieve internal consensus on its policy objectives. For the sake of at least nominal unity, cross-pressures arising from plural interests and competing affiliations must be accommodated by restricting and diluting the areas for collective political action. Particularly in the large peak associations of organized business and labour, the autonomy of the constituent groups has been promoted by different policy concerns. Employer and employee associations in one economic sector may, for instance, join forces to further their common policy interests against those of a similar alignment identified with another sector. The peak business organizations include associations of importers and exporters who may collaborate on some policy issues but compete on others. Occupational interests may sometimes unite public employees' organizations on policy matters relating to the salaries and pension rights of their members and at other times lead to conflicts within and between such associations.

Another major feature of conventional pressure group politics is that they exclude most West Germans and involve primarily inter-élite relations. The organizational rules and actual operation of the prevailing regime have served to institutionalize mutually advantageous exchange relationships among key interest group functionaries, party leaders, and public officials. As noted earlier, bargaining, reciprocal adaptation, and compromise have come to characterize interaction among various élites in a pluralist state and society; these patterns extend across occupationally segmented interest groups and make for basically harmonious relationships among their leaders, and between these and the manifest political decision-makers.

But though interest group élites may command extensive means for influencing public policies, they are constrained in the demands they can make and the means they can employ to realize them. One reason is the formal and informal 'rules of the game' for legitimate pressure group politics. A second reason is that cultural norms place the interest of state and community above those of special vested interests and establish public officials as the legitimate arbitrators among competing pressure group demands. There are also cross-cutting popular and élite allegiances, which may override identifications with 'non-partisan' interest groups and induce political participants to disregard such identifications for the sake of partisan objectives or party discipline. And, finally, there is the pluralism of competing élites involved in policy processes, which disperses rather than concentrates the power of organized interests.

These constraints tend to curb the political influence of even the most powerful pressure groups. They normally allow party leaders and high government officials to aggregate, balance, and, if need be, reject pressure group demands in the name of 'larger' public interests. And they enable these leaders to avoid commitments that would make them the instruments of any particular interest association or interest group alignment. Control over public policies rests in the last analysis with elected and appointed public officials, and the extensive intrusion of the authority of the state into West German society provides these officials with considerable power to curb pressure group demands.

It would seem then that the prevailing regime provides for effective checks and balances in the relationships between organized interest groups, political parties, and agencies of the state. Indeed, the apparent efficiency of the West German system for the regular representation of organized interests has been compared favourably with less tidy arrangements in other major European democracies. For instance the system has seemed to some observers far more conducive to the harmonized 'concertation' of competing interests in state and society than the much more fragmented system of rival social and economic pressure groups in France. And British commentators have seen in the collaborative relationship between business, labour, and government élites in the Federal Republic a better way to deal with the economic problems of capitalist democracies than the more adversarial relationship between management and trade union leaders in their own country.

More critical West Germans, however, do not agree that their regular interest associations are such admirable institutions for the orderly transmission of diverse demands from a pluralist society to a democratic state. Some assert, to the contrary, that the entire pressure group system has gotten out of hand or, at least, that some of its principal components exercise far too much influence at the expense of common public interests, particularly those of people who do not belong to interest associations. Critics of the prevailing arrangements point out that these strongly favour a few private interest groups with 'public status' under West German law, whereas the liberal democratic principles of the constitution call for all kinds of voluntary associations to have more or less equal access and influence. Such institutionalized inequities are said to be particularly pronounced where they matter most, on economic policy issues. Here big business, or organized labour, or both—the critics differ on that—are seen as enjoying undue advantages as privileged 'social partners' of the state.

In the Federal Republic, as in other Western democracies, conventional pressure group politics are generally held in rather low esteem by those who are not part of them. As we noted, most West Germans are at best only nominal members of regular interest associations and peripherally involved in their political activities. When influential opinion leaders resort to attacks on the 'excessive' power of particular interest groups in the heat of an electoral campaign or a battle over some policy decision, such charges are prone to tie in with popular hostility toward the regular pressure groups system in its entirety. But the most important groups are especially distrusted. Opinion polls show that big business and organized labour are widely believed to wield more influence than they deserve. Such sentiments are not new, but they have been reinforced in recent years by highly publicized revelations of corruption in trade union enterprises and of unsavoury financial deals between business leaders and prominent public officials. And as conventional pressure group politics have become more discredited, more unconventional ones have won more approval from the general public.

Unconventional pressure groups are relatively new phenomena in the Federal Republic. As we noted briefly at the beginning of this chapter, some West Germans have in recent times formed 'citizen initiatives' and 'citizens lobbies' for political action outside the regular parties and interest associations. The number and size of such civic action groups tend to fluctuate a good deal, but on the whole their active membership appears to take in only about 1 per cent of West Germans. Like various other so-called new social movements in the Federal Republic, such unconventional pressure groups operate outside the established system because they cannot or will not obtain influence through the regular institutional channels for interest representation.

Over the last decade or so civic action groups have proven to be surprisingly effective instruments of unconventional pressure group politics at the grass-roots level. For example, groups of parents have demanded and obtained more public funds for local schools, as well as blocked educational changes mandated by state authorities; neighbourhood associations have both prevented and promoted urban renewals projects of municipal governments; and pressure from environmental protection groups has led to tighter local controls over urban pollution and traffic patterns.

Much of the support for the Green party, and a good many of its activists and elected officials, came at first from such irregular civic action groups. However, their effectiveness and scope is quite limited at the local level since municipal and county governments do not have much power in the Federal Republic. As these irregular grass-roots groups became more concerned with regional and national issues they therefore joined forces for unconventional pressure group activities at the state and federal levels. A coalition of like-minded groups thus staged mass protest demonstrations in the late 1970s to prevent the construction of nuclear power plants and waste disposal facilities by various state governments; a similar alignment employed 'extra-parliamentary' direct action in an effort to keep the government of Hesse from building a new runway for West Germany's largest airport; and in the early 1980s such activities went national with mass rallies in Bonn and elsewhere to rally public opinion against the stationing of more powerful American nuclear missiles in West Germany.

A good many West German and foreign observers were alarmed by these protests against the decisions and commitments of properly elected public officials. While the demonstrations were on the whole peaceful and legal, their number and size were unprecedented in the Federal Republic. The predicted 'Hot Autumn' of 1983 did, however, not materialize; then as now West Germans have not shown the sort of propensity for militant direct action that has been a constant feature of interest group politics in France.

The loosely organized and quite heterogeneous national alignment of irregular cause groups and new social movements constitutes a highly unconventional form of interest aggregation in contemporary West German politics. It provides expression for the varied anti-establishment attitudes that we already noted for members and supporters of the Green party, and it reflects in large part the social discontent, the fears, and the pessimism we observed earlier among well-educated and politically interested young people. The reformist elements in the alignment generally press for more participatory democracy and for relatively moderate changes in current governmental policies; they include most of the peace movement, the environmentalist movement, and proponents of significant social reforms, such as the womens' movement. The ideologically more extreme elements consider the present socio-economic and political order with its 'élitist' institutions beyond reform. They include radical Marxists, as well as Utopian anarchists and romantic anti-technocrats of the counterculture 'alternative movement'. To the extent that these groups come to set the tone for the entire alignment it is likely to move on a collision course with a ruling establishment that is wedded to economic growth under capitalism, to military commitments under the Western NATO alliance, and to representative governmental institutions, parties, and interest associations.

Like the Green party that has given parliamentary expression to many of their demands, the grass-roots civic action groups and new social movements have grown into a political force that can no longer be dismissed by the dominant élites as constituting an unrepresentative minority of discontents given undue prominence by the media. At the same time these unconventional pressure groups do not threaten to topple the established political system, as some conservative critics have asserted; nor do they appear to signal a significant trend in West German socio-economic and political values for more personal liberty and collective democracy, as sympathetic commentators maintain. Their concrete achievements have been quite modest, especially above the local level of government, and their pressure group activities cannot compare with that of the regular interest associations. The impact of the irregular groups on the political system of the Federal Republic has evidently been more diffuse.

For the élites as well as for the political and general public the extra-parliamentary activities of unconventional pressure groups have become more or less acceptable, if not always legitimate forms of interest articulation and aggregation. These activities have moreover served to thrust previously ignored or neglected issues on the policy agenda of the ruling establishment. West German political leaders and would-be leaders have thus become more sensitive to public concern over environmental pollution and the threat of nuclear annihilation thanks largely to the mobilization of mass opinion by the peace and environmentalist movements.

13

INTEREST GROUPS IN THE EUROPEAN COMMUNITY

SONIA P. MAZEY AND JEREMY J. RICHARDSON

INTRODUCTION

As a general rule, interest groups in all industrialized countries have concentrated their energies hitherto upon influencing the content of national and/or local legislation rather than trying to influence supranational bodies. Since the early 1980s, however, growing numbers of organized interests—in non-EC countries and EC member states alike—have come to recognize the increasing importance of European Community legislation. It is no longer possible to understand the policy process in any of the twelve member states of the EC—and especially the role of pressure groups in that process—without taking account of the shift in power to Brussels. In this context, the 1986 Single European Act (SEA)—which significantly extended the scope of EC legislation and reformed the Community's decision-making process—marked an important turning-point. The result has been a sharp rise in the number of groups and levels of resources devoted to influencing EC policy outcomes. However, as several groups have discovered to their cost, lobbying the European Community is a far from simple task. Within Brussels, lobbying is widely regarded as a perfectly respectable and even necessary part of the EC policy process. Paradoxically, this very openness, along with the unique structural characteristics of the Community's decision-making processes, poses problems for groups more accustomed to working within a national politico-administrative system. In particular, groups have to contend at the EC level with the phenomenon of an especially competitive agenda-setting process and attendant problems of uncertainty and unpredictability. Thus, in order to be effective Euro-lobbyists, groups must be able to co-ordinate their national and EC level strategies, construct alliances with their European

© Sonia P. Mazey and Jeremy J. Richardson (1993). This chapter is part of a larger study of lobbying in the EC, funded by the Economic and Social Research Council as part of its Single European Market research programme.

counterparts, and monitor changing national and EC policy agendas.

The following analysis of interest group activity at the EC level is divided into three parts. We first examine the growth of Euro-lobbying in the wake of the SEA. Secondly, we provide a brief overview of the institutional framework and decision-making processes of the Community. Thirdly, we assess the implications of these structures not just for groups, but also for national governments and EC officials who are equally involved in the business of interest intermediation at the EC level.

THE SINGLE EUROPEAN ACT: A CATALYST FOR EURO-LOBBYING

The phenomenon of EC lobbying is not at all new. European-wide interest group federations have existed since the early 1950s in industrial sectors such as coal and steel and agriculture where responsibility for the formulation of Community policies had been granted to the European Commission (formerly the High Authority) by the 1951 and 1957 Paris and Rome Treaties respectively. By 1970 over 300 European Federations—colloquially referred to as 'Euro-groups'—existed; by 1980 this figure had risen to 439.[1] (European Federations are composed of national affiliated associations and are officially recognized by the European Commission as representative bodies having a right to be consulted over EC policies.) Nevertheless, prior to the 1986 Single European Act, much EC lobbying by national groups was conducted through national political and administrative channels. This pattern reflected the concentration of decision-making power within the Council of Ministers at the EC level. Since the 1966 Luxemburg Compromise effectively gave each national government a veto over proposals put to the Council by the European Commission, many groups relied upon national officials and ministers to defend their interests in Brussels. Moreover, prior to 1986, many groups had little interest in EC policy-making; though the principle of supremacy of EC law over national legislation had been established early on, the jurisdiction of the Community was, in practice, limited.

The adoption of the 1986 Single European Act by the twelve EC member states has effectively transformed this situation. As an amendment to the original Treaties, the Act has formalized and strengthened the European Commission's powers to initiate

---

[1] Economic and Social Committee, *The Right of Initiative of the Economic and Social Committee of the European Communities* (Brussels: Delta, 1980).

Community policies in a number of areas (notably environmental and social policies, research, and development) which were previously either wholly or in large part the responsibility of national governments. Signatories to the SEA have also agreed to the phased introduction of full economic and monetary union. Of more immediate importance, the Act committed member states to completion of the internal market (i.e. the free movement of goods, services, capital, and labour within the EC) by the end of 1992. This required the introduction of nearly 300 harmonization measures. Thus, at a stroke, the number and range of interests directly affected by EC policy-making has increased dramatically. In order to facilitate the attainment of these objectives, the SEA has also strengthened the legislative role of the European Parliament and removed the need for unanimity with the Council of Ministers from those decisions pertaining to the internal market. This reform of the EC policy-making process has reduced the EC policy-making influence of national governments, thereby increasing the need for interest group coalition-building at the EC level.

In consequence, there has been a steep rise in recent years in the volume and diversity of interests represented in Brussels. Latest figures indicate that there are now 525 officially recognized Euro-groups in Brussels, though the membership, status, resources, and influence of these associations vary enormously. There is also a significant imbalance between producer and consumer representation: industrial and commercial producer interests account for almost 50 per cent of the Euro-groups; 25 per cent are connected with agriculture and food production; and around 20 per cent are related to the service industry, with just 5 per cent of the Euro-groups representing trade union, consumer, and environmental interests.[2] Whilst some Euro-groups such as the ETUC (trade unions) and BEUC (European Bureau of Consumers' Associations) have a broad membership base, most—such as the European Button Industry Federation and the Union of European Manufacturers of Gas Meters—are more narrowly focused with fewer members, fewer resources, and a more selective interest in EC legislation.

Owing to their multinational composition and official status, the Euro-groups are the preferred interlocutors of Commission officials. A number of well-established European Federations also enjoy privileged status within the EC policy process. In this respect, the

[2] European Commission, *The Directory of the European Community Trade and Professional Associations* (Brussels: Delta, 1990).

most influential Euro-group is undoubtedly the Committee of Professional Agricultural Producers (COPA), which has been formally incorporated into the Commission where it plays a key role in the management of the EC Common Agricultural Policy. Similarly, Eurofer, the European Association of Steel Producers, has for many years enjoyed a quasi-institutional status within the Commission, whilst UNICE, which represents the interests of industrial employers from twenty-two countries, is—according to one EC official—widely regarded as 'an extension' of the Commission.[3] Increasingly influential are the various 'horizontal groupings' of leading European companies which have sprung up in recent years as European 'super-élite' lobbies alongside the European Federations. Of these, the most well known is the European Round Table of Industrialists which was founded in 1983 under the leadership of its first chairman, Peter Gyllenhammer, then head of the Swedish automotive group, AB Volvo. The Round Table currently unites thirty chief executives from Europe's biggest companies including Fiat, Philips, Sant-Gobain, Daimler-Benz, Plessey, Ferruzi, Nestlé, Telefonica, Norsk Hydro, and Nokia. The grouping—whose members include Giovanni Agnelli, head of the Italian Fiat company, François-Xavier Ortoli, chairman of the Total group, and Étienne Davignon, former President and vice-president of the EC Commission—has consistently promoted the internal market programme. Specific campaigns have included support for the building of the channel tunnel, a better European rail system, and the construction of trans-European business communication systems.[4] Other, more specialized groups of this kind include the European Information Technology Round Table, the European electronics industry's most influential lobby which was formed in the late 1970s at the initiative of the European Commission, and the Association for the Monetary Union of Europe. The latter was established in 1987 and has consistently lobbied for the free flow of capital within the Community and the establishment of a European central bank. Members include: Cornelius van der Klught, Chief Executive of Philips; François-Xavier Ortoli; Jacques Sovay, chairman of Belgium's Solvay chemicals company; and Jean René Fourtou, head of Rhône-Poulenc, the French, state-owned chemicals company. The political driving forces of the association are Helmut Schmidt, former Chancellor of the Federal Republic of Germany and Valéry Giscard d'Estaing, former President of France.[5]

[3] *Fortune* (June 1990).
[4] A. Krause, 'Many Groups Lobby on Implementation of Market Plan', *Europe* (July–Aug. 1988).
[5] Ibid.

In order to be effective, a European Federation (or horizontal grouping) must be well-resourced and united in its aims. In practice, most groups are chronically underfunded and on many issues internally divided. As one Euro-group member explained, though the European Federations are potentially influential, they are often paralysed by conflicting national interests:

We . . . try to influence policy through Euro-groups because we are of the opinion that statements brought forward by the Euro-groups will make a better impression on the EC Commission. Unfortunately, it is usually the case that national interests in our Euro-group ASSILEC (EC Dairy Trade Association) hinder the process of forming a consensus. It seems to us that these Euro-groups increasingly reflect national interests . . . But, if a compromise can't be found the Euro-group can't take the initiative.[6]

The recent dispute between EC electricity companies over how to introduce competition into international power distribution is a typical example of the problems Euro-groups face when trying to reconcile different national economic ideologies and industrial structures. British and Irish electricity suppliers have split from their continental European counterparts on this issue, refusing to sign a paper agreed by other members of Eurelectric (the industry's representative body), which warns that opening the EC market to greater competition could produce price rises and increased risk of power cuts. Significant structural differences lie behind this disagreement. In short, continental electricity suppliers practise more cross-border trade than their Irish and UK counterparts, added to which they are naturally keen to preserve their existing monopolies in electricity supply. But, as a British industry official commented, 'given that we have the [privatized] system that we have here, we are simply not able to sign that document'.[7]

Given the limitations of the Euro-groups, national federations increasingly lobby independently.[8] Since the mid-1980s several national federations such as the Italian employers' association *Confindustria*, the Permanent Assembly of French Chambers of Commerce and Industry (APCCI), and its German counterpart, the *Deutsche Industrie and Handelstag* (DIHT) have either opened or expanded their 'Brussels offices. Thus, the DIHT—whose Brussels office is sandwiched between those of the Bureau of Information of Swiss Cheeses and Greenpeace—recently increased the number of staff employed in Brussels from five to seven.[9] Similarly, the number

---

[6] Spokesman for the German Federal Association of Private Dairy Producers, postal survey response to authors, 20 August 1990.

[7] *Financial Times* (10 Apr. 1991).

[8] M. Petite, 'Les Lobbies européenes', *Pouvoirs*, 48 (1989).

[9] *Problèmes économiques* (1989), 25.

of people employed in the Brussels bureau of the French employers' association, the *Confédération National du Patronat Français* (CNPF) has quadrupled since 1988 from seven to thirty-one.[10]

Below this level, increasing numbers of multinational companies and economically powerful firms and organizations have either appointed a EC relations specialist or opened a so-called 'public relations' office in Brussels. Many large companies now have a permanent representation in Brussels—Elf-Aquitaine, Rhône-Poulenc, Bull, Philips, Exxon, ICI, Shell, IBM, Siemens, Mercedes, Unilever, and BASF. Whilst some companies such as Fiat, Ford-Europe, and Ferruzi have for many years maintained a Brussels office, others such as Daimler-Benz, Deutsche Bank, and Electricité-de-France are recent arrivals. It is also no coincidence that several leading multinationals such as BP, Nissan, and IBM are now moving their European headquarters to Brussels.[11] The importance of maintaining a presence in Brussels cannot be overestimated. As a spokeswoman for the British retail chain, Marks and Spencer commented, 'before he (an in-house EC specialist) started we didn't exactly miss anything, but we were constantly being taken by surprise at how far issues had gone . . . Now he's constantly going to Brussels and we're much better briefed'.[12] Likewise, an EC official acknowledged that the Commission's decision in 1987 to drop plans to deregulate air transport owed much to the persuasive arguments put forward by the Brussels-based Director of International Affairs for Air France.[13]

In addition to private producer interests, regional and local authorities throughout the EC have also become more active in Brussels. All the German *Länder*, five Spanish autonomous communities, eleven French regions, and four British local authorities have recently opened offices in Brussels. A variation on this theme is the Brussels office of Breiz Europe, a regional lobby for farming, banking, fishing, and food-processing industries of Brittany. Three factors help to explain this trend: the growing policy-making importance of sub-national levels of government in several EC countries; the expansion of EC regional and social policies and the concomitant growth in the size of the Community's structural development funds; and the direct impact upon local and regional interests (including authorities themselves) of the internal market programme.

---

[10] *Fortune* (June 1990).
[12] *Financial Times* (9 Apr. 1984).
[11] European Commission, *Directory*.
[13] *Le Monde Affaires* (8 Apr. 1990).

Increased interest in EC legislation is not confined to the member states. Concern on the part of non-EC groups and governments that completion of the EC internal market might create a protectionist 'fortress Europe' has prompted widespread interest in the 1992 legislative programme among non-EC groups. Whilst Eastern European and Chinese interests continue to rely largely upon diplomatic representation in Brussels, Japanese and American groups are among the most effective EC lobbyists. There is a permanent delegate from the Japanese employers' association in the Japanese mission to the EC and both the Japanese steel federation and association for Japanese machine-tool exporters have been represented in Brussels for several years. More recent arrivals from Japan are companies such as Nissan, Toshiba, Hitachi, Mitsubishi, and Sony.[14]

American companies have been in Brussels for many years and according to one source 'regard themselves as partners of the EC by virtue of the 125 billion US dollars invested in Europe by US firms and their 10 million employees'.[15] This is the principal argument of AMCHAM, the extremely influential EC Committee of the American Chamber of Commerce which represents nearly one hundred US groups including multinationals such as ITT, IBM, Allied Signal Inc., Colgate, Kodak, Palmolive, General Electric, General Motors, etc., all of which have EC subsidiaries.[16] Individual US companies are also powerful lobbyists in their own right. IBM-Europe, for instance, organized what is widely regarded as one of the most effective—and most controversial—lobbying promotion campaigns in Europe. By means of open letters to the EC Commission, informal talks with EC leaders and journalists in national capitals, and publication of detailed reports, IBM has sought (with some success) to accelerate the telecommunications deregulation process. The underlying objective of the campaign is to open the market to US suppliers—including IBM.[17] The 1992 programme has also triggered the establishment of an inter-agency task force in Washington, headed by the Office of the Special Trade Representative. In the words of one senior US embassy official in Paris, 'we are not going to sit and watch 1992 go by—we will be lobbying for US interests'.[18] Within Brussels, the effectiveness of US groups is often attributed to the fact that for many years large American companies have regarded Europe as a single market. As

[14] A. De Vogüé, 'L'Eldorado des lobbies', *Dynasteurs* (Nov. 1990), 97–103.
[15] *Fortune* (June 1990), 78. [16] Ibid.
[17] Krausse, 'Many Groups Lobby'. [18] Ibid. 24.

one professional lobbyist remarked, 'in business the Americans are the best Europeans. They immediately grasped the significance and advantages of the single market'.[19]

Most groups, however, cannot afford to employ their own 'EC watcher' in Brussels. Hence, one of the most spectacular developments since the mid-1980s has been the explosion of professional lobbyists, financial consultants, and law firms locating in Brussels. At the start of 1988 there were just five UK law firms with offices in Brussels, with US law firms just as thin on the ground. But by October 1990 there were thirty UK and eighteen US law firms with offices in Brussels, plus increasing numbers of German, Dutch, French, Scandinavian, and Belgian lawyers with offices in the vicinity of the Commission.[20] In the absence of any official register of EC lobbyists it is impossible to calculate just how many paid consultants of one form or another are based in Brussels. However, one estimate put the figure for 1990 at 3,000—three times that of two or three years ago.[21]

Just as in many national political systems, *pantouflage* is widespread; there are numerous examples of Commission officials leaving the Berlaymont building in order to become lobbyists. One source cites the case of the Director-General of the European Regional Development Fund, who subsequently became Director of the Brussels office of the European agro-food industries association. Other examples include a French, former EC official from Directorate-General (DG) VI (Agriculture) who now represents the interests of Breton co-operative societies in Brussels and a former Dutch Commission official from DG XIII (Telecommunications) who is now Director of a Brussels-based organization established by the Japanese electronics company Sony to monitor EC telecommunications policy.[22] Such practices are not confined to the private sector; for example, the Brussels office of one German Land, is headed by a former vice-president of the EC Commission.[23]

British and American groups are widely regarded as being among the most enthusiastic EC lobbyists. That this should be the case is possibly not surprising, bearing in mind the long tradition in these countries of an often symbiotic relationship between groups and government at the national level. Many producer interests in Britain and the United States have been well organized into national policy-making processes for many years and it comes naturally to them to

---

[19] *L'Express* (6 Apr. 1990).
[21] *Fortune* (June 1990).
[23] *Problèmes économiques.*

[20] *Financial Times* (19 Oct. 1990).
[22] *L'Express* (6 Apr. 1990).

seek a similar relationship with bureaucrats in Brussels. Other national groups have only recently begun to follow the Anglo-Saxon lead in Euro-lobbying. In France, for example, lobbying à l'Americaine is generally frowned upon by groups who are, for the most part, less accustomed to being consulted by national civil servants over government policies. French groups have thus tended more than their Anglo-Saxon counterparts to rely upon 'l'État' to protect their interests in Brussels.[24] Indeed, as recently as March 1990, the then French Minister for European Affairs, Edith Cresson, was urging French firms and organizations to be more assertive in lobbying Brussels direct.[25]

As highlighted above, there has been a marked increase both in the number and type of groups lobbying the EC. The overall picture which emerges is that of a honeycomb of closely integrated interests. Vertical linkages between the horizontal groupings, European Federations, national associations, companies, and professional consultants provide a multi-layered lobbying framework. Equally important, however, are the horizontal linkages (often based upon informal relationships) which exist at regional, national, and EC levels between organized interests and those officials and politicians involved in the formulation and implementation of EC policies. Thus, the problem facing groups is not how to gain access to the EC policy process, but how to maximize the range of lobbying conduits available to them. Resources play an important role in this calculation; multinational companies which can afford to combine membership of several EC and national level associations with co-ordinated company campaigns throughout EC capitals have an important advantage over smaller firms and voluntary organizations.

THE DECISION-MAKING FRAMEWORK OF THE EUROPEAN COMMUNITY

Whatever cultural attitudes govern pressure group behaviour, there is no doubt that institutional and structural factors are also of considerable importance in determining group behaviour. This is as true for the EC as it is for national systems. What follows, therefore, is a brief overview of the EC decision-making structures and processes which together constitute the EC policy-making environment within which groups must operate.

[24] *Le Point* (28 Nov. 1988).   [25] *Le Monde Affaires* (8 Apr. 1990).

The European Commission

Based in Brussels, the European Commission is the executive arm of the EC. Perceived by the founding fathers as an embryonic European government and the motor of European integration, it is guardian of the Treaties and formally responsible for the initiation and implementation of all EC policies. The Commission is headed by the seventeen political commissioners—two from the UK, France, Germany, Italy, and Spain and one from each of the other member states. Appointed by their national governments for a four-year (renewable) period, commissioners cannot be individually dismissed (though, in theory, the Commission *en bloc* may be censured by the European Parliament). Upon appointment, all commissioners swear an oath of allegiance to the EC in which they promise not to put national interests before those of the Community. In practice, groups and governments alike do expect their commissioner(s) to defend their interests within the context of EC policy-making. The commissioner(s) is also an important source of information regarding EC developments.

Each commissioner has his/her own *cabinet* headed by an influential *chef de cabinet*, who acts as 'gatekeeper' for groups seeking access to the commissioner. The commissioners, who are collectively responsible for determining EC policy are served by the Commission bureaucracy. This is a multinational administration comprising some 15,500 officials (including translators, clerical assistants, and researchers) drawn from the member states. The Commission is divided according to policy area into twenty-three Directorates-General (DGs), each of which is subdivided into a number of policy divisions. Each DG is headed by a Director-General who is accountable to the commissioner with overall responsibility for that particular policy sector(s). Clearly, some DGs such as DG III (Internal Market) and DG VI (Agriculture) are more important than others such as DG X (Information and Culture) and there is intense (though discreet) lobbying by member governments for their commissioners and senior officials to be placed in the more influential positions. In practice, the President of the Commission (appointed by the commissioners for a four-year (renewable) period) allocates responsibilities among the commissioners, bearing in mind unwritten conventions regarding the relative size and importance of the member states and the need for rotation of posts.

An important feature of the Commission is the 1,000 or so working groups and consultative committees, many of which are *ad hoc* in nature. These bring together EC officials, national experts (often from national administrations), and interested parties (typically from national associations and companies), and play an important role in the formulation and drafting of EC policies. Not surprisingly, membership of these groups is highly valued by groups seeking to influence the content of EC legislation. Close examination of the membership of such committees typically reveals the presence of sectoral and/or company interests. For instance, the seven-member Committee headed by the Dutch Finance Minister, Mr Otto Ruding, to examine the issue of corporate tax harmonization includes Mr Jean-Louis, President of the French Clothing and Shoe group and Mr Carolo Gatto, Director of the Italian Fiat company.[26] Given the central importance of the internal market programme, two of the most important groups at present are the European Normalization Committee (CEN), which brings together all the national standards bodies within the Community and the European Association for Free Trade (AELE), and its counterpart for the electronics industry, CENELEC. The purpose of CEN and CENELEC is to harmonize technical and safety standards for products and services.[27]

The European Parliament

Commission proposals, once drafted, are sent to the European Parliament (EP) and the Economic and Social Committee for consideration. (The Economic and Social Committee is a corporatist assembly comprising 183 selected representatives of industry, commerce, agriculture, trade unions, consumers, etc. It enjoys consultative status over most EC legislation, but wields little policy-making influence.) The Parliament is an itinerant body—plenary sessions are held in Strasburg whilst meetings of the eighteen standing committees are held in Brussels. Since 1986, the EP has become a more influential actor in the EC policy-process, and following the Maastricht Summit in December 1991 is likely to become more influential in future years. Prior to the SEA, the EP had no legislative powers whatsoever; though the 518 directly elected MEPs were consulted over legislative proposals, the Council of Ministers was under no obligation to take their views into account. In an attempt to redress the so-called 'democratic deficit' within the EC, the SEA introduced a new co-operation procedure (see Fig. 13.1) which grants the EP the right to a second reading of all Community legislation relating to the internal market. This provides MEPs with a further opportunity to propose amendments

---

[26] *Financial Times* (20 Dec. 1990).
[27] J. Monon, *Agir pour ne pas subir* (Paris: Ministry of European Affairs, 1989), 5.

to the 'common position' adopted by the Council of Ministers which can then be overridden by the Council only by a unanimous vote.

First Reading

Second Reading

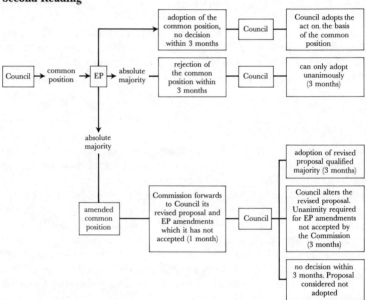

FIGURE 13.1   Co-operation Procedure (Pre-Maastricht 1991)

The co-operation procedure has undoubtedly provided MEPs with additional leverage over the details of legislation relating to the internal market. Since 1987, the Commission has accepted 1,052 of the Parliament's 1,724 amendments to single market laws, and of those the Council has agreed to 719.[28] For groups, the EP has thus become a useful means of achieving amendments to certain categories of legislation with the result that groups and lobbyists

[28] *The Economist* (10 Nov. 1990).

have begun to devote more time to courting the support of MEPs (especially those in the key standing committees responsible for scrutinizing legislative proposals). Nevertheless, the legislative powers of the EP remain—for the moment at least—limited. It has no right to initiate legislation, no legislative powers with regard to policies unrelated to the internal market, and no powers to override decisions taken by the Council of Ministers. Moreover, parliamentary amendments to the common position require the support of an absolute majority of MEPs. Obtaining such support is far from easy given the absence of party discipline within the Parliament. Though MEPs sit in ten recognized transnational party groupings (the largest of which are the Socialist and Christian Democratic groups) within the assembly, these are without exception internally divided along national and doctrinal lines. However, the Maastricht agreement of December 1991 provides for an increase in the powers of the European Parliament, giving it a veto in certain policy areas. The new Treaty introduces a procedure of co-decision-making between Parliament and Council which involves two readings and provides for Parliament to table amendments to proposed legislation, as can happen at present under the co-operation procedure. Whereas under the existing co-operation procedure Parliament's amendments at second reading can only stand if the Council is divided, the new procedure provides for the convening of a conciliation committee comprising equal representation as a last resort, allowing Parliament the right to reject the legislation if it is still not satisfied. Co-decision will apply to those areas where the Council takes a decision through qualified majority voting, namely, internal market rules, free circulation of workers, right of establishment, including the treatment of foreign nationals, the recognition of qualifications, and general environment programmes. In addition it will also apply to the new areas of competence—education and training, trans-European networks, health action, and consumer protection. Also included are the research framework programme and culture where Council decisions are taken by unanimity.[29]

The Council of Ministers

The most powerful EC decision-making body thus remains the Council of Ministers which is composed of national government ministers and which is, formally speaking, the legislative branch of the Community. Its principal function is to accept or reject

[29] *EP News* (9–13 Dec. 1991).

proposals put to it by the Commission, taking into account the views of the EP. In contrast to the European Commission and the European Parliament, both of which are in a sense 'European' bodies, the Council of Ministers is an 'intergovernmental' body where national officials and ministers, working behind closed doors, seek to secure the best possible deal for their government. It does not have a permanent membership; participants change according to the subject under discussion. The presidency of the Council of Ministers also changes every six months, rotating among the member-states in (French) alphabetical order. In addition to ordinary Council meetings, the twelve heads of government meet three times a year in European Summit meetings to discuss unresolved problems, foreign affairs, and broader constitutional issues affecting the Community. In fact, most routine negotiations within the Council are conducted by national officials (from relevant ministries) in the technical and specialist working groups and above these, by the Committee of Permanent Representatives (COREPER). Established in 1958, the COREPER—of which there are in fact two—comprise civil servants of ambassadorial rank from the member states. Their role is to negotiate mutually acceptable policy compromises—usually in the form of complicated 'package-deals'—in advance of Ministers' meetings. For groups, these officials constitute the principal means of access to the Council.

The original Treaties specified that voting in the Council was to be either by a unanimous vote or by a qualified majority (54 out of 76 votes. The UK, France, Germany, and Italy each have ten votes; Spain has eight votes; Belgium, Greece, Portugal, and the Netherlands have five votes each; Denmark and Ireland each have three votes and Luxemburg has two). However, in the past, each member state could effectively block proposals which might in theory have been adopted in the form of a qualified majority by invoking (or more usually by threatening to invoke) the right of national veto granted by the Luxemburg Compromise. The SEA has removed the need for unanimity within the Council from those decisions pertaining to the internal market, but left intact the Luxemburg Compromise. In practice, however, the extension of majority voting to new policy sectors (further extended at Maastricht to such areas as some aspects of environmental policy, development aid, public health, consumer protection, trans-European networks, individual research programmes, some aspects of transport and competition policy, some social policy, and the implementation of the social fund) has been accompanied by a diminution in the use of the Luxemburg Compromise. There appears to be agreement among the member states that it should not be invoked with respect to those policy areas brought under the Community's jurisdiction for the first time in the SEA (e.g. the environment, research, and development). In addition, member states have been generally reluctant to appear to be holding up legislation relating to the internal market. Thus, the extension of majority voting (54 out of 76 votes) to those sectors covered by the co-operation procedures has major implications for interest groups. By reducing the extent to which national governments within the Council are willing or able to obstruct proposals, the greater use of majority voting has increased the incentive for groups to seek allies in other member states in order to achieve either a blocking minority or a qualified majority.

The European Court of Justice

Though not directly involved in the EC policy-making process, the European Court of Justice, which is responsible for interpreting and enforcing EC legislation, is of crucial importance for EC lobbyists. In recent years, environmental organizations and women's groups, especially have used the Court (whose appellate powers resemble those of the US Supreme Court) as a means of forcing recalcitrant national governments to implement EC legislation concerning the quality of drinking water and equality between male and female workers.[30] More generally, the supremacy of EC law over national legislation means that no group (or government) can afford to ignore EC legislative developments which might undermine policy compromises being negotiated nationally. In 1990, for instance, the French government had to take back 12 billion FF (£1.26 billion) paid in subsidies to the car manufacturer, Renault, and in Britain, British Aerospace was also threatened with having to repay subsidies which it received from the Government, but subsequently won its case in the European Court. In both cases the subsidies were deemed by the (British) Commissioner responsible for EC Competititon Policy, Sir Leon Brittan, to contravene EC competition rules. These examples illustrate the dynamic interrelationship between national and EC policy-making; as the scope and volume of EC legislation expands, national governments and groups alike will increasingly have to operate within legal parameters set by the EC.

The EC legislative structures and processes are open in the sense that lobbyists have little difficulty in gaining access to them. This openness is generally welcomed by groups. Yet paradoxically, as

---

[30] S. P. Mazey (1988), 'European Community Action on behalf of Women: the Limits of Legislation', *Journal of Common Market Studies*, 27/1, 63–84.

highlighted in the following section, it is this feature of the EC policy-making process which makes EC lobbying such a complex and uncertain task. In order to be effective a group must lobby key EC policy-actors (including other groups and national governments) at all stages of the legislative process.

INTEREST GROUPS AND EC POLICY-MAKING:
COPING WITH UNCERTAINTY

In some respects, EC lobbying is not so dissimilar to national lobbying. In both cases the most successful groups tend to be those which exhibit the usual professional characteristics—namely resources, advance intelligence, good contacts with bureaucrats and politicians, and an ability to provide policy-makers with useful information and advice. Just as at the national level, informal contacts, working lunches, and telephone briefings are the stock in trade of the EC lobbyist. However, the distinctive nature of the EC policy-making structures and processes—notably the openness of the decision-making process, its multinational character, and the considerable weight of national politico-administrative élites within this process—create an unstable, multi-dimensional environment within which groups have to operate.

A major problem for groups is the unpredictability of the EC policy agenda compared to national agendas which are in most cases determined largely by the executive. As highlighted in the previous section, this is much less true within the EC where policy-making power is dispersed and where there are several policy initiators. Though the Commission announces its own legislative programme at the beginning of each year, other more pressing items may be added as a result of European Summit decisions. Indeed, there has been an increasing tendency on the part of the heads of government to use the Summit meetings to launch major initiatives (e.g. political and economic union) which the Commission is then requested to implement. In addition, every national government uses its six-month presidency of the Council of Ministers (during which period it also chairs and sets the agenda of all the Council working groups) to push favoured projects to the front of the agenda (e.g. the promotion of the 'social dimension' of the internal market by the French government and political union by the Italian government) whilst MEPs, individual commissioners, ambitious ministers and interest groups all seek to push the Commission in certain directions. Keeping track of EC policy initiatives is therefore a major undertaking for groups.

A second reason for the less certain agenda is the existence of different national political agendas which, in turn, leads to a degree of competitive agenda-setting within the EC itself. While many Community issues will be common across national boundaries, others may be country specific or there may be cross-national variations in the position of common issues. The environmental issue is perhaps the classic example of the differing emphases found in EC states and of the EC's own agenda being pushed along by certain enthusiastic actors. The Danes and the Germans, acting in concert with the small, but active, parliamentary grouping of Green MEPs (and sympathetic Socialist and Christian Democratic MEPs) have successfully forced the pace and content of EC environmental legislation on exhaust emissions, the quality of drinking water, the use of cadmium, packaging, and recycling. Indeed, legislation adopted by the German Parliament in April 1991 on packaging and recycling has dismayed other EC retailers and members of the packaging and recycling industries. The legislation will force German retailers and the packaging industry to operate and finance recycling schemes for all used packaging and containers for drinks, household cleaners, and paints. In addition, by the middle of 1995, the government insists that 42 per cent of all packaging must be collected and recycled. (The proportion rises to 64 per cent for plastics, paper, and board, and to 72 per cent for glass, tinplate, and aluminium.) What worries the affected industries most is the possibility that the Commission, which is currently preparing legislation on packaging and recycling, will adopt the German model as the basis of the EC Directive. The ambitious recycling targets outlined in early versions of the Directive—reductions in the amount of packaging of 10 per cent between 1990 and 2000 and of recycling half the rest—have done little to allay these fears.[31] National issues can thus suddenly be translated into cross-national issues via the EC. So, not only must the lobbyist monitor the relevant national policy networks in her/his own country, but she or he must also monitor the developing policy agendas in Brussels and in the other community states.

The relative unpredictability of the EC policy agenda is also in part due to the distinctive nature of the European Commission. Within the Commission, policy-making is highly compartmentalized with little horizontal co-ordination between different DGs which have a shared interest in an issue. For instance, DG VI (Agriculture), acting in the interests of farmers, has drafted

[31] *The Economist* (13 Apr. 1991).

Directives on pesticides and plant breeders with no prior consultation with the producers. Although the final decisions within the Commission are taken on a collegiate basis, there is nevertheless a risk that once a Directive has become the property of a particular DG and set of interests, other groups are not consulted.[32] The internal market programme has also exacerbated long-standing rivalries between DGs, each of which is keen to preserve its patch. The recent battle between DG VI (Agriculture) and DG III (Internal Market) Food Division is a case in point. DG III attempted to introduce 'horizontal' legislation (which sets general standards on a range of basic issues which then apply across a range of products) on sweeteners to replace individual regulations (known as 'composition law' or 'vertical legislation' which relates to a single product such as jam) dealing with the basics of food production (like hygiene, additives, and flavourings). The proposals were immediately challenged by DG VI. Resentful about the fact that DG III has usurped part of its traditional role, DG VI has been trying to sneak bits of composition law into the original proposals.[33] Conflicting policy proposals can thus emerge from different parts of the Commission (often from within the same DG), relating to the same area. In order to avoid being taken by surprise groups have to be able to monitor simultaneously policy developments in more than one Directorate-General. This task is rendered more difficult by the high turnover of Commission personnel and the considerable variation in the internal organization, culture, and working methods of different Directorates-General. These differences, which are in part attributable to national differences in the training and background of the officials, also extend to the ways in which officials manage the business of group consultation.

Of course, groups face similar difficulties to those listed above when dealing with national bureaucracies. The difference is one of degree and familiarity. Also, at the EC level, the problem is compounded by the relative openness of the Commission and the fact that groups from at least twelve countries have an input into the policy process. Commission officials are generally acknowledged by groups to be more accessible than most national officials. The Staff Regulations for European officials impose no particular constraints on contacts between officials and lobbyists, so long as the latter's function is limited to being one source of information among others. Thus, on the whole, the EC administration is open to the exterior. A

[32] D. Hudig, 'EC Legislation and European Industry's International Competitiveness', *European Affairs* (Spring, 1990), 84–7.

[33] *Daily Telegraph* (1 May 1991).

principal reason for this openness is the fact that the Commission, despite being 'technocratic', is relatively small (with just 4,000 senior policy-makers) and inexpert in the sense of lacking detailed technical knowledge, especially across twelve nations. It is therefore reliant upon external evidence from groups or 'experts'. As one official explained, 'we're isolated in our offices, we don't move much. How can we appreciate the diversity of particular cases in a Community of Twelve if no one comes and explains it to us?'[34]

However, the desire on the part of Commission officials to consult as wide a range of groups as possible, means that it is virtually impossible for any single interest or national association to secure exclusive access to the relevant officials. Thus, draft proposals are often revised several times following diverse representations from different groups and member states. Similarly, new ideas and policy initiatives can emerge from 'nowhere' with little or no warning simply because the Commission has seen fit to consult a particular group of experts. This can happen because stable and predictable 'policy communities'[35] have generally not been developed at the EC level. As Smith[36] has pointed out, a notable exception to this rule is agriculture, where EC policy-making has, until recently, at least, been dominated by a narrow range of interests (notably farmers and food manufacturers) who have successfully excluded other groups (e.g. consumers and environmentalists) who might have conflicting policy objectives. In most other sectors, however, EC policy-making is more pluralistic, characterized by less cohesive, larger 'issue networks' within which there are a wider range of conflicting policy objectives.

There are signs, however, that this situation may be changing. The extension of the Community's sphere of competence with the resultant increase in the volume and scope of EC legislation has placed considerable strain on an increasingly overloaded administration and presented EC officials in several policy sectors with a clear dilemma. On the one hand, the increased scope and amount of EC legislation has increased their need for interest group consultation. Yet, on the other hand, officials are becoming overwhelmed by the increased number and range of interest groups requesting an audience. As one EC official in DG XI (Environment)

[34] *Le Monde Affaires* (8 Apr. 1990).

[35] See e.g. Jeremy J. Richardson and A. G. Jordan (eds.), *Governing Under Pressure: the Policy Process in a Post-Parliamentary Democracy* (Oxford: Martin Robertson & Co., 1979), and R. A. W. Rhodes, *Beyond Westminster and Whitehall: the Sub-Central Governments of Britain* (Hemel Hempstead: Unwin Hyman, 1988).

[36] M. Smith, *The Politics of Agricultural Support in Britain: The Development of the Agricultural Policy Community* (Aldershot: Dartmouth, 1990).

complained, 'We are continually disturbed by consultants who are becoming more pressing . . . They shower us with tons of paper, but practise the art of selective quotation'.[37] In order to overcome this problem, senior officials in the more 'crowded' policy-sectors such as DG XI (Environment) are becoming more discriminating in their attitude to different groups. In particular, increasing numbers of officials have made clear their preference for working with those European Federations and national associations and organizations which are truly representative and which are really able to keep pace with and contribute to the EC policy process.

This attitude is in keeping with the essentially 'pragmatic' and consensual approach of Commission officials to EC policy-making. Their primary aim is to establish a practicable policy which is acceptable to all interested parties. Ideological objections and nationalistic pleas for special treatment generally cut little ice within the Commission, where informed debate, constructive negotiation, and compromise form the basis of the policy-making process. As one British observer, likening the Commission to a 'factory of ideas' remarked, 'this institution adores the art of negotiation. Here you are judged on your intellectual merits.'[38] The failure of Jacques Calvet, head of the French car manufacturer, Peugeot, to persuade the Commission to drop plans to fit catalytic converters on small cars is frequently cited within Brussels as the clearest illustration of how *not* to lobby the Commission. Calvet flatly opposed the proposed legislation, refusing to sign a memorandum prepared—at the suggestion of the French Minister for European Affairs—by other members of the European Committee of Automobile Constructors (CCMC), choosing instead to express outrage at what he perceived to be an attack on French car producers.

The memorandum in question requested, in return for producers' support for the introduction of catalytic converters on small cars, a substantial transition period, tougher EC controls on Japanese car imports, and more EC funds for research. However, according to the CCMC's own rules, Calvet's refusal to sign the memorandum prevented it being sent to the Commission. In the event, the combined influence of German car manufacturers—who, given their technological advantage, supported the proposals—and the environmental lobby, both within the EP and the Council (where national Environment ministers were only too aware of the high level of public support for the proposal), ensured that the legislation was adopted by a qualified majority in the Council without the

---

[37] A. De Vogüé, 'L'Eldorado des lobbies', 98.
[38] Ibid. 100.

concessions requested in the CCMC memorandum.[39] Shortly afterwards, the CCMC was disbanded following the refusal of the Directors of Peugeot and Citroën to accept changes in the federation's voting rules which would have abolished the need for unanimity.[40] As a lawyer working for the Brussels office of the UK law firm, Coopers & Lybrand explained, 'One has to learn the language of influence, sensitivity and pragmatism, the need for compromise, and demonstrate to the official that you are pursuing the same goal as him, but by other means.'[41] In short, in order to be successful at the EC level, groups must be able to build alliances and negotiate compromises with their EC counterparts.

Whilst it is obviously important for groups to lobby Commission officials (and MEPs), the final decision on all EC policies is, of course, taken by *national* officials and politicians in the Council of Ministers—whose meetings are secret and closed. Groups at this stage therefore have little option but to rely upon the negotiating skills and the support of national administrators and government ministers. Thus, somewhat paradoxically, the growing importance of EC legislation has in many cases reinforced the dependency which exists at the national level between groups and 'their' ministries, since the latter are effectively *intermediaries* between groups and the EC in the final stages of Community decision-making.

The degree of co-operation between groups and national administrations in this respect varies considerably both between countries and between groups—not all of which enjoy the same degree of political legitimacy. Within Brussels the UK is frequently cited as a member state where there is, generally speaking, close collaboration between major producer groups and the government (both at the level of individual ministries and within the Cabinet office which is responsible for the co-ordination of EC policy) with regard to EC policy. As Robert Fries, director of the Brussels office of the French employers' association, the CNPF ruefully remarked, 'British MEPs and officials adopt a position only after consulting the relevant industrial or commercial interests. In Anglo-Saxon countries there is an informal interventionism which is much more acknowledged than in France where the administration considers itself to be self-sufficient.'[42] In France, EC policy is co-ordinated within the Secretariat Général du Comité Interministeriel (SGCI), which is part of the Ministry of European Affairs, but which is, in practice, directed to a large extent by the Elysée Palace. In an

[39] *Le Monde* (11/12 June 1989).   [40] *Le Figaro* (29 Dec. 1990).
[41] *Libération* (4 May 1990).   [42] *Quotidien de Paris* (15 Nov. 1988).

attempt to improve the co-ordination of French interest group activity and government strategy within the Community, the French Minister for European Affairs, Edith Cresson, set up in 1988 a number of 'mobilization groups' (*Groupes d'Étude et de Mobilisation* (GEM)), based around major EC policy themes (Transport, Energy, . . .), designed to facilitate the exchange of information between groups, officials, and ministers at the national level.[43]

This initiative on the part of the French government is an indication of the fact that national governments as well as groups are having to adjust to the growing importance of EC policy-making and the consequent need to liaise with groups who are unable to present their own case in the Council of Ministers. The public exhortations of the UK Minister for Corporate Affairs, Mr John Redwood, urging British companies, City institutions, and others to lobby the EC in an attempt to alter the draft EC Directive on take-over panels is further evidence of this trend.[44] Government support does not, however, guarantee success for groups at the EC level either because national officials might fail to appreciate a group's interests, or because its interests are sacrificed in the Council as part of a much bigger package deal.

CONCLUSION

In many respects the art of EC lobbying is not so dissimilar to national lobbying—informal discussions, telephone briefings, lunches, good documentation, etc. are just as important in Brussels as in London, Washington, or Paris. The crucial difference which makes EC lobbying such a complex activity is the policy-making environment. Compared to most national political and administrative systems the EC is a very open system. At first glance, this is often perceived by groups to be an attractive characteristic. Yet, in practice, these 'opportunity structures' cause problems for groups seeking to control the EC policy agenda. In particular, the absence of any single decision-making centre and the fact that twelve member-states and sets of interests have an input into the EC policy process creates uncertainty and competitive agenda-setting. In order to be successful, groups must therefore be able to build alliances with their European counterparts and acknowledge the need for compromise (win–win strategies). But groups must also take care not to neglect the national dimension of EC lobbying since

[43] Monon, *Agir pour ne pas subir*, 22.   [44] *Independent* (23 Feb. 1991).

the final decisions on policies are taken not by a directly elected European government, but by national officials and ministers.

Just as the European Community is itself still developing its institutions and policies, so the interest group system surrounding the EC has yet to reach a stable state. We are still in the relatively early stages of group adjustment to a shift in the locus of power and it, therefore, is not surprising that the process of interest intermediation at the EC level is for the moment in a state of flux. However, it is already clear that just as at the national level, EC lobbying is not neutral between groups; producer interests with a long-standing direct interest in EC policies—farmers, steel producers, car-manufacturers, and employers' associations—are the most effective EC lobbyists. At the other end of the spectrum, voluntary organizations, consumer associations, and environmental groups often lack the necessary resources and political clout required to influence the formulation of EC policies. For these groups, the European Court of Justice has in the past proved a more fruitful means of exerting pressure upon EC policy-makers. For the moment, EC officials, groups and national governments alike are still striving to manage what has for all parties now become a major activity. Whilst groups seek to devise effective EC lobbying strategies, EC officials whose job it is to manage the business of interest group consultation are looking for ways of containing the 'problem' of lobbying. Some officials have already begun to be more discriminating with regard to which groups they deal with. It remains to be seen as to whether the EC structures will accommodate this corporatist logic.

14

THREE FACES OF ASSOCIATIONAL POLITICS: INTEREST GROUPS IN POLITICS IN ISRAEL

As pointed out by Hayward, relations between interest groups and political institutions can follow any of the following *three* broad patterns: group domination, when associations persuade, manipulate, or cajole decision-makers into action or inaction; co-operation between interest groups and official policy-makers; authoritative domination, when governments manipulate or cajole interest groups into conformity with the national or public interest.[1]

These three patterns correspond in broad terms to three models of interest politics. The pluralist model, prevalent mainly in the US, describes a system where groups wield a significant amount of power and play a vital role in determining policy outcomes.[2] The second and third categories are narrower than those described by Hayward. Co-operation characterizes the corporatist model, where groups are granted the privilege of 'integrated participation'[3] found in some Western European and Scandinavian countries. The third, only sparsely discussed in the interest group literature, is the partyist model, where the citizenry is mobilized to fulfil a national cause. This situation is typical in countries that have adopted forms of institutional democracy but are still coping with severe problems of social integration, economic development, and/or nation-building. The torch of the public interest is carried mainly by one or more political parties acting as a major socializing agency. India may serve as one example for this partyist model of interest politics.[4] A

Reprinted in slightly amended form by permission of Blackwell Publishers, Journals Department.

[1] J. E. S. Hayward, *Private Interests and Public Policy* (London: Longman, 1966), 1–2.

[2] G. Wootton, *Interest Groups: Policy and Politics in America* (Englewood Cliffs, NJ: Prentice Hall, 1985); K. Lehman Schlozman and J. T. Tierney, *Organized Interest and American Democracy* (New York: Harper & Row, 1986).

[3] J. P. Olsen, *Organized Democracy: Political Institutions in a Welfare State: The Case of Norway* (Oslo: Universitetsforlaget, 1983).

[4] M. Weiner, *Politics of Scarcity* (Chicago, Ill.: University of Chicago Press, 1968); S. P. Huntington and J. M. Nelson, *No Easy Choice: Political Participation in Developing Countries* (Cambridge, Mass.: Harvard University Press, 1976).

partyist model of interest politics, however, is not confined to developing countries but is prevalent in 'party-democracies' where political parties hold the centre of power. Italy provides a good example.[5] . . .

ORGANIZATIONAL STRUCTURE: CORPORATIST PATTERNS

From an organizational perspective the Israeli interest-group arena seems to fit the corporatist model, with little variation between sub-categories of interest group. In fact, Schmitter's classical analysis of the neo-corporatist structure describes the Israeli scene with almost photographic accuracy.[6] There are limited numbers of organizations, a single group often dominates its interest domain, and density of membership is high. The corporatist model seems particularly evident in the economic domain. Labour, business, farmers, and professionals are represented by a limited number of interest groups monopolizing their respective sectors. All 45 Israeli trade unions, for example, are organized under the umbrella of the Histadrut, Israel's Labour Federation.[7] The Histadrut is a unique association. Owing to its size and diversity, it can hardly be called a 'group': because of its all-encompassing objectives, it can hardly be perceived as promoting an 'interest'.[8] Although much of its activity has strong partisan overtones (the Labour Federation's leadership is nominated by party organs and its governing institutions are elected on a partisan basis), the Histadrut is not a political party but a highly influential association. Workers join the Histadrut rather than the individual unions and are assigned to a union according to their employment. The Labour Federation's monopoly even extends to non-members. By law, anyone employed in an 'organized workplace', a third of whose members are unionized, is willy-nilly represented by the Histadrut. Theoretically the Labour Federation has such a hold over the unions because funds flow from its centre to the sub-units rather than the other way around.

The business sector in Israel is also organized under an umbrella association, the Co-ordinating Office of Economic Organizations

[5] J. LaPalombara, *Interest Groups in Italian Politics* (Princeton, NJ: Princeton University Press, 1964); id., *Democracy Italian Style* (New Haven, Conn.: Yale University Press, 1987).

[6] P. C. Schmitter, 'Still the Century of Corporatism?', *Review of Politics*, 36 (1974), 85–131.

[7] D. Shimshoni, *Israeli Democracy: The Middle of the Journey* (New York: Free Press, 1982).

[8] S. N. Eisenstadt, *Israeli Society* (London: Weidenfeld & Nicolson, 1967).

(CO). The CO is dominated by the 'big four': the Manufacturers' Association, the Chamber of Commerce, the Centre for Builders and Contractors, and the Farmers' Union (comprising the small private agricultural sector). Its remaining 11 members cover the whole spectrum of the business sector. Despite conflicting interests (between, say, importers and manufacturers) the CO is a 'comprehensive association', drawing members from most sectors of business and seeking to address general problems facing business.[9] The CO monopoly in representing the business sector was partly disrupted in the early 1980s, when the organization of the self-employed (Lahav) was established. Lahav remained outside the CO but its lack of effectiveness in terms of influence on economic policy testifies to the closed circuit of the Israeli associational arena.

Most professional associations also contain constituent units that are organized into a limited number of singular, non-competitive, centralized, differentiated categories. Only one interest group, the Bar Association, has thus far been granted full statutory recognition by the Knesset (1962). Other groups, however, monopolize their professional domains, without formal state acknowledgment. For example, all Israeli physicians belong to the Israeli Medical Association; all engineers, architects, and technical workers belong to the Bureau of Engineers. Centralization is evident even in such fragmented domains as agriculture. Thus the farmers, though belonging to many different settlement movements affiliated with political parties from different ideological camps (such as the Labour-affiliated Takam and Herut-affiliated moshav movement), operate under a peak organization, the Agricultural Centre. These settlement organizations together embrace over 90 per cent of those living in agricultural localities. Although each settlement movement has a political party as patron, the tendency of the groups to co-ordinate activities on the interest level has recently increased. Farmers' associations of all political colours tend to act in concert to defend their material interests, regardless of their ideology and party affiliation.

Economic interest groups also rank high in membership density, with more than half reporting at least 85 per cent of their constituencies as members. The Histadrut, for example, claimed in 1988 to have enrolled some 90 per cent of the country's salaried workers. This figure is strikingly high by international standards.[10]

---

[9] W. D. Coleman and W. Grant, 'The Organizational Cohesion and Political Access of Business: A Case Study of Comprehensive Association', *European Journal of Political Research*, 16 (1988), 467–87.

[10] The figures for Europe were: France 20%, West Germany 41%, UK 50%, Sweden 80%. Quoted from Wilson, *Interest Group Politics in France*, 142.

The proportion of members of the business community in their respective associations is impressive: 77.8 per cent of the associations reported a membership of over 70 per cent of those eligible to join. Agricultural groups are also extremely comprehensive, for they involve not merely an organizational affiliation but a way of life: all those residing in a settlement belong to their association.

An important factor in both the monopoly character and the high membership density among Israeli sectional interest groups is the state's practice of granting the title of 'representative group' to a single organization in any given domain. The government has the authority to decide whether or not a group meets certain qualifications, which are legally set only for trade unions.[11] Many other groups were also granted the title of 'representative'. By means of an 'extension order' the Manufacturers Association was designated the only group eligible to represent the interests of industrialists; professional associations have gained a similar privilege. Thus title 'representative group' does not entail material benefits, eligibility for government funds, or positions on a formal advisory board. However, the sense of legitimacy conferred upon the group and the official confirmation that this group possesses sufficient weight that must be taken into consideration afford it important assets. Most important, 'representative' status militates against splits and withdrawals because the splinter group is bound to lose the advantages of being recognized by the state. Members cannot break away because there is no competing organization to join and the costs of forming a new one are too high for individual members to carry.

Harmony among the groups is another feature of Israeli interest politics. Associations of all types and shades emphasize they do not compete in a free market. When asked to identify their adversaries, interest groups seemed to find it a difficult task. The figures are striking. When asked about their relationship with other interest groups, 89.1 per cent of the party-affiliated associations and 78.5 per cent of the economic groups stated they are 'harmonious'. Of course, some associations, such as the organizations of landlords and tenants, are clearly pitted against each other. However, contrary to what might be expected, the business community and the Histadrut have maintained a great degree of accord. Co-ordinating bodies of workers and employers, besides fostering close personal contact,

---

[11] A union is recognized as representative when its membership includes a plurality of workers to whom the labour agreement applied, on condition that they comprise not less than one-third of the total employees in the work-place. See A. Shirom, *Introduction to Labor Relations in Israel* (Tel Aviv: Am Oved, 1984) (Mavo Lehahasei Avoda).

defuse emerging tensions and settle differences. One factor contributing to conciliation between these traditional adversaries is Histadrut's dual nature. It is the sole representative of the workers; at the same time, it is one of the country's biggest industrialists and thus shares many interests with manufacturers in the private sector.

In contrast, fragmentation and conflict are the rule among public interest groups, which tend to proliferate and rival each other. Four or five ecological movements compete for the extremely limited public concern over Israel's environment. There are no fewer than five consumer groups, at least half a dozen women's associations, a multitude of groups promoting religious causes, and many associations attempting to forge co-operation between Jews and Arabs. Proliferation is greatest in relation to Israel's most salient political issue, its future boundaries. The best-known groups are Peace Now, advocating territorial concessions in return for a peace settlement, and Gush Emunim, the major proponent of Greater Israel.[12] There are two major camps but there is no unanimity within them. Some 30 groups endorse compromise and demand prompt dialogue with the Palestinians, while more than a dozen associations advocate a harsher Israeli stand toward the Arab population. Despite this diversity there have been repeated attempts to enhance inter-group co-operation among public interest groups and to co-ordinate activities. For example, a peak organization—the Lobby (Shdula)—represents the interests of some dozen women's associations.

The differences between the sectional associations and the cause groups are evident also in regard to other structural characteristics, especially the degree of centralization. The majority of the party-affiliated groups (72.3 per cent) and half of the economic associations reported a centralized organizational structure, compared with only 39.2 per cent of the cause groups. Although internal dissensions do erupt, more than half the interest groups in all categories reported no 'serious challenge to leadership'.

STRATEGIES OF ACTION: PLURALIST PATTERNS

From the foregoing, one might expect that Israeli interest groups would operate within the corporatist model. The government has to deal with only one interest group per constituency; it may and often does grant recognition to representative associations: harmonious

---

[12] Y. Yishai, *Land or Peace: Whither Israel?* (Stanford, Calif.: Hoover Institution Press, 1987).

TABLE 14.1 Reported Frequency of Recourse to Strategies of Influence (Often and Occasionally) (percentages)

	Interest-group category				
	Party-affiliated	Economic	Promotional	Other	n
Demonstrations and strikes	30.5	17.5	19.5	16.0	147
Litigation	21.2	23.1	20.0	12.5	141
Lobbying Parliament	57.6	56.5	50.0	46.0	142
Contacts with government	79.4	82.1	67.4	76.0	147
Personal contacts	81.9	86.9	65.9	65.5	141
Media	60.6	68.6	74.0	76.0	146
Membership in joint bodies	72.7	83.9	43.8	30.0	143
Contacts with parties	33.6	23.7	21.7	33.4	141

relations among groups may also enhance the prospects for an 'institutionalized dialogue'. Surprisingly, however, Israeli interest groups tend to choose strategies (presented in Table 14.1) prevalent mostly in countries classified as pluralist, although they have acquired a particular Israeli style.

Although Israel is a party democracy, contrary to expectations interest groups do not, as a rule, direct their attempts to influence public policy at partisan institutions or personnel. Only a minority of associations (16.9 per cent) reported requesting a political party to include a plank favourable to their cause in its electoral platform. Contacts with parties are more prominent among party-affiliated associations. Over half of the settlement organizations reported interaction with political parties as part of their daily routine. Over a third of both agricultural groups and trade unions conduct their internal elections on the basis of partisan lists. The proportion of party-affiliated groups that select a candidate for a partisan position is far higher than that of cause groups (16.6 per cent and 3.7 per cent, respectively). Yet even among the party-affiliated groups there is a growing tendency to break away from parties. All Israeli interest groups, including those traditionally linked with political parties, tend to intensify their contacts with the administrative branch of government and to decrease their interaction with political parties.

The paucity of contacts with parties as a means of securing influence is surprising in view of the fact that an overwhelming majority of respondents (96.7 per cent) unequivocally agreed that political parties constitute the major source of power in the country. The claim of party dominance is thus still deeply ingrained but if, as suggested by Beer,[13] interest-group strategies serve as a yardstick for measuring influence, power in Israel actually lies beyond the inner party circles. This gap between what interest-group activists do and what they think may be explained in part by the fact the political parties are perceived as powerful but as the least trustworthy among political institutions.[14]

The lack of formal interaction with political parties is compensated for, in any case, by a pattern of friendly personal relations between party politicians and interest-group leaders.[15] In fact, more than half of the members of all boards of associations are party activists. This is true not only for the party-affiliated organizations,

[13] S. H. Beer, 'Group Representation in Britain and the United States', *The Annals of the American Academy of Political and Social Science*, 119 (1958), 130–40.

[14] Y. Peres, 'Most Israelis are Committed to Democracy', *Israeli Democracy*, 2 (1987), 11–19.

[15] A. Arian, *Politics in Israel: The Second Generation* (Chatham: Chatham House, 1985).

such as trade unions or settlement movements, but also for politically 'neutral' associations in the business community. The pattern of 'accumulated roles' produced by joint membership in both political parties and interest groups does not necessarily imply party infiltration of associations. It may, instead, confirm the universal rule of reinforcing patterns of political participation.[16]

As to corporatist strategies, data show that a large proportion of both party-affiliated groups and economic associations (72.7 per cent and 83.9 per cent, respectively) delegate representatives to joint state group bodies. We should bear in mind, however, that corporatism does not imply mere membership in consultative bodies. Rather, it constitutes an institutionalized exchange in which groups are incorporated into the policy process. As noted by Cawson, 'what makes corporatism distinctive is the fusion of representation and intervention in the *relationship* between groups and state',[17] In Israel these relationships are rarely institutionalized. Formal representation in joint state group commissions is fairly uncommon. Only the farmers deviate from this rule. Their incorporation into formal decision-making bodies is unique on the Israeli political scene. The tendency of farmers to participate in corporatist structures is not universally acknowledged. According to one opinion, organized agriculture is less frequently included in corporatist arrangements than the business sector.[18] Others argue that agriculture shows a marked propensity for corporatism. The peculiarly vulnerable nature of agriculture and the strategic importance of food production have produced corporatist patterns in the farming sector.[19] This is the case in Israel where an institutionalized dialogue goes on within the framework of 14 agricultural councils for marketing and production, staffed by representatives of the Ministry of Agriculture and the settlement movements. The councils have comprehensive formal authority over production, marketing, dealing with surpluses, setting quotas, awarding incentive bonuses, and dispensing funds. In short, the agricultural councils were vested with far-reaching policy-making authority. Corporatism, however, was never achieved because the councils fell into one of the traps of corporatist

[16] S. Verba, N. H. Nie, and J. Kim, *Participation and Political Equality: A Seven-Nation Comparison* (Cambridge: Cambridge University Press, 1978).

[17] A. Cawson, *Corporatism and Politics of Theory* (Oxford: Basil Blackwell, 1988), 39.

[18] G. Lehmbruch, 'Liberal Corporatism and Party Government', in P. C. Schmitter and G. Lehmbruch (eds.), *Trends Toward Corporatist Intermediation* (London: Sage, 1979).

[19] J. T. S. Keeler, *The Politics of Neo-Corporatism in France: Farmers, The State and Agricultural Policy: Making in the Fifth Republic* (New York: Oxford University Press, 1987), 258.

politics: the agenda was determined by the state actors, or matters of concern to the farmers were 'crowded out' by items placed on the agenda by the bureaucracy.[20] Members representing the agricultural groups were excluded from direct influence over decisions affecting them and soon refused to comply with the councils' decisions. There have been recurrent attempts to break away from the councils' authority and to introduce more privatization into the farming sector. The fundamental requirement for successful corporatist strategies, acquiescence of rank-and-file members, was thus not fulfilled.

As distinct from daily interaction, 'institutionalized dialogue' is not a characteristic strategy of business of labour sectors in Israel. There have been repeated attempts to establish some form of socio-economic deliberating forum but the efforts have not produced a body that even approximates corporatist practices in Western Europe. One of the more recent versions of such a council was constituted in December 1988, comprising representatives of the state, the business sector and the Histadrut. The Social-Economic Council gives its members the opportunity to air differences, vent grievances, and settle controversies. Its role in the policy process, however, remains insignificant. Major issues, such as how the economic sector will share in the nation's resources, are not discussed by the council, whose mainly symbolic function does not qualify it as a corporatist structure.

Group strategies are thus neither partisan nor corporatist. In some respects they are also different from those practised in classic pluralist societies. To begin with, direct action is not prevalent. Although some interest groups, typically those concerned with issues of foreign and defence policy, have frequently mobilized large crowds, demonstrations were not considered a major strategy even by cause groups (only 19.5 per cent of which reported medium or high frequency). Israel has evinced a considerable growth of political protest since the Six Day War[21] but the organized interest groups studied here do not often resort to direct action. By international standards, Israel has also ranked low in strikes.[22]

---

[20] W. Streeck, 'Between Pluralism and Corporatism: German Business Associations and the State', *Journal of Public Policy*, 3 (1983), 265–84; P. C. Schmitter, 'Reflections on Where the Theory of Neo-Corporatism has Gone and Where the Praxis of Neo-Corporatism May be Going', in G. Lehmbruch and P. C. Schmitter (eds.), *Patterns of Corporatist Policy-Making* (Beverly Hills, Calif.: Sage, 1982).

[21] G. Woltsfeld, *The Politics of Provocation: Participation and Protest in Israel* (Albany, NY: State University of New York Press, 1988).

[22] The index was based on lost workdays per 1,000 employees: See A. Michael and R. Bar-El, *Strikes in Israel* (Ramat Gan: Bar Illan University Press, 1970) (Shvitot Beyisrael).

Litigation, another typical pluralist strategy, is also not widespread, although it is growing both in volume and in impact. As the data show, it has been used mostly by professional associations appealing to the Labour Court in wage disputes. Recourse to litigation by these groups was spurred by the unionization of the professional labour force in Israel, 95.1 per cent of those employed in the public sector.[23] With the relaxation of demands for a personal stake of the appellant in the case under concern (*locus standi*), increasing numbers of public interest groups have attempted to influence policy through litigation. Finally, structured parliamentary lobbying, a traditional pluralist strategy, is largely missing. Although over half the interest groups do appeal to the legislature and often testify before a Knesset committee, the practice of establishing a profes- sional lobby working in Parliament is rare.

What, then, justifies the conclusion that the behaviour of Israeli interest groups is reminiscent of pluralism? The answer lies in the daily forms of activity that are clustered around three strategies: formal contacts with the bureaucracy, informal interaction with the state's leadership and recourse to the media. The immense power amassed by state authorities necessitates continuous negotiation with the bureaucracy. This is true for all segments of sectional associations. The need to secure licences and to bargain on the terms of dozens of regulations restricting or assisting producers and consumers has prompted intensive interaction with the authorities, an interaction that has more to do with pressure politics than with accommodation. Promotional associations are not excluded from the scene. In fact, the data indicate that access to decision-makers is widely available. Only in extremely rare instances did a Knesset committee, a government official, or even a minister refuse outright to listen to a group's plea.[24] A meeting between the prime minister and a petitioning group is not unusual. This intensive and frequently effective interaction between group representatives and public authorities, mainly in the civil service, is the first indication of pluralist strategies.

Interest groups, particularly in the economic sector, are not content with 'formal' contacts but tend to develop personal relationships with senior politicians. As noted by Arian, the pyramidal structure of Israeli political life and the relatively small number of people at the apex of the pyramid enhance the

[23] *Statistical Abstract of Israel* (1990), 335.

[24] 19% of the research interest groups were denied a meeting by an official, 14.7% were denied a meeting by a minister, and 9.1% were denied access by a Knesset committee.

opportunities for frequent meetings in both official and unofficial capacities.[25] In addition (in the case of public interest groups often as a substitute), groups attempt to influence policy decisions through the media. Recourse to the media is perceived by an overwhelming majority of groups as both an effective and a legitimate strategy. It is the most popular strategy among public interest groups but it is frequently employed by other categories as well. Publicity, in fact, may substitute for other forms of influence because it poses a direct threat to decision-makers, who would much rather bargain with interest groups behind closed doors. Finally, the pluralist attributes of Israeli interest politics are enhanced by a realization, shared by close to half (48.8 per cent) the responding interest groups, that 'pressure' was the crucial factor in influencing specific decisions. 'They [policy-makers] understand only the language of power' was a recurring statement in the interviews held with group activists.

NORMS AND VALUES: THE PARTISAN PATTERN

Ideologies and norms sustaining partisan attributes of interest politics in Israel are evident both in legal arrangements and in norms adhered to by interest-group activists. Faced with enormous tasks of absorbing mass immigration, building an economy and, particularly, withstanding external belligerency, the Israeli political leadership has come to believe not only in its own indispensability but also in the infallibility of its judgement.[26] Social engineering and intrusion into citizens' lives have resulted from these attitudes. The fact that Israel is a 'garrison democracy'[27] engaged since its inception in an armed struggle with the Arab and Muslim world, has fed paternalism.

A manifestation of this paternalistic attitude is the Associations Law (1980), which places interest groups under state scrutiny. Freedom of association is a basic tenet but this freedom needs the state's approval. The law compels associations to register with the Ministry of Interior Registrar. The law also places some restrictions on associative freedom. Registration is granted only when the objectives of the organization do not negate the existence of the state or its democratic form of government, or serve as a cover for unlawful activities. Although rejection of an application may be

---

[25] Arian, *Politics in Israel*, 193.

[26] A. Elon, *The Israelis: Founders and Sons* (New York: Penguin Books, 1981), 311.

[27] J. C. Hurewitz, *Middle East Politics: The Military Dimension* (New York: Praeger, 1969).

overruled by a District Court, the law, which has been very controversial[28] does establish a form of 'debilitated pluralism'.[29] It allows the establishment of voluntary associations but at the same time enables the state to keep a close eye on their activity. The law also prescribes state intervention in the internal affairs of associations. Thus a registered association is obliged to convene a general meeting, to elect committees, to adhere to democratic rules and to keep financial records. Associations are required to present a copy of their balance sheet as well as reports on the elections of their governing bodies to the Registrar. Such regulations reflect the pervasive norm of the state's supremacy and its dominant role in safeguarding the well-being of its citizens. The 'state', in this regard, it should be noted, is not coterminous with the administrative élite but rather with the political leadership associated with party politics. It should also be noted that the Associations Law has so far not resulted in any association being denied registration. Groups that did not comply with the language of the law negotiated with authorities until agreement was reached; the financial records of the associations have largely escaped state scrutiny; and administrative slackness has precluded the implementation of other regulations on organization life.[30]

Partisan features were evident also on the attitudinal level. Asked about reasons for their achievements, association activists were given three alternatives compatible with the three models of interest politics: accumulation of resources (pluralism), functional role in society (corporatism), and contribution to advancing a national cause (partyism). The answers (presented in Table 14.2) clearly reflected the partisan paradigm. The secret of success, activists asserted, lies in adherence to and fulfilment of national objectives. Adherence to national goals was strikingly higher among the issue-orientated groups than among the party-affiliated and the economic groups. For example, the activists of the Society for the Protection of Nature, the largest environmental group, believed that teaching the people (many of whom are newcomers)[31] a love of the country and

---

[28] Three drafts of the Association Law were presented to the Knesset: in Dec. 1954, in Mar. 1964, and in Dec. 1979. Only the last was enacted into a law, after a highly contentious Knesset debate. See Y. Yishai, 'Land of Paradoxes. Interest Politics in Israel' (Albany, NY: University of New York Press, 1991), 139–49.

[29] R. Bianchi, *Interest Groups and Political Development in Turkey* (Princeton, NJ: Princeton University Press), 114.

[30] State Comptroller, *Annual Report*, 39 (1989).

[31] In 1988 more than one-third (36.7%) of the Jews in Israel were not native-born: only one-fifth (21.5%) were second-generation Israelis: see *Statistical Abstract of Israel* (1989), 83.

TABLE 14.2   Most Important Factor Determining Interest-Group Influence (percentage reporting)

	Interest-group category			
	Party-affiliated	Economic	Promotional	Other
Resources	25.9	22.2	8.0	29.1
Functional role in society	19.3	13.9	12.0	4.2
Contribution to national goals	54.9	63.9	80.0	66.7
n	31	36	50	24

its landscape is the main source of their achievements. Associations advocating defence-related issues, precisely because the issue they advocate is divisive and controversial, argued that their adherence to the national cause is unalloyed. This is particularly true of Peace Now, whose activists took pains to establish their dedication to Israel's security. Legitimacy, on the basis of adherence to 'Zionist goals', was sought even by the feminist movement, generally associated with anti-state radicalism. This identification with national interests is not confined to cause groups. Even the industrialists evaluate their influence in terms of 'contribution to the national economy' rather than to the immense organizational power they have accumulated. Contribution to a national cause has always been valued in Israel as symbolic of good citizenship and participation in the common endeavour. The identification with collective goals enables associations to counteract the perjorative term 'interest group', signifying concentration on selfish goals rather than on the good of the nation as a whole. The answers of interest-group activists, as well as the language in which they phrased their objectives, indicate that the public good may no longer be a guideline for action but it nevertheless looms large in the declared attitudes of interest group activists.

CONCLUSIONS

Israel's interest politics present a confusing complexity for any student of associational theory. The organizational attributes of interest groups qualify the country as corporatist, with a high degree of concentration, monopolization, and cohesion. Against this background, however, adversarial politics take place, with interest groups negotiating with the authorities and pressing them to yield to their demands. The pluralist aura of Israeli interest politics is dimmed, however, by strong strands of partyism. Not only is there a law subjecting associations to strict state supervision, but the groups' own norms reflect successful mobilization by party élites. What light can these paradoxical attributes of Israeli associational politics shed on interest group theory?

First, both pluralist and corporatist models have been treated in the literature as *Gestalts*,[32] that is, these two models are most valuable as analytical tools when their various components are examined in terms of their interrelationships. Interdependence between variables

---

[32] P. C. Schmitter, 'Corporatism is Dead: Long Live Corporatism', *Government and Opposition*, 24 (1989).

has been emphasized particularly in regard to structures and modes of behaviour, between the ways in which interests are organized, and the ways in which decisions are made and implemented. The Israeli case reveals that the variables of a given model need not co-vary. It demonstrates that concentrated structures do not necessarily lead to concerted state group collaboration and that pluralist strategies do not, perforce, generate liberal norms associated with free-market politics. The utility of interest group theories may thus lie not only in their applicability to the meso or micro levels,[33] but in their relevance to various dimensions of the polity as a whole.

Secondly, the causal relations between environmental conditions and the attributes of interest-group politics appear to be less solid than believed. Corporatism, for one, has been considered to be a product of socio-economic and political developments, its emergence instigated *inter alia* by growing social complexity and an increased role played by the state in socio-economic life. The Israeli soil seemed ripe for corporatism. Yet, this form of interest politics has largely failed to develop because the cultural orientation sustaining institutionalized co-operation between state authorities and outside contenders was lacking. Organizational structures thus do not necessarily lead to predicted forms of behaviour. They may do so only if normative orientations sustain this linkage.

Finally, the pluralist and corporatist theories of interest politics were presented as alternatives. One of the purposes for developing corporatist theory was to challenge the pluralist paradigm of interest politics which, until the mid-1970s, completely dominated North American political science.[34] However, much criticism has been raised against the purported distinctiveness of the corporatist model. It has been argued that the lines separating it from the pluralist model are superficial at best.[35] The proponents of corporatism nevertheless maintain that the theory 'not only provides a valuable alternative framework through which to examine organized interests in contemporary liberal democracies'.[36] It has also been suggested that corporatism does not supplant pluralism but rather supplements it and reduces the scope of its applicability.[37]

[33] A. Cawson, 'Varieties of Corporatism: The Importance of the Meso-Level of Interest Intermediation', in id. (ed.), *Organized Interest and the State* (London: Sage, 1985).

[34] Schmitter, 'Still the Century of Corporatism?'.

[35] G. Jordan, 'Pluralist Corporatism and Corporate Pluralism', *Scandinavian Political Studies*, 7 (1984), 137–51.

[36] P. J. Williamson, *Corporatism in Perspective: An Introductory Guide to Corporatist Theory* (London: Sage, 1989), 192.

[37] Cawson, *Corporatism and Politics of Theory*, 4.

Be the theories complementary or competing, advocates of both pluralism and corporatism have largely ignored the role political parties can play in mobilizing support for the public interest. Corporatists believe that such an interest is a product of the state-group alliance. Even parliamentary influence on policy-making is minimal, confined to rubber-stamping decisions reached by negotiations between the state and interest groups. Pluralists can envisage a situation where interest groups would be willing to subordinate their sectional ends to what they accept as the public interest,[38] but this would be a result of their incorporation into the machinery of government. Pluralists do not distinguish between the state as a political-administrative entity and the state as a political-ideological entity guided by the principles forged by political parties.

The Israeli case introduces parties into the interest-group scene, not as transmitters of petitions but as sources of values that shape the nature of these petitions. Parties do not mediate between interest groups and state authorities, as suggested by pluralist analysts; neither do they yield to powerful interest groups, as suggested by corporatist analysts. The 'invisible hand' of political parties may thus play a greater role in shaping interest politics than presumed by either the pluralist or the corporatist proponents. Partyism is a form of interest politics that does prevail in societies facing major national endeavours, ruled by a dominant party and/or confronting external enemies. The partisan version of interest politics is not akin to state corporatism. It is a configuration of interest politics which prevails in democracies leaning, because of particular circumstances, towards emphasis on collective, national goals.

[38] J. Hayward, 'Interest Groups and the Demand for State Action', in J. Hayward and R. N. Berki (eds.), *State and Society in Contemporary Europe* (Oxford: Martin Robertson & Co., 1979), 37.

15

AUSTRALIAN INTEREST GROUPS

TREVOR MATTHEWS

DETERMINANTS OF STRATEGY AND TACTICS

What determines how an interest group goes about attempting to influence public policy? What channels is it likely to use? Which policy makers will it set its sights upon? Three broad strategies of influence are available to interest groups: persuasion, coercion, and inducement. Despite the connotations of 'pressure' in the term 'pressure group', most groups choose to persuade rather than to threaten, to convince rather than to coerce. They present submissions, give testimony, supply evidence, and make requests.

None the less, threats are often embedded in arguments. A warning about the consequences of a policy may also be a warning that the group will make life difficult for the government. Once this happens, coercion takes over from persuasion. For example, the group may threaten to challenge a decision in the High Court; to campaign against the government at the next election; to close down a factory; to move investment overseas; to sabotage the implementation of a programme; or to go public with information that will embarrass the government.

Sometimes groups will seek to sway decision-makers by promising rewards. This is the strategy of inducement. Some inducements are administrative: the promise to assist in the smooth administration of a scheme. Others clearly smack of bribery and corruption. Given these broad strategies, the particular tactics or techniques that a group will use and the target it will attempt to influence depend on four factors. Two of these relate to stable features of the political system:

- the structure of the decision-making processes which groups seek to influence; and
- the characteristic style of a country's decision-making and the general attitudes towards legitimate political behaviour.

Trevor Matthews, 'Australian Interest Groups', in R. Smith and L. Watson, *Politics in Australia* (Sydney: Allen & Unwin, 1989), 211–44. Reprinted in abridged form by permission of Allen & Unwin Pty Ltd.

Two are situational:

- the issues at stake and the stage they have reached in the policy process; and
- the resources that the group has at its disposal.

Of these the most important are the first two: the structure and operating style of the decision-making system. Interest groups gravitate to where effective decision-making lies. If the Executive dominates the legislature and if the permanent bureaucracy is a key factor in policy-making, interest groups will try to influence ministers and their departments. If, on the other hand, the legislature share power with the Executive (as occurs in the United States), groups will direct their lobbying as much to Congress as towards the Presidency. Likewise, in federal countries (such as Australia), where significant powers are shared with state governments, groups have a broader range of targets to aim at than do groups in unitary countries. One of these targets in Australia is the High Court, which has the power to rule on the constitutionality of actions of Federal and state governments.

Interest groups will also tend to conform to generally accepted political values that give legitimacy to certain types of activity (such as preparing well-researched submissions and giving evidence to official committees). Similarly they will steer away from those activities deemed to be illegitimate (such as violent protests) or illegal (such as bribery, fraud, and blackmail). Political values also shape the predominant style of policy-making in a country.[1] The bias towards bureaucratic decision-making involving consultation with knowledgeable, 'responsible', 'useful' insider groups is based in part on a cultural norm that governing should be built on consent. In their efforts to generate support for their work, bureaucrats take steps to foster contact with their 'clientele'. One result, in Canberra as well as elsewhere, has been the rise in significance of what political scientists refer to as 'policy communities', 'issue networks', and 'subgovernments'. For an interest group to be an integral part of a policy community—to be accorded 'insider status'—is a sign that it conforms to the bureaucratic standards of 'responsible' behaviour. Some interest groups are as much concerned with securing (and keeping) this status as they are with pursuing substantive policy goals.

While a country's structure of government and predominant style of policy making will set the broad constraints on interest groups' strategies, the actual tactics a group will adopt will also be shaped

---

[1] Jeremy J. Richardson (ed.), *Policy Styles in Western Europe* (London: Allen & Unwin, 1982).

by two situational factors: the character of the issue and the resources at the group's disposal.

Certain features of an issue will deflect an interest group away from bureaucratic channels. The first of these is if the issue is not yet on the political agenda. Getting an issue on to the political agenda—i.e. placing it on the list of problems that politicians and officials are paying serious attention to—is the first stage in the policy-making process. Second, the issue may belong to the realm of 'high' rather than 'routine' politics. Routine politics deals with the normal, day-to-day decision-making and administration in a policy area. It is concerned with technical matters and with detail. Solutions often lie in incremental adjustments to existing policy. High politics, in contrast, deals with issues of principle and consequence, with major questions concerning the nation's economy and its place in world politics, and with issues that fundamentally divide the political parties. Even if it is conceded that a matter of detail for one person can be a matter of high principle for another, the two types of issues tend to be settled in different political arenas. The former in bureaucratically-dominated policy communities; the latter in top-level interdepartmental committees, in Cabinet, in the Prime Minister's office, or in Parliament. An interest group will find itself being drawn into these arenas if it is embroiled in an issue of high politics.

The third feature occurs when the issue has already been decided and the interest group has suffered defeat. If the group wishes to challenge the decision it will find it has to use quite different tactics to those that are appropriate when discussing an issue with officials in a government department. The group may ask an MP to raise the issue in Parliament; it may protest against the decision in public; it may fight the issue during an election campaign (as the gun lobby did during the 1988 New South Wales elections); or it may challenge the decision in the courts.

Similarly, the resources at the group's disposal may determine the tactics it uses and the target it focuses upon. In general, the fewer resources available to a group, the narrower the menu of strategies and tactics it can choose from. For example, if a group lacks 'insider' status and a reputation among policy makers for reliability and credibility, it may not be able to use the strategy of bureaucratic persuasion; if it lacks a geographically concentrated and politically aroused membership, it will not be able to mobilize its members electorally; and if it lacks funds it will not be able to undertake an ambitious advertising campaign or to engage in expensive litigation.

The Executive

At the present time in Australia most interest groups that seek to influence public policy direct their activities toward the Executive branch of government. This is because most of the decisions that concern interest groups are made by ministers (the political executive) or public servants (the bureaucratic executive). The best way to influence ministers is to influence the advice they receive. For that reason the public service has become a key target for most interest groups. The bureaucracy's significance for interest groups is reinforced by its policy-making and policy-implementing roles. Many 'routine', 'technical', and 'less-important' decisions of vital concern to interest groups are actually made by public servants.

But the relationship between interest groups and the Executive is not all one-sided. Ministers and bureaucrats also need the groups. Groups can tell the government how a proposed policy is likely to affect or be regarded by certain sections of the population. They not only furnish opinions: some can supply facts, figures, and research results that a department might lack. In addition, an interest group's co-operation may be essential for the smooth implementation of a programme and its approval may be crucial in selling a policy to the public. They are useful sounding boards.

To solicit this information, governments employ a variety of advisory devices. There are, for instance, formal, continuing committees on which groups are represented. An example is the National Labour Consultative Council representing the ACTU and the Confederation of Australian Industry. There are also *ad hoc* committees set up to report on particular topics. They include Royal Commissions, task forces, and inter-departmental committees. These committees frequently invite interest groups to present submissions, although such invitations tend to elicit responses only from the organized and the articulate.

There is marked bias in favour of producer groups on Commonwealth advisory committees.[2] Not only is representation on advisory committees biased in favour of clientele producer groups. So too is access to departments. Moreover, the two are mutually reinforcing. Groups that have access are frequently appointed to advisory committees; and groups that are appointed to such committees gain

---

[2] T. V. Matthews, 'Interest Group Access to the Australian Government Bureaucracy', in Royal Commission on Australian Government Administration, *Appendices to the Report*, ii. (Canberra: AGPS, 1976), 339–42.

official contacts and a certain 'standing', which further facilitates their access.

Trade unions have not enjoyed this kind of patron–client access. Except for the RSL, Aboriginal, and conservation groups, all of which have patron departments, no non-producer associations have been able to establish quite the sort of close, institutionalized client relations with departments that trade associations and farmers' groups possess. This is largely because they lack the socio-economic leverage of producer groups. It is also because they lack other resources: particularly large, stable memberships and money.

Quasi-Judicial Tribunals

If the structure of decision-making in Australia has a distinctive character, it lies in the prominent place occupied by adjudicative tribunals and boards. The Arbitration Commission and the Industries Assistance Commission are two such bodies. Given the significance of the decisions of the Arbitration Commission (not only on wage levels but also on such questions as working hours, paid leave, and superannuation), it is a major target for the ACTU and the CAI.

Parliament

One result of Parliament's eclipse by the Executive as a maker of public policy has been the decline in the importance and frequency of parliamentary activities in the strategy of most interest groups.

Parliament is now used mainly as a second resort when efforts to influence ministers or the bureaucracy have failed. Intensive lobbying against a bill generally indicates that the hostile pressure groups have been unsuccessful in their representations to the relevant minister. In Canberra such lobbying tends to focus on the Senate, where the government's control has on occasion been weaker. The Whitlam Government, for example, lacked a majority in the Senate.

Most parliamentary activity by pressure groups in Canberra, however, relates not to legislation but to two of Parliament's other functions: criticizing the Executive and gathering information. Some groups use the services of friendly MPs to question a minister about administrative and policy issues during question time. Others give evidence and present submissions to inquiries that are held by parliamentary committees. The Senate gave a boost to the information-gathering function of parliament in the late 1960s with its greater use of select committees and its decision to set up a number of standing committees.

Litigation

Going to court is a tactic sometimes used by interest groups. The court system is available as a channel for interest-group activity mainly because the constitution gives the High Court the power of judicial review; that is, the power to rule on the constitutionality of legislation and decisions of the Federal and state governments. This gives interest groups whose claims have been rebuffed by Parliament, Cabinet, or the bureaucracy a further decision-making arena to turn to.

Not surprisingly, High Court litigation has been used by groups who wish to challenge a governmental decision. Employers' groups successfully used this tactic in the early decades of the century by sponsoring challenges to the constitutional validity of awards and rulings of the Commonwealth Arbitration Court as well as to industrial legislation passed by the Commonwealth Parliament.

Two considerable barriers exist to limit interest-group use of litigation. One is cost. Litigation can be extremely expensive, especially as the losers must generally pay the costs of the winning side as well as their own. The second is standing. This refers to the rules that determine whether a person or body initiating legal proceedings is an appropriate party to do so. These rules in Australia have required that the instigator must establish some personal stake or material interest in the subject matter of the case. If this cannot be done, the proceeding fails. The relevance of these rules is to make it difficult for groups (especially public interest groups) to initiate proceedings. The High Court, for instance, recently ruled that the Australian Conservation Foundation lacked standing to take action under environmental protection legislation to restrain Alcoa from erecting a smelter at Portland in Victoria.

Voters

Except for trade unions affiliated to the ALP, it is now rare for sectional groups to campaign openly for one political party at elections. When they do, it is almost always to oppose the party in office and it indicates a high level of dissatisfaction with the government. A recent example was the National Farmers' Federation's opposition to ALP candidates in twenty-two marginal rural electorates at the 1987 federal election.

In general, promotional rather than sectional groups employ electoral tactics. Causes promoted in this way have included opposition to state aid for private schools and to Australia's participation in the Vietnam War (in the 1960s); to uranium mining (in the 1970s); and to dams, legalized abortion, and gun control (in the 1980s). Single-issue groups have used the technique of asking their supporters to vote only for the candidates who have 'acceptable' views on the issue. The Victorian Right to Life Association has recently given a new twist to the technique: using what it calls 'punishment politics' it has campaigned intensively *against* candidates with pro-abortion views.

Public Campaigns

When a pressure group's direct approaches to the government or Parliament are unsuccessful, it often resorts to a public campaign in the hope that public opinion will achieve what it, through direct channels, was unable to secure. There are two types of public campaign. The first is a short-run campaign to influence a decision about to be taken or to a decision recently taken. The second is a longer-run campaign to create a favourable public image or slogan for a group, or to create a public demand for a certain type of policy.

The first of these types is most graphically illustrated by the campaign waged in 1947 against the Chifley Labour Government's proposed legislation for nationalizing the private banks. This was probably the most intense and concentrated campaign ever experienced in Australia.

The second type of campaign has been waged in the 1980s by the National Farmers' Federation. With a budget of $3.8 million, the NFF launched a massive series of advertisements stressing that agriculture affects the lives of all Australians. Its jingle 'You Can't Take the Country Out of Our Country' was heard in 40,000 radio and TV advertisements. The campaign was launched to counter what opinion polls showed to be an outdated and unsympathetic public image of farming.[3]

Small promotional groups often attempt to create the semblance of intense support for their cause by writing letters to newspapers and participating in talkback radio programmes. One index of the use of letter-writing campaigns is the size of the Prime Minister's morning mail. Not only is the number staggering (133,000, or over 500 letters each working day, in 1985–86) but a good proportion is orchestrated. In 1978, 40 per cent of the letters were 'campaign' letters dealing with such issues as uranium mining, pensions, family allowances, and whaling.[4]

---

[3] National Farmers' Federation, *Australian Agriculture* (Camberwell: National Farmers' Federation, 1987).

[4] See Dept. of the Prime Minister and Cabinet, *Annual Report 1985–86* (Canberra: AGPS, 1986), 27; *Annual Report 1978–79* (Canberra: AGPS, 1979), 25.

Political Parties

The only interest groups that are formally affiliated to a political party in Australia are the trade unions. Although the ACTU is not affiliated to the ALP, about 60 per cent of unionists belong to unions that are ALP-affiliated.[5] In New South Wales and Western Australia farmers' groups were formally affiliated to the Country Party until the 1940s. By then, however, these groups had come to view their affiliation as a hindrance to their pressure group activities with other parties. Likewise the Country Party itself realized that its organizational dependence on primary producers' associations was preventing it from becoming more broadly based. Accordingly the two sides agreed upon a friendly separation. Since then no farmers' groups have been formally affiliated to the successor of the Country Party—the National Party.

The Liberal Party and its predecessors, unlike the ALP and the National Party, have never had outside organizations as formal affiliates. There were, however, a number of clandestine cabals of big businessmen, which collected and distributed political funds for the Liberal Party's predecessors. This practice ended in 1945.

From time to time interest groups that are not affiliated to a political party will attempt to influence public policy indirectly by working through the party channel. An example was the Australian Council of Churches' successful campaign to get the ALP's Federal Conference to adopt a policy resolution recognizing aboriginal land (and mineral) rights.

HOW INFLUENTIAL ARE INTEREST GROUPS?

The concepts 'power' and 'influence' are among the most debated in political science. Because of these disputes, any question about interest-group influence hides a minefield of methodological difficulties. Each path towards a possible answer has its own risks. All that can be done here is to signpost some of these dangerous paths.

Inferring Influence from Outcomes

This is the sort of argument that says that the government's adoption of a policy demonstrates the influence wielded by the interest groups which had been campaigning for that policy. But

[5] D. W. Rawson, *Unions and Unionists in Australia*, rev. edn. (Sydney: Allen & Unwin, 1986), 49.

does it? Not necessarily, for the interest-group input may not have been the decisive factor that 'caused' the government to act. More important may have been a party's own policy commitment; the arguments put forward by departmental advisers; the climate of opinion; the views of foreign governments; and so on. Indeed, the government may well have used the group to give the appearance that it acted in accord with organized opinion. Arguments that infer influence from outcomes neglect to consider the full context of a decision; forget that pressure groups are often 'pressured groups'; and commit the logical fallacy of *post hoc ergo propter hoc* (i.e. of reasoning that if *Y* follows *X*, *Y* is therefore caused by *X*).

Inferring Influence from a Group's Internal Resources

This is the sort of argument that says trade unions are powerful: just look at the ACTU's massive membership and its annual income; its personal links with Prime Minister Hawke; its cohesion; and its highly professional staff and leadership. But arguments like these run into difficulties. First, God is not always on the side of the big battalions. To concentrate only on a group's aggregate resources would not enable us to explain cases where an asset-rich Goliath is defeated by a puny David. Second, it is not self-evident how different sorts of resources are to be measured and then totalled or how one group's 'total' is to be compared to another group's 'total'. How, for example, is membership to be compared with expertise, and expertise with cohesion? Third, the value to a group of certain resources depends on the strategy that group wishes to pursue in the political contest. It is a case of horses for courses. A reputation for always producing accurate scientific data may be more important than sheer membership size when giving evidence to a technical commission of inquiry. But membership size may be of crucial importance if the group is contemplating a letter-writing campaign. An intimate relationship with one political party may be counter-productive if that party's opponents are in office. Fourth, a focus on the group's internal assets (membership, wealth, staff expertise, cohesion, members' commitment) overlooks two assets that are external: access to government and socio-economic leverage.

Inferring Influence from Access

This is the sort of argument that suggests that 'insider' groups are more effective than 'outsider' ones. It is the argument that accounts for the political influence of big business by pointing to its representation on governmental advisory committees.[6] But access does not equal influence. Mere representation on advisory committees neither demonstrates nor guarantees that the interests represented share in the exercise of state power. There are a number of reasons for this. First, all the committees are multi-partite. Business representatives, for example, have to compete not only with bureaucrats but with the representatives of other interests. Secondly, their proceedings can be used by departmental officials to engineer support for departmentally formed policies. In the 1960s the Manufacturing Industry Advisory Council 'became as much a departmental arm as a voice of industry within the government'.[7] Thirdly, having access to one's 'own' department or membership on a high-level standing advisory committee does not ensure that the group will be listened to (or consulted), even on issues of fundamental importance to its members.

Inferring Influence by Observing who Prevails in Decision-Making

According to Dahl,[8] A has power over B if A can get B to do something B would not otherwise do. If an interest group (A) can, despite governmental resistance, get the government (B) to shift its position, the group can be said to have exercised influence. This behavioural interpretation has come under much criticism. One criticism concerns the difficulty of gaining conclusive evidence: 'Although we can discover that A wanted B to take a certain action, and we can observe that A has certain resources of potential power and used the available means to bring them to bear on B, and we can observe that B took the action that A intended, we still cannot be sure that B would not have taken the action without A's efforts.[9] This criticism is obviously less valid in cases where a government is forced to back down. Here it is more certain that the government would not have suffered the humiliation of conceding defeat were it not for A's efforts.

Another criticism concerns influence that cannot be observed by considering only the formal decision-making process. An interest group may, for example, be able to prevent a threatening issue from even getting on to the political agenda. Another group may have influence although it does not participate in the decision-making

[6] J. Playford, *Neo-Capitalism in Australia* (Melbourne: Arena, 1969), 7.

[7] L. Glezer, *Tariff Politics* (Melbourne: Melbourne University Press, 1982), 247.

[8] R. A. Dahl, *Modern Political Analysis*, 4th edn. (Englewood Cliffs, NJ: Prentice Hall, 1983), chs. 3 and 4.

[9] M. Derthick, *The National Guard in Politics* (Cambridge, Mass.: Harvard University Press, 1965), 7.

process. This occurs when a government takes that group's interests into account by anticipating what would happen if those interests were ignored. To deal with such situations, some political analysts have rejected behavioural interpretations of power in favour of ones that give priority to a group's socio-economic leverage.

Inferring Influence from Structural Position in the Economy

This is the sort of argument that says that the political power of producer groups lies in the strategic positions they occupy in the economy. This structural position gives them the ability to disrupt economic life and causes governments to be mindful of the threat of such action. Such arguments have been applied to trade unions[10] and to business.[11] Unions exercise socio-economic leverage by threatening to strike; business by threatening an 'investment strike'. More generally, business exercises structural influence because its employment and investment decisions affect the health of the economy, which in turn affects the government's electoral chances. Governments consequently anxiously court 'business confidence'.

Useful as these contributions are in pointing to a structural bias in the politics of interest groups, they fail to account for variations in business (or trade union) power over time and between countries. Their analysis is too blunt for this. These problems have led a number of Marxist analysts to examine the mechanisms whereby the class interests of capital are accorded disproportionate weight by governments. In doing so they have brought organizational questions and interest groups back into their analyses, particularly in their discussions of corporatism.[12]

Corporatism and Interest Group/Government Relations

Some commentators assert that interest group/government relations in Australia are now corporatist. Katharine West[13] writes of a corporatist 'revolution' having occurred under the Hawke Government. Other commentators, while avoiding the impression that the

[10] S. E. Finer, 'The Political Power of Organised Labour', *Government and Opposition*, 8/4 (1973), 391–406.
[11] C. Lindblom, *Politics and Markets* (New York: Basic Books, 1977), 170–233.
[12] See L. Panitch, 'The Development of Corporatism in Liberal Democracies', in P. C. Schmitter and G. Lehmbruch (eds.), *Trends Towards Corporatist Intervention* (Beverly Hills, Calif.: Sage, 1981); and C. Offe, *Disorganised Capitalism* (Oxford: Polity Press, 1985), chs. 7 and 8.
[13] K. West, *The Revolution in Australian Politics* (Ringwood, Victoria: Penguin, 1984).

Hawke Government has wrought a wholesale shift from pluralist to corporatist politics, use the idea of corporatism to explain aspects of recent policy-making, such as the prices and income Accord between the ACTU and the ALP.[14]

Two basic uses underlie most political science discussions of corporatism. One treats corporatism as a way in which producer interests are structured: here the stress is on each functional area (e.g. business, agriculture) possessing a peak organization that has the authority to commit its members and is granted a representation monopoly by the state. The other treats corporatism as a way in which interest groups are incorporated into the policy-making process: here the stress is on collaboration between antagonistic producer interests and their joint participation with government officials in the making and administering of public policy (the typical form involving tripartite co-operation between the state, business, and labour).

Corporatist analysis has been valuable in focusing attention on the links between economics and politics; on the interpretation of governments and interest groups; on interest group collusion and collaboration; on the unequal participation and influence of producer groups in the making and implementation of public policy; and on the ways groups (especially trade unions) are co-opted by governments to exercise control over their members. To this extent a corporatist approach has been a valuable corrective to much pluralist imagery of a multiplicity of competing groups, each 'representing' its members, and exerting one-way pressure on governments.

How valid is it to portray interest group/government relations in Australia as 'corporatist'? Three aspects need to be examined: 'consensus politics', preconditions for corporatism, and the shift from pluralism.

The Hawke Government's 'consensus politics'

'Corporatists' point to the Accord, the Economic Summit, and the Economic Planning Advisory Council (EPAC) as evidence of corporatist structures and arrangements in Australia. Superficially these arrangements seem to illustrate Panitch's notion of corporatist practices—ones that 'integrate trade unions with the state/executive bureaucracy and associations of business in forming legitimating

[14] See R. Stewart, 'The Politics of the Accord: Does Corporatism Explain It?', *Politics*, 20/1 (1984), 26–36; and R. Gerritsen, 'The Necessity of "Corporatism": The Case of the Hawke Government', *Politics*, 21/1 (1986), 45–54.

and administering public policy'.[15] But closer examination shows these arrangements hardly support a corporatist interpretation.[16]

- business is not a party to the Accord;
- thus the Accord is not an instance of mutual collaboration among interest groups;
- business was not represented by a single group at the Summit or on EPAC;
- EPAC does not make and administer economic policy: it advises on policy and legitimizes policy made elsewhere;
- EPAC is not strictly tripartite: consumers and the welfare sector are represented; business representation is fragmented; and government representation is divided between federal, state, and local governments;
- EPAC is prevented by the Accord from considering incomes policy (said to be a 'core domain' of corporatism);
- business is unwilling for political reasons to be a partner to tripartite arrangements between the ACTU and a *Labour* government;
- the Accord is essentially an agreement between organized labour and a *political party* (not 'the state'); and it has been legitimized 'through the party and parliamentary system' (not through private tripartite interaction).[17]

The Preconditions for Corporatism

Corporatism as a form of policy formation presupposes a strong, cohesive government able to negotiate with producer groups. As a form of interest mediation it presupposes single, cohesive peak organizations able to negotiate on behalf of their constituents. In Australia, however, governmental and group structures are in many ways incompatible with corporatism:

- federalism fractures and divides 'the state'. Many powers are shared between the Commonwealth Government and the states
- the constitution limits the Commonwealth Government's powers over incomes policies. This is because the principal agency for a national wages policy is not the government but

---

[15] L. Panitch, 'The Development of Corporatism in Liberal Democracies', in P. C. Schmitter and G. Lehmbruch (eds.), *Trends Towards Corporatist Intervention* (Beverly Hills, Calif.: Sage, 1981), 27.

[16] See G. Singleton, 'The Economic Planning Advisory Council: The Reality of Consensus', *Politics*, 20/1 (1985), 12–25; D. McEachern, 'Corporatism and Business Responses to the Hawke Government', *Politics*, 21/1 (1986), 19–27.

[17] Singleton, 'The Economic Planning Advisory Council', 22–4.

the Arbitration Commission, whose quasi-judicial status gives it an independence from governmental direction
* many other statutory bodies are also independent of government (i.e., Cabinet or ministerial) direction
* the Arbitration Commission's use of adversarial procedures and public hearings is inconsistent with the collaborative, closed-door, tripartite procedures characteristic of corporatism
* the High Court and the Senate have the constitutional power to check and balance the government of the day
* business is organizationally disunited. No single group has achieved the authority to speak for business.

A Shift from a Pluralist Pattern

It is factually wrong to argue that, until the Hawke Government, Australia had a 'pluralist kind of pressure group politics' where groups 'were clearly separate from the government they were trying to pressure'.[18] Such an assertion ignores the close (and often closed) clientele relations that have existed between some government departments and 'their' interest groups; the Department of Veterans' Affairs and the RSL; and, during the Menzies years, the Department of Health and the Australian Medical Association. Far from being 'clearly separate', these groups were said to be in 'co-operative partnership' with their sponsor departments. It also ignores the distinctive place in Australian politics of special bodies designed to cater to the needs of interest groups. Examples include the numerous bodies established to market Australian primary products. In all cases, the relevant farmers' groups are represented on, and in some cases they control, the board.

To treat interest group/government relations as being *either* pluralist *or* corporatist is misleading in three ways. First, many frequently observed group/government relations cannot be easily labelled as pluralist or corporatist because they share characteristics of both. Examples include policy committees, bargaining between producer groups and governments, and clientele relations between departments and the groups they serve. Pluralism and corporatism are not mutually exclusive. More useful is the image of group/government relations as a continuum with competitive pressure-group 'contestation' at one end and collaborative corporatism at the other, with various forms of 'corporate pluralism' lying between.[19]

[18] K. West, *The Revolution in Australian Politics* (Ringwood, Victoria: Penguin, 1984), 3.
[19] C. Crouch, 'Pluralism and the New Corporatism: A Rejoinder', *Political Studies*, 31 (1983), 452–60.

Second, pluralist and corporatist relations can coexist in the same political system. Corporate arrangements might apply, for example, to trade unions and business on questions of incomes policy, while pluralist politics will characterize other issues such as abortion, gun control, and conservation. Finally, to think of interest group/ government relations as either pluralist or corporatist runs the risk of exaggerating the role of interest groups in the policy process. In some policy areas interest groups may play *no* significant role at all. Defence, foreign policy, and fiscal policy are such areas in Australia.

16

PRESSURE GROUPS IN JAPAN

KAREL VAN WOLFEREN

PRESSURE GROUPS IN JAPAN

A popular theory about how government policies develop holds that 'interest groups' or 'pressure groups' manage to 'capture', as it were, the segment of the public service whose co-operation they need. One Japanese group that, quite exceptionally, has done exactly this is the Japan Medical Association (JMA), which since the 1950s has won great prominence among Japan's pressure groups by functioning as such groups are expected to function outside Japan—only more so. Unlike most of its fellows, it has tended to confront the bureaucrats rather than accommodate them in exchange for favours.

Led until 1982 by a forceful personality, Takemi Taro, it created an obedient rank and file while using aggressive methods such as lambasting the government in full-page newspaper advertisements in order to dominate decision-making concerning medical matters. It has had a major voice in banning oral contraceptives, thus preventing any decline in the lucrative abortion industry. It has run its own candidates in national elections, and bankrolls a number of regular LDP candidates.

The JMA can stop the import of particular medical equipment, if this threatens to eliminate the need for lucrative cures; it can, on arbitrary grounds, prevent the use of medicines and methods of treatment; and it protects the widespread racketeering made possible by the health insurance system. Not only is the income of Japanese doctors from the health insurance scheme calculated partly by the quantity of medicine they prescribe, but they themselves have the right to sell this medicine in their offices. This has led to corrupt relations with the pharmaceutical industry, to an alarming degree of over-medication and to some very rich doctors.

Since the departure of Takemi Taro, the power of the JMA has declined, but it is one of the minor components of the System.

Reprinted in abridged form from Karel van Wolferen, *The Enigma of Japanese Power: People and Politics in a Stateless Nation* (London: Macmillan, 1989), pp. 53–7. Permission requested.

Health and Welfare Ministry officials have become so used to bowing to the wishes of the association that the laws they draft still seem to have been formulated by the doctors themselves. It is significant that the one major exception among Japanese pressure groups, functioning the way Westerners expect pressure groups to function, should do this in an extreme fashion. The practitioners of medicine have taken over the very area of government that ought to be controlling them in order to safeguard medicine as a public service.

Post-war society saw a mushrooming of pressure groups: of housewives, families of the war dead, veterans, wounded veterans, former landlords (who lost their property in post-war land reform), returnees from former colonies, and brothel owners—to mention only the best known. They became a familiar subject of newspaper comment in the mid-1950s, especially after brothel owners formed the All-Japan Association for Prevention of Venereal Diseases in an attempt to block passage of the Anti-Prostitution Law (they failed, so that roughly half a million ladies of the night had to find new descriptions for their profession). A very successful pressure group, drawing press attention, was Chuseiren, later to become the main federation of small and medium-sized companies.

These new actors on the political stage caused mixed feelings. In 1958 two veterans' groups succeeded in having the budget for war pensions increased by 30 billion yen, while the JMA managed to reserve an extra 21 billion yen. Japanese political commentators and editorial opinion interpreted such things as undermining the democratic political process; the pressure groups were accused of lack of concern for the general welfare, and of selfishly pushing measures from which only they would benefit. Ironically enough, at the very time in the 1960s when Japanese were seeing the pressure groups as undemocratic, Western observers were citing them as the best proof that 'democracy' was finally gaining a foothold in Japan. Even in the 1980s they are still seen as a force for greater pluralism.

A closer look reveals that it is a rather odd kind of pluralism they serve. With the exception of the doctors, the 'capturing' in Japan takes place largely in the wrong direction, with officials and the LDP making use of the groups in exchange for certain subsidies and a minimal degree of accommodation. When all groups that have close organizational ties with the administrators are eliminated, the category of genuine pressure groups is very small. It diminishes still further if one excludes those with semi-official ties to other major components of the System. Finally, one is left with a core of groups the majority of which have one leg in the camp of the openly anti-System activists and occasionally battle with riot police to demonstrate the fact that they will not be bought and cannot be incorporated in any way. The farmer–radical-activist coalition which continues to block expansion of the new Tokyo International Airport at Naita is a prime example.

POLLUTION ACTIVISTS

Among the post-war pressure groups that have stayed outside the System, the most successful—measured by the extent to which the System has had to accommodate them—are those that have fought on behalf of the victims of industrial poisoning. Even so, it took some ten years before pollution problems received serious consideration in Japan. Only when cats that had eaten mercury-laden fish began to have spasms and jump into the sea did the problems of Minamata (the municipality that was later to become a symbol of environmental pollution the world over) first attract some limited attention from the press. Several years more passed before the plight of the human victims became a national issue. They had been rapidly increasing in number, dying sometimes of sheer exhaustion as a result of the spasms caused by their injured nervous systems.

The corporation responsible for dumping mercury waste into the sea maintained that there was no connection, and hired gangsters to manhandle petitioning victims and their families. The victims themselves, mainly from poor villages, were ostracized. The bringers of bad tidings—doctors who were studying the Minamata cases and similar mercury-poisoning cases in Niigata—were at first discredited. The Kumamoto University research team saw their findings suppressed and research money cut off. A campaign was waged against a certain Dr Hagino Noboru who was treating patients in Toyama prefecture for the so-called *itai-itai* ('ouch, ouch') disease, a mysterious affliction in which bones became so brittle, owing to cadmium that had been allowed to seep into rice paddies, that they fractured at many places. The suppression of evidence and the hiring of doctors to claim lack of scientific grounds for the complaints were repeated in other parts of Japan until riots, the storming of the factory responsible for the mercury waste in Minamata, a national press campaign, and foreign publicity finally made such approaches untenable.

The first lawsuit on behalf of pollution victims, filed in 1967 by leftist lawyers, was quickly followed by three more. In the early 1970s, prodded by this legal action and popular discontent with the badly polluted air of the capital region, officialdom, together with some politicians and businessmen, concluded that some measures

had become inevitable. Strict industrial regulations were introduced; overnight, it became fashionable to decry industrial expansion achieved at the expense of the living environment. Courts of
justice, too, though they took ten or more years to conclude trials,
were beginning to award damages to victims. But experience in most
cases showed the judiciary playing only a subsidiary role; the
System had responded to pressure caused by an outcry greatly
amplified by the press. Its response was evidence that it can be
moved to right wrongs, provided the wrongs are sufficiently eye-
catching and can awaken widespread public indignation.

In the late 1970s the anti-pollution campaign seemed to portend a
new kind of opposition to the way Japan was being managed, and
citizens' movements were thought to have created permanent
changes by stimulating political awareness on the regional level.
Opposition mayors were elected. But in the mean time oppositionist
policy programmes were adopted by LDP-run municipalities. In
LDP eyes, the opposition had been absorbed. By the mid-1980s the
activist groups were comparing themselves to 'wind-chimes in
winter'—an allusion to the small bells hung outside windows in
summer, whose tinkling, thought refreshing at the time, becomes
irritatingly irrelevant in winter. The number of cities with opposition mayors declined from 136 in 1974 to 60 in 1988. Hasty anti-
pollution measures, an adjustment of election rhetoric by local LDP
candidates and a reconfirmation of the LDP as the sole fount of
plenty with regard to costly projects had brought to an effective halt
grass-roots opposition to the status quo.

PRESSURE GROUPS AS ELECTION CAMPAIGN STAFF

While the consumer and anti-pollution activists have gradually
faded out of the political picture, other types of pressure group have
remained politically important, not because of any changes in the
political process achieved by their 'pressure', but for the work they
do on behalf of LDP politicians.

Since the government party has almost no grass-roots organization, candidates for parliamentary elections must rely on personal
organizations of supporters, known as *koenkai*. In most cases the
chances of an incumbent staying in parliament relate first and
foremost to the membership and influence of the *koenkai* that he
keeps going between elections. And almost from the moment that
pressure groups made their appearance it was clear that they would,
if properly treated, make ideal *koenkai*. Thus it comes about that
pressure groups are right up front in Japanese political life,

canvassing votes, collecting funds, and performing all manner of odd jobs for individual LDP candidates.

For the LDP parliamentarian friendly connections with various ministerial bureaux are crucial in achieving such a relationship with a pressure group, since the politician must prove, by at least token measures, that he is doing something in return. In speaking to his constituents the incumbent rarely beats around the bush. Should they want a new airport, they are assured that he has the best entrée, or *paipu* (from the English word 'pipe'), to the Transport Ministry and the Finance Ministry; if wider roads are needed, or a new bridge, then he has more friends at the Ministry of Construction than any other candidates. In the multi-member constituency, the LDP politician compares his access to bureaucrats with that of his fellow LDP members; and everyone understands that the minority parties do not have a *paipu* into the ministries.

The party 'colleagues' against whom an LDP candidate fights in parliamentary elections almost always belong to different LDP *habatsu* (cliques). Thus it is important for *habatsu* leaders to cultivate good relations with national umbrella organizations controlling local pressure and petition groups. This is why the veterans' organizations, the association of war wounded and the organization of the families of war dead continue to be a significant force pressuring the LDP to endorse and participate in controversial symbolic activities extolling the military past. A politician whom I accompanied on his initial round of a hamlet recently added to his constituency made a special point of first seeking out the house of a man without legs—the local representative of the association of war wounded.

BUREAUCRATIC EXTENSIONS

Many pressure groups will start by going directly to the officials whose co-operation they need for their original purposes. Relatively weak regional industrial and trade associations have used the bureaucracy 'to help them strengthen their organizational foundations through government legislation legalizing their status and providing for compulsory membership'. Pressure groups, established to promote specific agricultural or other economic interests, will find open doors at the ministries that must deal with those interests. If a group appears large and potentially powerful enough, it will be actively courted by the officials. In return for having its wishes taken into account it provides detailed information about conditions, personalities, and important events in its locality.

It thus becomes part of the 'radar' whereby the bureaucrats effectively steer the System as a whole. Since the information moves in only one direction, towards Tokyo, the administrators gain firmer control over segments of Japanese life that have hitherto been less effectively incorporated in the System. And this increased control is often exercised through the pressure groups in question.

NOTES ON CONTRIBUTORS

ARTHUR BENTLEY published *The Process of Government* in 1908. He is often regarded as the founder of pressure group studies because of his thesis that groups are central to the governmental process.

JACOB A. BUKSTI was formerly Associate Professor of Political Science at the University of Århus and has directed several research projects on Danish interest organizations, agricultural politics, and labour market politics. He then spent a period as Senior Political Advisor to the leadership of the Danish Social Democratic Party and was Head of the party's Political and Economic Staff. He has written several books on interest groups in Denmark, including *Et enigt landbrug? Konflict og samarbejde mellem landbrugets organisationer* (1974), *Danske Organisationers Hvem-Hvad-Hvor* (with L. N. Johansen), (1977), and *Organisationer under forandring* (1980).

TERRY COX is Senior Lecturer in Sociology at the University of Strathclyde, and has specialized in the study of the sociology of Eastern Europe. He is currently analysing the politics and sociology of privatization in Eastern Europe. He is the author of *Rural Sociology in the Soviet Union* (1979), *Kritsman and the Agrarian Marxists* (1984) (with Gary Littlejohn), and *The Peasants, Class and Capitalism* (1986).

LEWIS J. EDINGER was formerly Professor of Government and a member of the Institute on Western Europe, at Columbia University. He has written several books on German Politics including *West German Politics*; *West German Armament*; *Germany Rejoins the Powers*; *Politics in Germany*, and *Politics in West Germany*.

PETER HALL is a Professor in the Centre for European Studies, Harvard University, and is a specialist in political economy, comparative politics, and the politics and sociology of Western Europe. He is the author of *The Politics of State Intervention in Britain and France* (1986).

GRANT JORDAN is Professor of Politics at the University of Aberdeen. Together with Jeremy J. Richardson he initiated a series of research projects on policy communities in the late 1970s and they have co-authored a number of works utilizing the concept, including *Governing Under Pressure* (1979), *British Politics and the Policy Process* (1987), and *Government and Pressure Groups in Britain* (1987). He is also editor of *The Commercial Lobbyists* (1991) and author of *Engineers and Professional Self-Regulation: From the Finneston Committee to the Engineering Council* (1992).

RICHARD KIMBER is a Lecturer in Politics at the University of Keele. He is co-editor of the *Journal of Theoretical Politics* (with Jan-Erik Lane and Elinor Ostrom). He has undertaken empirical studies of interest groups (with Jeremy J. Richardson) and more recently has been involved in conceptual and empirical work on democracy and democratization using artificial intelligence techniques. He also takes an active interest in political science computing within the three main professional organizations: APSA, ECPR, and PSA, and is a member of the Advisory Committee of SocInfo.

LUCA LANZALACO teaches Political Science and Organization Theory at the Bocconi University of Milan and the University of Bologna and has conducted research on political parties, election strategies, and interest groups in Italy. He recently published a book about the Italian Confederation of Industry in a comparative and historical perspective.

TREVOR MATTHEWS is Associate Professor in the Department of Government and Public Administration at the University of Sydney. His recent publications have dealt with organized business in Australia, Astralia's trade policy, and élite attitudes to Australian foreign policy. He is the co-author of *The Japanese Connection: Australian Leaders' Attitudes towards Japan and the Australia–Japan Relationship* (1988). His current research is on the Japanese and South Korean experience with strategic trade policy.

SONIA MAZEY is a lecturer in Politics and Fellow of Churchill College, Cambridge. She is a specialist in French politics and European integration and is co-editor (with M. Newman) of *Mitterand's France* (1987), co-author (with V. Lintner) of *The European Community: Economic and Political Aspects* (1991), and co-editor (with Jeremy J. Richardson) of *Lobbying in the European Community* (1993). Together with Jeremy J. Richardson she is currently directing a project on interest groups and European integration.

MANCUR OLSON is Professor of Economics of the University of Maryland. He is the author of several works including what is probably the most important modern theoretical study of pressure groups, *The Logic of Collective Action, Public Goods and The Theory of Groups* (1965), and an equally important work on the causes of the decline of nations, *The Rise and Decline of Nations: Economic Growth, Stagflation and Social Rigidities* (1982).

A. PAUL PROSS is Professor of Political Science at the University of Dalhousie, Nova Scotia. He is the author, co-author, and editor of a number of books and various articles on Canadian policy processes, natural resource administration, pressure group behaviour, and government publishing. His most recent books are *Group Politics and Public Policy* (1992), (with Susan McCorquodale), *Economic Resurgence and the Constitutional Agenda* (1987), and (with I. Christie and J. A. Yogis) *Commission of Inquiry* (1990).

JEREMY J. RICHARDSON is Director of the European Public Policy Institute and Professor of European Integration at the University of Warwick. He has collaborated with Richard Kimber on empirical studies of interest groups. Together with Grant Jordan, he initiated a series of research projects on policy communities in the late 1970s and they have co-authored a number of works utilizing the concept, including, *Governing Under Pressure* (1979), *British Politics and the Policy Process* (1987), and *Government and Pressure Groups in Britain* (1987). He is also the editor of

Policy Styles in Western Europe (1982), co-editor (with E. Damgaard and P. Gerlich) of *The Politics of Economic Crisis—Lessons from Western Europe* (1989), and co-editor (with Sonia Mazey) of *Lobbying in the European Community* (forthcoming). Together with Sonia Mazey, he is currently directing a project on interest groups and European integration.

GRAHAM WILSON is Professor of Political Science of the University of Wisconsin-Madison and was formerly at the Department of Government, University of Essex. He is the author of several books on British and American politics, including *Interest Groups in the USA* (1981), *Business and Politics: A Comparative Introduction* (1985), and *Interest Groups* (1991).

KAREL VAN WOLFEREN has lived and worked as a foreign correspondent in Japan for over twenty-five years and is a correspondent for NRC Handelsbad.

YAEL YISHAI is Professor of Political Science at the University of Haifa and has conducted many studies of the role and influence of interest groups in Israel. She is the author of several books on interest groups including *Land of Paradoxes: Interest Groups in Israeli Politics* (1991).

SELECT BIBLIOGRAPHY

In addition to those works reproduced in this volume, the following texts are useful sources of both theory and empirical material relating to pressure groups:

1. THEORETICAL WORKS

Group Theory

ALMOND, Gabriel, 'A Comparative Study of Interest Groups and the Political Process', *American Political Science Review*, 52 (1958), 270–82.
—— 'Corporatism, Pluralism and Professional Memory', *World Politics*, 25/2 (1983).
DAHL, R. A., *A Preface to Democratic Theory* (Chicago, Ill.: Chicago University Press, 1956).
—— *Who Governs?* (New Haven, Conn.: Yale University Press).
—— *Dilemmas of Pluralist Democracy* (New Haven, Conn.: Yale University Press, 1982).
—— and LINDBLOM, C. E., *Politics, Economics and Welfare* (New York: Harper & Row, 1976).
GARSON, David G., *Group Theories of Politics* (Beverly Hills, Calif.: Sage, 1978).
KEY, V. O. (Jr.), *Politics, Parties and Pressure Groups*, 5th edn. (New York: Thames Crowell & Co., 1965).
LINDBLOM, C. E., *The Intelligence of Democracy* (New York: Free Press, 1965).
—— *Politics and Markets* (New York: Basic Books, 1977).
OLSON, Jr., Mancur, *The Rise and Decline of Nations: Economic Growth, Stagflation and Social Rigidities* (New Haven, Conn.: Yale University Press, 1982).
SCHATTSCHNEIDER, E. E., *The Semi-Sovereign People: A Realist's View of Democracy in America* (New York: Holt, Rinehart & Winston, 1960).

Studies on Corporatism and Policy Networks

ATKINSON, Michael M. and COLEMAN, William D., 'Strong States and Weak States: Sectoral Policy Networks in Advanced Capitalist Economies', *British Journal of Political Science*, 19 (1989), 47–67.
GRANT, Wyn (ed.), *The Political Economy of Corporatism* (London: Macmillan, 1985).
HECLO, Hugh, 'Issue Networks and the Executive Establishment', in A. King (ed.), *The New American Political System* (Washington, DC: American Enterprise Institute, 1978).

HEISLER, Martin O., 'Corporate Pluralism: Where is the Theory?', *Scandinavian Political Studies*, NS, 2/3 (1979).

LEHMBRUCH, Gerhard, 'The Organization of Society, Administrative Strategies and Policy Networks: Elements of a Development Theory of Interest Systems', in Roland M. Czada and A. Windhoff-Heritier (eds.), *Political Choice: Institutional Rules, and the Limits of Rationality* (Frankfurt: Campus Verlag, 1991).

—— and SCHMITTER, P. (eds.), *Patterns of Corporatist Policy-Making* (London: Sage, 1982).

SCHMITTER, P. C. and LEHMBRUCH, G. (eds.), *Trends Towards Corporatist Intervention* (London: Sage, 1979).

—— 'Still the Century of Corporatism?', *Review of Politics*, 85 (1970), 85–131.

—— 'Corporatism is Dead! Long Live Corporatism!', *Government & Opposition*, 24/1 (1989), 54–73.

STREECK, Wolfgang and SCHMITTER, Philippe C. (eds.), *Private Interest Government: Beyond Market and State* (London: Sage, 1985).

2. COMPARATIVE STUDIES

BALL, Alan R. and MILLARD, Frances, *Pressure Politics in Industrial Societies: A Comparative Introduction* (Atlantic Highlands, NJ: Humanities Press, 1987).

BAUMGARTNER, Frank R. and WALKER, Jack L., 'Educational Policy-making and Interest Group Structure in France and the United States', *Comparative Politics* (Apr. 1989).

BERGER, Suzanne D. (ed.), *Organizing Interests in Western Europe: Pluralism, Corporatism and the Transformation of Politics* (Cambridge: Cambridge University Press, 1981).

ERHMANN, Henry, *Interest Groups on Four Continents* (Pittsburgh, Pa.: Pittsburgh University Press, 1958).

HEISLER, Martin O. and KVAVIK, Robert B., 'Patterns of European Politics: The European Polity', in Martin O. Heisler (ed.), *Politics in Europe: Structures and Processes in Some Postindustrial Democracies* (New York: David McKay & Co., 1974).

LEHMBRUCH, Gerhard, 'Concertation and the Structures of Corporatist Networks', in John H. Goldthorpe (ed.), *Order and Conflict in Contemporary Capitalism* (Oxford: Oxford University Press, 1989), 60–80.

LIJPHART, Arend and CREPAZ, Markus, 'Corporatism and Consensus Democracy in Eighteen Countries: Conceptual and Empirical Linkages', *British Journal of Political Science*, 21 (1991), 235–56.

LYNN, Leonard H. and MCKEOWN, Timothy J., *Organizing Business: Trade Associations in America and Japan* (Washington, DC: American Enterprise Institute, 1988).

RICHARDSON, Jeremy J. (ed.), *Policy Styles in Western Europe* (London: Allen & Unwin, 1982).

WILSON, Graham K., *Interest Groups* (Oxford: Basil Blackwell, 1991).

3. WESTERN EUROPE (COUNTRY STUDIES)

United Kingdom

GRANT, Wyn, *Pressure Groups, Politics and Democracy in Britain* (London: Philip Alan, 1989).

JORDAN, A. G. and RICHARDSON, J. J., *Government and Pressure Groups in Britain* (Oxford: Clarendon Press, 1987).

RICHARDSON, Jeremy J. and JORDAN, A. G. (eds.), *Governing Under Pressure: The Policy Process in a Post-Parliamentary Democracy* (Oxford: Martin Robertson & Co., 1979).

France

ASHFORD, D., *Policy and Politics in France: Living with Uncertainty* (Philadelphia, Pa.: Temple University Press, 1982).

HOFFMAN, Stanley, *et al.*, *In Search of France* (New York: Harper & Row, 1963).

MÉNY, Yves, *Government and Politics in Western Europe: Britain, France, Italy, and West Germany* (Oxford: Oxford University Press, 1990), ch. 3.

WILSON, F. J., 'The Trade Unions and Economic Policy During the Mitterrand Presidency 1981–84', in H. Machin and V. Wright (eds.), *Economics ad Politics in Mitterrand's France* (London: Pinter, 1985).

WILSON, Frank, *Interest Group Politics in France* (Cambridge: Cambridge University Press, 1987).

WRIGHT, Vincent, 'The State and the Pressure Groups', in Vincent Wright, *The Government and Politics of France* (London: Unwin Hyman, 1989), 254–93.

Germany

BEYME, K. VON, 'The Changing Relations between Trade Unions and the Social Democratic Party in West Germany', *Government and Opposition* (Autumn, 1978).

DYSON, K., 'The Politics of Economic Management in West Germany', in W. Paterson and G. Smith, *The West German Model: Perspectives on a Stable State* (London: Frank Cass, 1981).

ESSE, Joseph, 'State, Business and Trade Unions in West Germany after the "Political Wende" ', *West European Politics*, 9 (1982), 198–214.

SMITH, Gordon, *Democracy in West Germany* (Aldershot: Gower, 1986), 211–35.

Italy

LAPALOMBARA, J., *Interest Groups in Italian Politics* (Princeton, NJ: Princeton University Press, 1964).

MARTINELLI, A., 'Organized Business and Italian Politics: Confindustria and the Christian Democrats in the Postwar Period', *West European Politics* (Oct. 1979), 67–87.

Austria

GERLICH, P., GRANDE, E., and MÜLLER, W., 'Corporatism in Crisis: Stability and Change of Social Partnership in Austria', *Political Studies*, 36/2 (1982), 209–23.

Norway

OLSEN, Johan P., *Organized Democracy: Political Institutions in a Welfare State: The Case of Norway* (Oslo: Universitetsforlaget, 1983).

European Community

MAZEY, Sonia P. and RICHARDSON, Jeremy J. (eds.), *Lobbying in the European Community* (Oxford: Oxford University Press, 1993).

STREECK, Wolfgang and SCHMITTER, Philippe C., 'From National Corporatism to Transnational Pluralism: Organized Interests in the Single European Market', *Politics & Society*, 19/2 (1991), 133–64.

4. UNITED STATES AND CANADA

United States

FRITSCHLER, A. Lee, *Smoking and Politics: Policymaking and the Federal Bureaucracy* (Englewood Cliffs, NJ: Prentice Hall, 1969).

GAIS, Thomas L., PETERSON, Mark A., and WALTER, Jack L., 'Interest Groups, Iron Triangles, and Representative Institutions in American National Government', *British Journal of Political Science*, 14 (1984), 161–85.

HREBENAR, Ronald J. and SCOTT, Ruth K. (1990), *Interest Group Politics in America*, 2nd edn. (Englewood Cliffs, NJ: Prentice Hall, 1990).

LOWI, Theodore J., *The End of Liberalism: The Second Republic of the United States*, 2nd edn. (New York: W. W. Norton, 1979).

McFARLAND, Andrew S., *Common Cause: Lobbying in the Public Interest* (Chattan, NJ: Chattan House Publishers Inc., 1984).

—— 'Interest Groups and Theories of Power in America', *British Journal of Political Science*, 17 (1987), 129–47.

—— 'Interest Groups and Political Time: Cycles in America', *British Journal of Political Science*, 21/3 (1991), 257–84.

SALISBURY, Robert H., 'Interest Representation: The Dominance of Institutions', *American Political Science Review*, 78 (1984), 64–76.

—— HEINZ, John P., LAUMAN, Edward O., and NELSON, Robert L., 'Who Works with Whom? Interest Group Alliances and Opposition', *American Political Science Review*, 81 (1987), 1217–34.

SCHLOZMAN, Kay L., 'What Accent the Heavenly Chorus? Political Equality and the American Pressure System', *Journal of Politics*, 46 (1984), 1006–32.

—— TIERNEY, John T., *Organized Interests and American Democracy* (New York: Harper & Row, 1986).

TRUMAN, David B., *The Governmental Process: Political Interests and Public Opinion* (New York: Knopf, 1951).

WALKER, Jack L., 'The Origins and Maintenance of Interest Groups in America', *American Political Science Review*, 77 (1983), 390–406.

Canada

PROSS, A. Paul, *Group Politics and Public Policy* (Toronto: Oxford University Press, 1986).

5. OTHER COUNTRIES AND SOCIAL MOVEMENTS

DAHLERUP, D. (ed.), *The New Women's Movement: Feminism and Political Power in Europe and the USA* (Beverly Hills: Calif., Sage, 1986).

HASE, Toshio, 'Japan's Environmental Movement', in T. O'Riordan and K. Turner (eds.), *Progress in Resource Management and Environmental Planning*, ii. (Chichester: John Wiley, 1980).

PEMPEL, J. J. and TSUNEKAWA, K., 'Corporatism without Labour? The Japanese Anomaly', in P. Schmitter and G. Lehmbruch (eds.), *Trends Towards Corporatist Intervention* (London: Sage, 1979).

RÜDIG, W. (ed.), *Green Politics* (Edinburgh: Edinburgh University Press, 1991).

INDEX

ex-Communist Party (Italy) 123
executive branch 91, 132, 173, 184, 231,
    233-4
  devolution of 133
  fusion with legislature 89

factions 27, 78, 82, 173, 180
Fareri, P. 127 n.
Farm Bureau (US) 139, 140
farmers 4, 133, 140, 141, 221, 236
  angry 166
  benefits to, at the expense of
    consumers 6
  collective/common interests 26, 137
  large 164
  movements/organizations 8, 25, 59
  radical-activist coalition 247
  Socialist-leaning unions 165
Farneti, P. 118 n.
Fascists 114, 115, 117
FDP (Free Democratic Party) 183
Fedele, M. 124 n.
Federal Diet, see parliaments
Federal Elections Commission
    (US) 131, 132
federalism 3, 13, 15, 231
Fédération des Conseils de Parents
    d'Élèves 170
Federation of Danish Industries 102,
    104, 107
feminism 114, 227
FEN, see France (unions)
Ferraresi, F. 124 n.
Ferrari, G. 123 n.
Ferrera, M. 128 n.
Financial Times 98 n., 195 n., 196 n.,
    198 n., 201 n.
Finer, S. E. 240 n.
Finland 103
First Catholic Association 87
First World War 101, 106
Fisichella, D. 113 n.
Fleron, F. 72 n.
FN (Front National) 171
FNSEA/FO, see France (unions)
Folketinget 104
Fortune 194 n., 196 n., 197 n., 198 n.
Fourton, Jean René 194
fragmentation 116, 120, 122-3, 127,
    140, 144
  and conflict 218
  extreme 115
  high level of 128
France 15, 216 n.

Chambers of Agriculture 166
EC membership 198, 199, 200, 204,
    205, 211-12
fragmented system of pressure
    groups 187
pluralism and pressure
    politics 159-74
unions 4, 161-71, 196, 211
Franklin, Grace A. 63, 152 n.
free-riders 40, 43, 46
Freeman, J. L. 63, 64
Friedgut, T. H. 72 n.
Fries, Robert 211
Fritschler, A. Lee 8
Froman, L. A. 107 n.

Galeotti, M. 80 n.
gangsters 247
Gatto, Carolo 201
Gaulle, Charles de 159, 160
Gaullists 160, 164, 165, 167, 173, 174
GEM (Groupes d'Étude et de
    Mobilisation) 212
Gerlich, P. 95 n., 111 n.
Germany 15, 139, 172, 216 n.
  EC membership 200, 204, 207
  federation of trade unions (DGB) 163
  interest group representation in
    legislatures 183
  lawyers 198
  pressure group politics 175-90
  relations between state and organized
    interests 163
Gerritsen, R. 241 n.
Gestalts 227
Giscard D'Estaing, Valéry 194
Giscardians 171
Gladstone, A. 114 n.
Gladstone, W. E. 87
glasnost 76, 78, 81
Glezer, L. 239 n.
Goble, P. 82 n.
Golden, M. 120 n., 121 n.
Goldthorpe, J. 65 n.
Gorbachev, M. S. 75, 76, 78, 79, 83, 84
government:
  bourgeois 105, 109, 111
  federal/unitary 3, 15, 231
  hierarchy 59
  influence of 147
  popular front 82
  pressure groups and 1-15
  process of 19-22
  proletarian 46

Index compiled by Frank Pert